AF568117

John Dryden

ALL FOR LOVE

John Dryden

ALL FOR LOVE

[Edited with Complete Introduction, Biography, Author's Background, Complete Text, Study Questions, Select Criticism and Bibliography]

Aditya Nandwani
B.A. English (Hons), Delhi University;
M.A. (English), IGNOU; Print Journalism (English) YMCA

ANMOL PUBLICATIONS PVT. LTD.
NEW DELHI - 110 002 (INDIA)

ANMOL PUBLICATIONS PVT. LTD.

H.O.: 4374/4B, Ansari Road, Darya Ganj,
New Delhi-110 002 (India)
Ph.: 23278000, 23261597

B.O.: No. 1015, Ist Main Road, BSK IIIrd Stage
IIIrd Phase, IIIrd Block
Bangalore - 560 085 (India)
Visit us at: www.anmolpublications.com

All for Love

First Published, 2009

PRINTED IN INDIA

Printed at Mehra Offset Press, Delhi.

Contents

Preface

John Dryden (1631-1700) was one of the major representatives of Restoration comedy. He was a remarkable English Poet, literary critic and dramatist. Marriage A-la-Mode (1672) was one his popular comic play. Another immnesly popular tragic play by John Dryden was All for Love (1678). He was the son of Erasmus Dryden and Mary Pickering. Of their fourteen kids, John Dryden was the eldest. He was born in Aldwinkle, Northamptonshire, England.

All for Love revolves around Mark Antony. He retired to Alexandria, Egypt, after defeating at Actium. He remained isolated for some time in the temple of Isis and also avoided Cleopatra, the queen of Egypt and also his mistress.

Author

Chapter 1

Introduction

The age of Elizabeth, memorable for so many reasons in the history of England, was especially brilliant in literature, and, within literatujre, in the drama. With some falling off in spontaneity, the impulse to great dramatic production lasted till the Long Parliament closed the theaters in 1642; and when they were reopened at the Restoration, in 1660, the stage only too faithfully reflected the debased moral tone of the court society of Charles II.

John Dryden (1631-1700), the great representative figure in the literature of the latter part of the seventeenth century, exemplifies in his work most of the main tendencies of the time. He came into notice with a poem on the death of Cromwell in 1658, and two years later was composing couplets expressing his loyalty to the returned king. He married Lady Elizabeth Howard, the daughter of a royalist house, and for practically all the rest of his life remained an adherent of the Tory Party. In 1663 he began writing for the stage, and during the next thirty years he attempted nearly all the current forms of drama. His"Annus Mirabilis" (1666), celebrating the English naval victories over the Dutch, brought him in 1670 the Poet Laureateship. He had, meantime, begun the writing of those admirable critical essays, represented in the present series by his Preface to the"Fables" and his Dedication to the translation of Virgil. In these he shows himself not only a critic of sound and penetrating judgment, but the first master of modern English prose style.

With"Absalom and Achitophel," a satire on the Whig leader, Shaftesbury, Dryden entered a new phase, and achieved what is regarded as"the finest of all political satires." This was followed by"The Medal," again directed against the Whigs, and this by"Mac Flecknoe," a fierce attack on his enemy and rival Shadwell. The Government rewarded his services by a lucrative appointment.

After triumphing in the three fields of drama, criticism, and satire, Dryden appears next as a religious poet in his"Religio Laici," an exposition of the doctrines of the Church of England from a layman's point of view. In the same year that the Catholic James II. ascended the throne, Dryden joined the Roman Church, and two years later defended his new religion in"The Hind and the Panther," an allegorical debate between two animals standing respectively for Catholicism and Anglicanism.

The Revolution of 1688 put an end to Dryden's prosperity; and after a short return to dramatic composition, he turned to translation as a means of supporting himself. He had already done something in this line; and after a series of translations from Juvenal, Persius, and Ovid, he undertook, at the age of sixty-three, the enormous task of turning the entire works of Virgil into English verse. How he succeeded in this, readers of the"Aeneid" in a companion volume of these classics can judge for themselves. Dryden's production closes with the collection of narrative poems called"Fables," published in 1700, in which year he died and was buried in the Poet's Corner in Westminster Abbey.

Dryden lived in an age of reaction against excessive religious idealism, and both his character and his works are marked by the somewhat unheroic traits of such a period. But he was, on the whole, an honest man, open minded, genial, candid, and modest; the wielder of a style, both in verse and prose, unmatched for clearness, vigour, and sanity.

Three types of comedy appeared in England in the time of Dryden-the comedy of humors, the comedy of intrigue, and the comedy of manners-and in all he did work that classed him with the ablest of his contemporaries. He developed the somewhat bombastic type of drama known as the heroic play, and brought it to its height in his"Conquest of Granada"; then, becoming dissatisfied with this form, he cultivated the French classic tragedy on the model of Racine. This he modified by combining with the regularity of the French treatment of dramatic action a richness of characterization in which he showed himself a disciple of Shakespeare, and of this mixed type his best example is"All for Love." Here he has the daring to challenge comparison with his master, and the greatest testimony to his achievement is the fact that, as Professor Noyes has said,"fresh from Shakespeare's'Antony and Cleopatra,'we can still read with intense pleasure Dryden's version of the story."

Chapter 2

Biography of John Dryden

John Dryden was born at the vicarage of Aldwinkle, Northamptonshire, on August 9, 1631, son of Erasmus Dryden and Mary Pickering. His family were Parliamentary supporters with Puritan leanings. He attended Westminster School as a king's scholar under Richard Busby, and was an avid student of the classics. While at Westminster, Dryden published his first verses, an elegy"Upon the Death of Lord Hastings", in Lachrymæ Musarum (1649). He entered Trinity College, Cambridge, in 1650, and took a BA in 1654.

Dryden moved to London around 1657, and first gained notice with his'Heroic Stanzas'(1659) on the death of Lord Protector Cromwell. In the Royalist climate of the Restoration, he sensibly wrote Astraea Redux (1660) to celebrate the return of King Charles II. For the coronation, Dryden wrote"To His Sacred Majesty, A Panegyric" (1661). In 1662, Dryden wrote verses"To My Lord Chancellor" Clarendon, and was elected to the Royal Society. The theatres had been reopened, demand for entertainments was high, and Dryden set to writing plays. In 1663, Dryden married Lady Elizabeth Howard, the sister of his theatrical partner Sir Robert Howard, and the eldest daughter of the Earl of Berkshire. His first play was the prose comedy of humours A Wild Gallant (1663), a wholly unremarkable piece, followed by the tragicomedy The Rival Ladies (1664) and The Indian Queen (1664). In 1665, the theatres were closed down because of the plague that raged in London, and the King's court relocated to Oxford. There, Dryden finally established a reputation as a playwright with The Indian Emperor (1665), a heroic drama.

The year 1666 was eventful in English history, including both the naval war with the Dutch, and the Great Fire of London. Dryden commemorated this'year of wonders" in his long poem, Annus Mirabilis, in 1667. This poem secured him the position of Poet Laureate on the death of William D'Avenant in 1668. The same year, he was also given the degree of M. A. by the Archbishop of Canterbury. As a fellow of the Royal Society, he was furthermore made Historiographer Royal in 1670, which brought him an annual income of £200.

In 1668, Dryden began a fruitful period of both critical and dramatic writing. His first major critical work was the Essay of Dramatic Poesy (1668), followed by A Defence of an Essay (1668), and Essay of Heroic Plays (1672). His plays from this period include the comedy Secret Love (1667); the heroic drama Tyrannic Love (1669); the two-part The Conquest of Granada (1670-71); and the comedy Marriage á la Mode (1672). In 1674, Dryden published a tribute to Milton in the form of a musical adaptation of Paradise Lost, entitled The State of Innocence-it was never performed. The tragedy Aureng-Zebe (1676) was Dryden's first play in blank verse, followed by his masterpiece All for Love (1678), based on the story of Anthony and Cleopatra.

The success and fame Dryden enjoyed naturally garnered him enemies. He was ridiculed in Buckingham's The Rehearsal (1671), and brutally beaten in an attack in Rose Alley, Covent Garden, on December 18, 1679. It has been suggested, though never proved, that Lord Rochester had a hand in hiring the ruffians responsible for the attack. Rochester had lampooned Dryden earlier, and had in turn suspected of Dryden for complicity in ridiculing him in Lord Mulgrave's Essay on Satire.

With the the unsuccessful prose comedy"Limberham" (1678), the poor adaptation of Troilus and Cressida (1679), and the play"Spanish Friar" (1681), Dryden left his career as dramatist for a time and turned his attention to satire. His political satire on Monmouth and Shaftesbury, Absalom and Achitophel, appeared in 1681. It is one of the great English satires, and it brought him further favour with Charles II, who was pleased at this attack against the Whigs during the Exclusion Crisis. Dryden dutifully wrote the Second Part of Absalom and Achitophel in collaboration with Nahum Tate, as well as another attack on Shaftesbury's supporters, The Medal (1682). These naturally provoked counterattacks, including Thomas Shadwell's The Medal of John Bayes. Dryden in turn responded Mac Flecknoe, full of ridicule for Shadwell, perhaps his most entertaining poem, pirated in 1682, and officially printed in 1684.

Dryden also had a keen interest in theology, and this resulted first in the publication of Religio Laici (1682). This work, the title of which translates as"A Layman's Faith", was a long religious poem arguing Christianity over Deism, the Bible as the guide to salvation, and the Anglican Church over the Catholic Church. This period saw some of Dryden's best poems, the Pindaric ode"Threnodia Augustalis" (1685) at the death of Charles II, the beautiful lyrical ode"To the Pious Memory... of Mrs Anne Killigrew" (1686) written to commemorate a painter who drowned in the Thames, and"A Song for Saint Cecilia's Day" (1687). Dryden had long grappled with religious uncertainty, and converted into Roman Catholicism in 1686, the year after the ascension to the throne of King James II, a Catholic. In 1687, Dryden published The Hind and the Panther, an allegorical fable criticizing the Anglican church. Dryden suffered for this almost immediately. The Revolution of 1688, which placed the Protestant William III on the throne, caused him to be deprived of his laureateship, and what was worse, he was replaced by his old enemy, Shadwell.

Dryden returned to the theatre. He wrote the libretto to Purcell's opera King Arthur (1691); a tragicomedy, Don Sebastian (1690); a comedy of errors, Amphitryon (1690); and Cleomenes: the Spartan Hero (1692). Dryden's Love Triumphant (1694), the prologue of which announced it as his last play, was a failure. Dryden turned to writing translations, including the satires of Perseus and Juvenal (1693) and Virgil's Aeneid (1697). He also wrote more poetry, including"An Ode, on the death of Mr Henry Purcell" (1696) commemorating the composer, a second ode for St. Cecilia's Day,"Alexander's Feast" (1697), which was later incorporated into his Fables Ancient and Modern (1700), paraphrases of Ovid, Boccaccio, and Chaucer.

Dryden died on April 30, 1700, soon after the publication of the Fables, of inflammation caused by gout. He was buried in Westminster Abbey. Dryden was a good playwright and poet, a fine translator, a solid critic, and an excellent satirist whose works are still worthy of much admiration.

Early Life

Dryden was born in the village rectory of Aldwincle near Oundle in Northamptonshire, where his maternal grandfather was Rector of All Saints. He was the eldest of fourteen children born to Erasmus Dryden and wife Mary Pickering, paternal grandson of Sir Erasmus Dryden, 1st Baronet (1553-1632) and wife Frances Wilkes, Puritan landowning gentry who supported the Puritan cause and Parliament. He was also a second cousin once removed of Jonathan Swift. As a boy Dryden lived in the nearby village of Titchmarsh where it is also likely that he received his first education. In 1644 he was sent to Westminster School as a King's Scholar where his headmaster was Dr Richard Busby, a charismatic teacher and severe disciplinarian. Recently enough re-founded by Elizabeth I, Westminster during this period embraced a very different religious and political spirit encouraging royalism and high Anglicanism. Whatever Dryden's response to this was, he clearly respected the Headmaster and would later send two of his own sons to school at Westminster. Many years after his death a house at Westminster was founded in his name.

As a humanist grammar school, Westminster maintained a curriculum which trained pupils in the art of rhetoric and the presentation of arguments for both sides of a given issue. This is a skill which would remain with Dryden and influence his later writing and thinking, as much of it displays these dialectical patterns. The Westminster curriculum also included weekly translation assignments which developed Dryden's capacity for assimilation. This was also to be exhibited in his later works. His years at Westminster were not uneventful, and his first published poem, an elegy with a strong royalist feel on the death of his schoolmate Henry, Lord Hastings from smallpox, alludes to the execution of King Charles I, which took place on 30 January 1649.

In 1650 Dryden went up to Trinity College, Cambridge where he would have experienced a return to the religious and political ethos of his childhood. The Master of Trinity was a Puritan preacher by the name of Thomas Hill who had been a rector in Dryden's home village. Though there is little specific information on Dryden's undergraduate years, he would have followed the standard curriculum of classics, rhetoric, and mathematics. In 1654 he obtained his BA, graduating top of the list for Trinity that year. In June of the same year Dryden's father died, leaving him some land which generated a little income, but not enough to live on.

Arriving in London during The Protectorate, Dryden obtained work with Cromwell's Secretary of State, John Thurloe. This appointment may have been the result of influence exercised on his behalf by the Lord Chamberlain Sir Gilbert Pickering, Dryden's cousin. Dryden was present on 23 November 1658 at Cromwell's funeral where he processed with the Puritan poets John Milton and Andrew Marvell. Shortly thereafter he published his first important poem, Heroique Stanzas (1658), a eulogy on Cromwell's death which is cautious and prudent in its emotional display. In 1660 Dryden celebrated the Restoration of the monarchy and the return of Charles II with Astraea Redux, an authentic royalist panegyric. In this work the interregnum is illustrated as a time of anarchy, and Charles is seen as the restorer of peace and order.

Later Life and Career

After the Restoration, Dryden quickly established himself as the leading poet and literary critic of his day and he transferred his allegiances to the new government. Along with Astraea Redux, Dryden welcomed the new regime with two more panegyrics; To His Sacred Majesty: A Panegyric on his

Coronation (1662), and To My Lord Chancellor (1662). These poems suggest that Dryden was looking to court a possible patron, but he was to instead make a living in writing for publishers, not for the aristocracy, and thus ultimately for the reading public. These, and his other nondramatic poems, are occasional- that is, they celebrate public events. Thus they are written for the nation rather than the self, and the Poet Laureate (as he would later become) is obliged to write a certain number of these per annum. In November 1662 Dryden was proposed for membership in the Royal Society, and he was elected an early fellow. However, Dryden was inactive in Society affairs and in 1666 was expelled for non-payment of his dues.

On December 1, 1663 Dryden married the royalist sister of Sir Robert Howard-Lady Elizabeth. Dryden's works occasionally contain outbursts against the married state but also celebrations of the same. Thus, little is known of the intimate side of his marriage. Lady Elizabeth however, was to bear him three sons and outlive him.

With the reopening of the theatres after the Puritan ban, Dryden busied himself with the composition of plays. His first play, The Wild Gallant appeared in 1663 and was not successful, but he was to have more success, and from 1668 on he was contracted to produce three plays a year for the King's Company in which he was also to become a shareholder. During the 1660s and 70s theatrical writing was to be his main source of income. He led the way in Restoration comedy, his best known work being Marriage A-la-Mode (1672), as well as heroic tragedy and regular tragedy, in which his greatest success was All for Love (1678).

Dryden was never satisfied with his theatrical writings and frequently suggested that his talents were wasted on unworthy audiences. He thus was making a bid for poetic fame off-stage. In 1667, around the same time his dramatic career began, he published Annus Mirabilis, a lengthy historical poem which described the events of 1666; the English defeat of the Dutch naval fleet and the Great Fire of London. It was a modern epic in pentameter quatrains that established him as the preeminent poet of his generation, and was crucial in his attaining the posts of Poet Laureate (1668) and historiographer royal (1670).

When the Great Plague closed the theatres in 1665 Dryden retreated to Wiltshire where he wrote Of Dramatick Poesie (1668), arguably the best of his unsystematic prefaces and essays. Dryden constantly defended his own literary practice, and Of Dramatick Poesie, the longest of his critical works, takes the form of a dialogue in which four characters-each based on a prominent contemporary, with Dryden himself as'Neander'-debate the merits of classical, French and English drama. The greater part of his critical works introduce problems which he is eager to discuss, and show the work of a writer of independent mind who feels strongly about his own ideas, ideas which demonstrate the incredible breadth of his reading. He felt strongly about the relation of the poet to tradition and the creative process, and his best heroic play"Aureng-zebe" (1675) has a prologue which denounces the use of rhyme in serious drama. His play All for Love (1678), was written in blank verse, and was to immediately follow Aureng-Zebe.

Dryden's greatest achievements were in satiric verse: the mock-heroic MacFlecknoe, a more personal product of his Laureate years, was a lampoon circulated in manuscript and an attack on the playwright Thomas Shadwell. It is not a belittling form of satire, but rather one which makes his object great in ways which are unexpected, transferring the ridiculous into poetry. This line of satire continued with Absalom and Achitophel (1681) and The Medal (1682). His other major works from this period are the religious poems Religio Laici (1682), written from the position of a member of the Church of England; his 1683 edition of Plutarchs Lives Translated From the Greek by Several Hands in which he introduced the word biography to English readers; and The Hind and the Panther, (1687) which celebrates his conversion to Roman Catholicism.

When in 1688 James was deposed, Dryden's refusal to take the oaths of allegiance to the new government left him out of favour at court. Thomas Shadwell succeeded him as Poet Laureate, and he was forced to give up his public offices and live by the proceeds of his pen. Dryden translated works by

Horace, Juvenal, Ovid, Lucretius, and Theocritus, a task which he found far more satisfying than writing for the stage. In 1694 he began work on what would be his most ambitious and defining work as translator, The Works of Virgil (1697), which was published by subscription. The publication of the translation of Virgil was a national event and brought Dryden the sum of ?1,400. His final translations appeared in the volume Fables Ancient and Modern (1700), a series of episodes from Homer, Ovid, and Boccaccio, as well as modernized adaptations from Geoffrey Chaucer interspersed with Dryden's own poems. The Preface to Fables is considered to be both a major work of criticism and one of the finest essays in English. As a critic and translator he was essential in making accessible to the reading English public literary works in the classical languages.

Dryden died in 1700 and is buried in Westminster Abbey. He was the subject of various poetic eulogies, such as Luctus Brittannici: or the Tears of the British Muses; for the Death of John Dryden, Esq. (London, 1700), and The Nine Muses.

Reputation and Influence

Dryden was the dominant literary figure and influence of his age.He established the heroic couplet as the standard meter of English poetry, by writing successful satires, religious pieces, fables, epigrams, compliments, prologues, and plays in it; he also introduced the alexandrine and triplet into the form. In his poems, translations, and criticism, he established a poetic diction appropriate to the heroic couplet-Auden referred to him as"the master of the middle style" -that was a model for his contemporaries and for much of the 18th century. The considerable loss felt by the English literary community at his death was evident from the elegies which it inspired. Dryden's heroic couplet became the dominant poetic form of the 18th century. The most influential poet of the 18th century, Alexander Pope, was heavily influenced by Dryden, and often borrowed from him; other writers were equally influenced by Dryden and Pope. Pope famously praised Dryden's versification in his imitation of Horace's Epistle II.i:"Dryden taught to join / The varying pause, the full resounding line, / The long majestic march, and energy divine." Samuel Johnson summed up the general attitude with his remark that"the veneration with which his name is pronounced by every cultivator of English literature, is paid to him as he refined the language, improved the sentiments, and tuned the numbers of English poetry." His poems were very widely read, and are often quoted, for instance, in Tom Jones and Johnson's essays.

Johnson also noted, however, that"He is, therefore, with all his variety of excellence, not often pathetic; and had so little sensibility of the power of effusions purely natural, that he did not esteem them in others. Simplicity gave him no pleasure." The 18th century did not mind this too much, but in later ages, this was increasingly considered a fault.

One of the first attacks on Dryden's reputation was by Wordsworth, who complained that Dryden's descriptions of natural objects in his translations from Virgil were much inferior to the originals. However, several of Wordsworth's contemporaries, such as George Crabbe, Lord Byron, and Walter Scott (who edited Dryden's works), were still keen admirers of Dryden. Besides, Wordsworth did admire many of Dryden's poems, and his famous"Intimations of Immortality" ode owes something stylistically to Dryden's"Alexander's Feast." John Keats admired the"Fables," and imitated them in his poem Lamia. Later 19th century writers had little use for verse satire, Pope, or Dryden; Matthew Arnold famously dismissed them as"classics of our prose." He did have a committed admirer in George Saintsbury, and was a prominent figure in quotation books such as Bartlett's, but the next major poet to take an interest in Dryden was T. S. Eliot, who wrote that he was'the ancestor of nearly all that is best in the poetry of the eighteenth century', and that'we cannot fully enjoy or rightly estimate a hundred years of English poetry unless we fully enjoy Dryden.'However, in the same essay, Eliot accused Dryden of having a"commonplace mind." Critical interest in Dryden has increased recently, but, as a relatively straightforward writer

(William Empson, another modern admirer of Dryden, compared his"flat" use of language with Donne's interest in the"echoes and recesses of words") his work has not occasioned as much interest as Andrew Marvell's or John Donne's or Pope's.

Poetic Style

What Dryden achieved in his poetry was not the emotional excitement we find in the Romantic poets of the early nineteenth century, nor the intellectual complexities of the metaphysical poets. His subject-matter was often factual, and he aimed at expressing his thoughts in the most precise and concentrated way possible. Although he uses formal poetic structures such as heroic stanzas and heroic couplets, he tried to achieve the rhythms of speech. However, he knew that different subjects need different kinds of verse, and in his preface to Religio Laici he wrote:"...the expressions of a poem designed purely for instruction ought to be plain and natural, yet majestic...The florid, elevated and figurative way is for the passions; for (these) are begotten in the soul by showing the objects out of their true proportion....A man is to be cheated into passion, but to be reasoned into truth."

Chapter 3

Major Works

Astraea Redux, 1660
The Indian Emperor (tragedy), 1665
Annus Mirabilis (poem), 1667
The Enchanted Island (comedy), 1667, an adaptation with William D'Avenant of Shakespeare's The Tempest
An Essay of Dramatick Poesie, 1668
An Evening's Love (comedy), 1669
Tyrannick Love (tragedy), 1669
The Conquest of Granada, 1670
Marriage A-la-Mode, 1672
Aureng-zebe, 1675
All for Love, 1678
Oedipus (heroic drama), 1679, an adaptation with Nathaniel Lee of Sophocles'Oedipus
Absalom and Achitophel, 1681
MacFlecknoe, 1682
The Medal, 1682
Religio Laici, 1682
The Hind and the Panther, 1687
Amphitryon, 1690
Don Sebastian, 1690
Amboyna, or the Cruelties of the Dutch to the English Merchants, 1673
The Works of Virgil, 1697
Fables, Ancient and Modern, 1700

Chapter 4

Dryden as Critic

Dryden was the major literary figure in both literature and criticism of during the Restoration and later 17th century, and the most influential critic of the whole century. Criticism during the Jacobean age and the Commonwhealth will fail to justly appraise or even recognize the great works of the age. It is an undeveloped genre, and the information about literature often consists of a"roll-call" of authors, a bare list of names and works with some laudatory comment appended to them. There is not even a single detailed study or commentary of a literary work. Dryden will do much to change this situation; his success is also the success of criticism in English letters.

Being a writer as well as a critic, Dryden always wrote criticism to some practical end concerning his own works. Much of his critical work is to be found in prefaces to his own works. Besides, he was a professional writer. He was not a nobleman writing for his pleasure: he had to live from his work and in the age he wrote in this meant that he had to find some patron or other to take him under his protection. He had to flatter, and this explains not only the nature of his writing, but also sometimes that of his criticism. Sometimes his reasoning is flawed by this need to flatter. As in the critics we have studied up to now, we find in Dryden an interest in the general issues of criticism rather than in a close reading of particular texts (although he will provide one of the first of such readings, that of Jonson's The Silent Woman). He wants to rely on both authority and common sense, and often seems at a loss when the two seem to go against each other. We call

Dryden a neoclassical critic, just as Boileau, although in fact there are wide differences between them. Dryden meditates on the neoclassical rules, which he feels to be right in the main, but then he also wants to find a critical justification for the great tradition of English poetry, which lay beyond those rules. It is to his credit that he thought over the principles of French neo-Classicism and did not apply them mechanically to the English letters. According to T.S. Eliot, Dryden's great work consists not so much in the originality of his principles as in having realized the need to affirm the native tradition, as opposed to the overwhelming French influence.

His best-known work, the Essay of Dramatic Poesy, partly reflects this tension in Dryden's commitments. Its dialogue form has often been criticised as inconclusive, but actually, as in most dialogues, there is a spokesman more weighty than the others. Dryden carries about his task with efficiency, stating his own ideas but leaving some leeway for difference of opinion. Neander's overall statement on the rules is that they can add to the perfection of a work, but that they will not improve a work which does not already contain some degree of perfection or genius in it.

And we may find writers like Shakespeare, Dryden believes, who did not follow the rules but are nevertheless obviously superior to any"regular" writer. Shakespeare disconcerts Dryden, who recognises his superiority but is more at ease with Ben Jonson. In Dryden, then, we find a"liberal" neoclassicist, although he is most coherent when he is dealing with that which can be understood and reduced to rule. His relaxation is to a great extent both a refusal to believe in the universal application in the neoclassic principles and an inability to provide new and more comprehensive principles. Because his most cogent statement on the rules (following Rapin) is that if the rules be well considered, we shall find them to be made only to reduce nature into method... they are founded upon good sense and sound reason, rather than on authority.

Dryden is not a great analyst of texts nor an important literary historian, but some of his works are significant steps in the development of both directions in criticism. Dryden's importance as a critic comes from his place in history at the start of the long neoclassical era, whose principles he helped determine; he contributed a great deal to raise the standards of criticism and to define the role of the discipline. As he says himself they wholly mistake the nature of criticism who thinks its business is principally to find fault. Criticism, as it was first instituted by Aristotle, was meant a standard of judging well; the chiefest part of which is to observe those excellencies which should delight a reasonable reader.And of course his ideas also give us insights into his own work.

The Poet and the Creative Process

The way the work is"moulded to shape" is through"fancy moving the sleeping images of things towards the light, there to be distinguished and then either chosen or rejected by the judgement." In Dryden, and indeed in all the 18th-century critics after him, fancy is sometimes synonymous with imagination and sometimes identified as a special kind of imagination."Wit" is also used to refer to this faculty. Fancy and imagination will become different concepts in Coleridge. So we have two opposite principles at work in the writer's mind: fancy and judgement (cf. the different accounts of the creative process in Sidney, Bacon, and Hobbes). We may note that fancy is subordinate to judgement, although it seems to be assigned a more relevant role than in Hobbes'theory. Fancy is synthetic, while judgement is analytic, as Hobbes had said and Locke will reaffirm.

Of course, Dryden has to give fancy its due in the composition of a work. But it is something he mistrusts. It is too lawless, and there is a danger that it may get out of hand. Strictures placed during the process of composition, such as the rules or the use of rhyme, are a good means to restrict the impulse of fancy and allow judgement to become dominant. While writing,"fancy, memory and judgement are then extended in the rack" (Orrery 2). Writing is a painstaking activity, one which demands the utmost of the writer's capabilities.

In the preface to his poem Annus Mirabilis (1667), Dryden gave an account of the phases of the creative process, which we can profitably compare with the inventio, dispositio and elocutio of classical rhetoric. To compose an epic poem, he says, a poet needs wit."Wit" in the eighteenth century did not suggest the gift of the quick repartee or the bon mot, as it does today; rather, it stood for the creative faculty of the human mind, above all the aspect defined by Hobbes as"fancy," the ability to see the resemblances between different objects. Dryden defines wit as imagination, as the ability to find the right memory or the right metaphor we are looking for:

But to proceed from wit in the general notion of it to the proper wit of an heroic or historical poem, I judge it chiefly to consist in the delightful imaging of persons, actions, passions, or things... it is some lively and apt description, dressed in such a colors of speech, that it sets before your eyes the absent object, as perfectly and more delightfully than nature. So then, the first happiness of the poet's imagination is properly invention or finding the thought; the second is fancy, or the variation, deriving or molding of that thought, as the judgment represents it proper to the subject; the third is elocution, or the art of clothing and adorning that thought so found and varied, in apt, significant and sounding words: the quickness of the imagination is seen in the invention, the fertility in the fancy, and the accuracy in the expression.

Writers in dramatic style, such as Ovid and all playwrights, must excel in invention and fancy; those speaking in his own voice, like Virgil, must cultivate their expression. So, there are different creative faculties in the human mind, and each kind of work may demand a special development of one or other. Dryden feels at times the need to specialise: he wrote works in practically all genres except the novel, but he seems to think that each writer excels in a particular kind of writing. He complains that the Ancients were either tragedians or comedians, and that it is easier to attain perfection in this way, writing only the kind of thing one does best. This natural gift has to be controlled by technique. The good writer must be a born genius (here Dryden refers us to Longinus), and he must know the emotions he is depicting. But he must not be carried away by them because probably the audience would not follow him. Dryden believes that poetry is an art for witty men, and not for madmen. Passion would blur the differences between characters, and it is judgment which keeps them separate. We can compare this analytical labour of the judgment to Hobbes once again. Dryden's interest in the successful objectification of the poet's emotions is an interesting prefiguration of later aesthetic theories (e.g. Schopenhauer's).

Of course we have the classical models to guide us. To copy their ways is not a fault, rather a virtue. In the Essay of Dramatic Poesy we find this phrase as a commendation of Ben Jonson:"He was not only a professed imitator of Horace, but a learned plagiary of all the others". But true imitation must be original and improve the models. Dryden believes that poetry has a historical development, and he wishes"that poetry may not go backward, when all other arts and sciences are advancing." We may profit from the models and the experience of the ancients and try to go beyond them. All great writers have borrowed from others, without their being less original for it. He traces the Homeric influence in Virgil, for instance. The neoclassical era is not particularly sensitive to originality and invention, but nevertheless Dryden believes that other things being equal, originality is to be preferred to good imitation, and is a greater proof of genius.

One word on the subject of progress in literature: Dryden, as many other critics of his time, seems to believe in a cyclical alternance of barbarian ages with ages of refinement and progress. They believe themselves to be in the equivalent of the Roman Empire. Shakespeare is Dryden's Homer, and Jonson is his Virgil. He does not seem to believe that the heights of the classical age can be reached again; even the language is too unstable for great works and inferior to Greek. Like Pope, Dryden believed that writing in English is like writing on sand, compared to the writing on marble of the Ancients.

Prosody and Diction

Rhyme is for Dryden something more than a mere

ornament. It is a way of consciously controlling the process of composition: because of the superior attention it requires, rhyme demands a greater consciousness on the part of the poet, and less abandonment to the inspiration of his fancy. Rhyme bounds and circumscribes the fancy.... The fancy then gives leisure to the judgment to come in, which, seeing so heavy a tax imposed, is ready to cut off all unnecessary expenses".

Rhyme, then, is not mere"embroidery of sense," it is a means of clarifying the thought.

We shall see that Dryden initially favored the use of rhyme in plays when the appropriateness of this convention coming from France is being debated. Verse is right; it is only unnatural when it is forced. Rhyme is superior to blank verse, which Dryden believed was invented by Shakespeare. Paradoxically, he recognizes that it is blank verse which is the tradition natural to English. However, Dryden's statement on rhyme does not end here. We may note that he accepts blank verse in the less serious types of plays. And in later years, he was to modify his views, and he came to recognize that blank verse was a suitable vehicle for serious drama. In the prologue to Aureng-Zebe (1676), he admits to growing"weary of his long-loved mistress, rhyme" and recognizes Shakespeare's superiority. And in the preface to All for Love (1678), an imitation of Shakespeare's Antony and Cleopatra, he admits that blank verse is more suitable for a Shakespearean imitation, even if it is a tragedy.

Maybe the neoclassical preference for the heroic couplet is the reason for this change: couplets of alexandrines, the staple of French classical drama, are all right for the French language, but the English heroic couplet does not lend itself so easily to the portrayal of conversation. It is best fit to long series of meditative or essayistic verses, and it is here where it will triumph; English drama reverts to blank verse and then to prose.

Dryden also writes a miniature history of modern prosody. Although he is a bit patronizing on Chaucer, he is readier than most people in his age to recognize his genius. However, at the time Chaucer's language was still unknown

(Dryden laughs at the first news of a reconstruction of Chaucer's regular metrics in the preface to his translation), so Dryden does not recognize his merits as a versifier, and considers Waller and Denham (who are minor poets from our point of view) to be the first great versifiers of the English language. Waller is the inventor of the couplet: he"first showed us to conclude the sense most commonly in diptychs" (Ornery 5). Dryden will insist on the connection between form and sense: in this way form will impose itself directly on sense. Couplets and quatrains must contain a unit of sense. On the other hand, he opposes the strict equality of syllables in all lines, a reasonable thing to do, since stressing certain weak syllables and making them count for measure is unnatural to English.

Dryden opposes Aristotle in believing that the soul of a play is not to be found in its plot, but rather in its author's language, in diction and thought. Dryden wants a literature written in a pure language, one which is free from neologism and pedantry alike. However, he accepts coinages from Latin. Like Swift whose complaints will be much the same, he longs for an academy with an authority to decide on linguistic matters.

We find in the age of Dryden a growing reaction against the Ramist conception of rhetoric. If rhetoric is just an addition of ornamental words, it is better to do away with it. The Cartesian and the empiricist ideas coincide here. Fancy will seen as something which plays with words, while judgment defines the real relationships between things. One of the most notable phenomena of the age is the definition of the language of science in opposition to rhetoric. The Royal Society inspires the works of John Wilkins (Essay towards a Real Character and a Philosophical Language, 1668) and Thomas Sprat, who advocates a"mathematical plainness" in style: one word, one thing. These ideas will be satirized in Swift's Gulliver's Travels, where the wise men in Laputa carry with them all the objects they want to speak about and merely point to them. For Locke, the most influential philosopher during the eighteenth century, eloquence misleads judgment, instead of directing it. All these writers mistrust literature, poetry, rhetoric, which they consider empty words. There is a growing emphasis on reason which will be felt in literary theory as well.

Character and Plot

Dryden discusses character and plot as technical difficulties faced by the writer, sometimes working one against the other. This conception is very characteristic of British criticism. We can compare it with E. M. Forster's account in Aspects of the Novel (1927), which describes how the plot seems to lead the writer in one direction and the characters in a different one. For both Forster and Dryden, it is the poet's art to respect both the decorum of the characters and the causally necessary, natural solution to the plot. The writer, Dryden says, is like a god to his characters, having prescience and power of determination. But it is difficult to use them in a way altogether convincing, working as a whole.

We may note that decorum and rule are for Dryden a means of giving formal integrity to the work: that is, they are not only content, but form as well; their aim is not to depict the world as it is, but to give unity to the work. Dryden, like many later critics, is conscious of two different tendencies present in a work: although he does not use these terms, we might call them the mimetic tendency (the relationship between an element in the work and reality) and the structural tendency (the coherence of the work imposing its own conventions, the concern for formal integrity).

He opposes the strongly conventionalized characters and plots of Roman comedies, asking for a wider imitation of nature, although he also appreciates the advantages of patterning and of structural simplicity in current French plays, and he believes some of Shakespeare's plays to be"ridiculously cramped" with incident. But the interest of the plot and the characters is also to be found in variety and not simply in a well-defined structure. In variety we recognize real life, and this is one of the advantages of the English approach to dramatic art.

The story itself is the least important part of a poet's work, the one which lends it most easily to imitation. It is a material which must be worked on, finding suitable characters and style. Aristotle, Dryden points out, placed plot first of all elements in a play as the basis on which the others are built, and not as the most important one to determine the quality of a play. For Dryden, it is the characters'language which is the most important element in a play.

Dryden repeats Aristotle's theory on the unity of action, but understanding it in a wider sense than many neoclassical critics. There can be unity in a play with two lines of action, if they are causally linked. Dryden introduces in English criticism the criterion of unity used by Corneille, the contrast between the suspense of the partial actions and the final repose of the mind of the audience when the whole of the action is completed. He demands that beginning, middle and end fo"ow each other in a necessary way: a fable ought to have a beginning, middle, and an end, all just and natural, so that that part which is the middle, could not naturally be the beginning or end, and so of the rest: all are depending on one another, like the links of a curious chain.

This does not happen, he says, in Spanish plots; as in perspective, so in tragedy there must be a point of sight in which all the lines terminate; otherwise the eye wanders, and the work is false ("Grounds" 167). It is the moral that directs the whole action of the play to one centre.

Dryden also repeats Aristotle's doctrine on characters. Manners must be apparent (shown in action and discourse), suitable, resembling, and constant. Characters derive from manners, but they must be a suitable composite of manners, and not be grounded on a single trait. We may compare this conception, once again, to E. M. Forster's well-known opposition between flat and round characters (Aspects of the Novel).

The Essay of Dramatic Poesy

In 1663, a Frenchman called Sorbière published a book on England, in which he made fun of the state of both the science and the arts in that country. Thomas Sprat, of the Royal

Society, answered back with a treatise on the new science which was being developed in England. Dryden wrote his Essay of Dramatic Poesy (1668), a meditation on the nature and conventions of drama which was an answer to Sorbière (who had criticized English drama for not following the unities) as well as to French dramatic theory and practice in general. It is a defence of the English theatrical ways, presenting them at least as an alternative to the classical and the French styles.

Something can be said for them, and not just against them, and we may well think that Meander's arguments for English drama are the strongest. However, it is not clear which is the drama Dryden is defending, because he answers Sorbière's attack against current English theatre with an appeal to Ben Jonson and Shakespeare, the writers of the"last age", fifty years his predecessors. Dryden's comments on earlier playwrights are important not only in themselves, but also because they are at the start of a tradition of valuation of English literature,"dearest moments in the history of national self-appreciation" for Sampson. Dryden set the rules for Shakespearean criticism for the next century and a half; and if his admiration for Ben Jonson seems excessive to us now, we still use many of his views of the differences between both writers, in whom he saw an entirely different force at work. For us, there is little doubt that French drama in Dryden's time was superior to whatever was being written in England and to anything written for the English stage for centuries afterwards; Molière, Corneille and Racine are far better playwrights than the Restoration comedians (Congreve, Vanbrugh, Sedley, Wycherley) and they are above Dryden himself as a tragedian.

In any case, Dryden expounds in a fair enough way the reasons for and against the dramatic practice of both countries, as well as of that of the Ancients, and re-states the classical doctrine on drama. Dryden retains openness to contrary argument which almost approaches skepticism, although it would be more accurate to define his views as probabilistic rather than skeptic (Wimsatt and Brooks 193). Dryden was accused of inconclusiveness, and he retorted with the Defence of an Essay of Dramatic Poesy (1668), and there he alludes to the Aristotelian difference between demonstrative and probabilistic arguments: the latter Aristotle had said to be proper to rhetoric. It is up to the talent of each fictional speaker to convince us of the rightness of his opinions. They are Cities, Eugenics, Siliceous, and Meander. Although Meander is generally recognized as Dryden's spokesman and as the more cogent speaker of all, all are allowed to have their say, and the dialogue is not brought to a conclusion through the victory of Meander's argument: we leave the four friends still debating the issues. And in the Defence of the Essay of Dramatic Poesy,

Dryden says that his argument is not demonstrative but probabilistic: it is up to the reader to decide which of the speakers he will side with. Crites defends and extreme Classicist position, although he is not blind to the merits of modern versification. Siliceous and Eugenics accept the same Classical premises as Crites, but say that modern poets have profited from the experience and imitation of the Classics and follow rules more exactly. Siliceous adds that the rules have been best followed by French drama, which is to be regarded as the model. Meander ("new man") insists on the need of liveliness-which he feels is lacking in Classical and French plays-rather than plain verisimilitude. He approves as well of Corneille's phrase,"il est facile aux speculatifs d'estre severes," and he is concerned with the excessive rigidity that critical principles, divorced of actual dramatic practice, tend to impose on drama.

The Dramatic Unities of Time and Place

The three unities, Dryden observes, ought to be followed in all regular plays. But he is tolerant enough with plays which are moderately irregular. In the Essay of Dramatic Poesy, Crites repeats the account of the unities given by Corneille (without his qualifications on the difficulty of the enterprise). The unities aim at verisimilitude; the space and time of representation must be as close as possible to those of the feigned action. Any distortion must be supposed to fall between the acts, plots have to begin"in medias rest", narration must be restricted to events simultaneous with the action if possible, etc. In time we find that the coincidence of times works all right in dealing with the precipitate events at the conclusion of a play, but makes the complication seem artificial or else rely too much on narrative. Dryden follows Corneille in showing how the unities of space and time are mutually related and regularity in one favors regularity in the other. This may be helped through the"liaison des scenes." Place (and time, too) remains the same inside each act, and that you may know it to be the same, the stage is so supplied with persons that it is never empty all the time.

But the view of the question give by Crites is much qualified in the debate by the advocates of the moderns. The disadvantages of regularity are pointed out: there is a danger of narrowness and monotony. The"liaison des scenes" is only possible in French plays because their plots contain little action and their scenes are very long. This also demands an excessive use of monologue, which is unnatural. One main end of theatre, delight, is not sufficiently attended to in Greek or French plays.

Rhyme and Verisimilitude

Dryden held an interesting debate with his brother-in law, Sir Robert Howard, on the property of rhyme in plays and its relationship to verisimilitude. Howard opposed the use of rhyme, which he believed to break the illusion of reality which any play ought to produce. Dryden defended the use of rhyme. He believes that the end of a play is not so much to give a faithful imitation of human life as to give a heightened image of reality. Rhyme works in that way: it guides the attention and gives greater tightness to speeches.

Besides, Dryden says, blank verse (which was proposed by Howard as a substitute for rhyme) is not"natural," either. Howard based his attack on rhyme on the principle that if a play is to trick our minds into a fictive reality, then the use of rhyme worked against that, because men do not speak in rhyme; we will not believe that it is the character who is actually speaking. Dryden's answer is categorical: we are never tricked in a play into believing that we are facing a real scene; and it is the author, not the characters, whom we consider to be speaking in the last analysis. In the Essay of Dramatic Poesy, even Crites acknowledges that dramatic verisimilitude deceives us because we desire to be deceived, and that we know all the time that we are being deceived. We will have to keep this in mind when we discuss the definition of the audience's role as a"willing suspension of disbelief" in nineteenth-century criticism. Howard was also against following of the three unities, also for the sake of verisimilitude: he believed that too much use must be made of coincidence to concentrate an action in so restricted a space and time. Paradoxically, Dryden holds the opposite: the unities produce an effect of verisimilitude.

Actually, Dryden's position is not incoherent; only, verisimilitude as such is not the only thing at stake here. Howard, we may note, is for a relaxation of the formalities of theatre: no rhyme, no rules, whereas Dryden appreciates the value which they have in the making of a work of art, because of the tightness they impose on experience, the concentration, the dramatic intensity, the heightened attention of the audience. Dryden sees that the essence of art is more than just imitation of real life. Drama is not trompe-l'il, that extreme of mimetic trickery. Verisimilitude is all right, it is relevant to the question, but we need something more than just verisimilitude, something which rhyme and a concentrated action help to shape. A tragedy is always natural as a tragedy:

The plot, the characters, the wit, the descriptions, are all exalted above the level of common converse, as high as the imagination of the poet can carry them with proportion to versatility. Verse, then, is natural to tragedy, even if it is not natural to life: Verse,'tis true, is not the effect of sudden thought; but this hinders not that sudden thought may be represented in verse.

Delight and Instruction

In his definition of a play in the Essay of Dramatic Poesy,

Dryden says it is "a just and lively image of human nature, representing its passions and humors, and the changes of fortune to which it is subject, for the delight and instruction of mankind."

So, once again we meet a version of the Horatian""productive delight." Elsewhere Dryden writes: "these two ends may be thus distinguished. The chief end of the poet is to please, for his immediate reputation depends on it. The great end of the poet is to instruct, which is performed by making pleasure the vehicle of that instruction; for poetry is an art, and all arts are made to profit."

But in later pronouncements, Dryden asserts that "delight is the chief, if not the only end of poesy; instruction can be admitted but in the second place, for poesy only instructs as it delights, or that instruction is the end of tragedy, but in comedy it is not so; for the chief end of it is divertissement and delight, and that so much, that it is disputed... whether instruction be any part of its employment."

Dryden does not believe comedy to be grounded on any serious principle such as moral instruction. Here Dryden sides with Heinsius in declaring that comedy has amusement and delight as its only aim, far from the serious concerns of tragedy. Comedy works not on the best impulses of the audience, but on the worst, making them laugh. The pleasure coming from comedy is a"malicious pleasure"; comedy may instruct, but it is a secondary purpose: its main duty is to please. But he often changed opinions on this subject, alternately stressing or playing down the responsibilities and moral requirements of drama. In this sense he is not the typical neoclassical critic. The general attitude towards comedy is that it ought to provide moral instruction. Sidney and Jonson had even defended comedy without laughter. Others defend, of course, laughter, such as Molière and Pope. Dryden affirms that Ben Jonson did not require creative wit, being satisfied with humour. He believes that as far as wit is concerned, modern playwrights are superior to Jonson. His characters are funny, but not witty. They do not make us laugh willingly: we laugh at them. They are at once more realistic, and more approximate to real conversation. Dryden distinguishes between a comedy of wit and a comedy of humors, and he prefers a mixture of the two.

In A Discourse Concerning the Original and Progress of Satire, written in his old age (1693), Dryden asserts that pleasure is only a secondary end to poetry. It is only a means to the real end, which is instruction. Conversely, the aim of the poet is to please, but not everything that pleases is good. Dryden believes that the quality of a work is inherent to it, that it comes from its having certain qualities; he mistrusts to some extent the judgment of the audience. The dramatist must not be a slave to the taste of the audience. So we find in Dryden all the gamut of combinations between the poles of delight and instruction. Instruction comes unconsciously from the admiration produced by the events in the plot. The soul of the spectator is wound insensibly into the practice of that which it admires.

In the late 1670s, Dryden receives strong influence from the French critics Boileau, Rapin and Le Bossu, and also from the extreme classicism of another Englishman, Rymer. In his Tragedies of the Last Age, Thomas Rymer had introduced the term"poetic justice" and had insisted that it had to be respected in all plays. Many were ready to agree with him for a long time, such as Dennis, and Addison, who still exaggerate the concept. Rymer launched some silly attacks on Shakespeare, criticizing him for his moral faults and his ignorance of the unities. Dryden had a respect for Rymer which we cannot understand today: but then we must not forget that Dryden himself was a great rewriter and"improver" of Shakespearean plays (All for Love, The Tempest, Troilus and Cressida, etc.). But Dryden, while accepting poetic justice, is not an extreme advocate of it.

And he makes some interesting observations on the conflicts it arises in tragedy, when it runs against sympathy. The aim of tragedy is to instruct by example. Dryden proposes love as the most suitable theme to move the pity of the audience, a subject which"was almost unknown to the Ancients." The poet must labour to arouse pity for the criminal, and not for the victim, and terror must come from the punishment of the criminal we pity: this idea introduces some complexity beyond the simplicity of poetic justice.

We may note that the favourite theatrical emotions of the Neoclassic age, when a new ethics of benevolence is developing, are poetic justice, pity, melodrama, the pleasure of compassion of injured innocence. All are in direct opposition to Aristotle's catharsis and his basic requirements for tragedy. Now a sentimentalized version of catharsis is fashionable: it is understood to be the abating of pride and anger through fear and pity. The stage is ready for the development of sentimental drama and bourgeois tragedy or melodrama (George Lillo, The London Merchant, 1731; Richard Steele, The Conscious Lovers, 1722).

Satire

Dryden wrote a long essay on satire: A Discourse Concerning the Original and Progress of Satire (1693). He follows Horace and the French critic Dacier, who had undertaken a similar enterprise before.

Satire is a kind of poetry, without a series of action, invented for the purging of our minds; in which human vices, ignorance and error, and all things besides, which are produced from them, in every man, are severely reprehended; partly dramatically, partly simply; but for the most time figuratively and occult.... It ought only to treat of one subject; to be confined to a particular theme, or, at least, to one principally.

Satire is not libel or slander: it is concerned with the castigation of universal vice through its manifestation in individuals (cf. A's comedy vs. lampoon or poetry vs. history). Nevertheless, satires will still be concerned with attack to particular persons on concrete occasions.

Dryden traces the independent development of satire in Greece and Rome, the similar restrictions placed by law upon it, the influence on Roman satire not of Greek satire, but of Greek Old Comedy. He classifies the types of satire, following those previous writers, according to the poet who first developed them. We have then Menippean (or Varronian) satire, which mixes verse with prose and serious philosophical matters with pleasantries, parodies and obscenity. The term became popular once more with Northop Frye's Anatomy of Criticism. Frye expands the term to include works of intellectual or philosophical parody and disquisition such as Rabelais'Gargantua and Pantagruel, Burton's Anatomy of Melancholy, Montesquieu's Lettres persanes, Voltaire's Candide, Swift's Tale of a Tub and Gulliver.

The other main styles in satire were developed by Persius, who writes invective and insults against vice rather than satire, and above all by Horace and Juvenal. Horace is more profitable, and Juvenal more delightful. Also, they castigate different things: Horace folly, Juvenal vice. Horace's instructions are more general:

[Horace] had found out the skill of Virgil, to hide his sentences to give you the virtue of them without showing them in their full extent, which is the ostentation of a poet, and not his art".

However, Dryden finds that Horace's wit is insipid, and that Juvenal is sharper. Horace specialises in fine mockery, Juvenal is more direct and pungent. Dryden's conclusion is that although Horatian satire is the best kind of satire, both in tone and in objects, Horace has carried it to less perfection than Juvenal, who writes more successfully an inferior kind of satire.

Chapter 5

Restoration Drama

FROM 1642 onward for eighteen years, the theaters of England remained nominally closed. There was of course evasion of the law; but whatever performances were offered had to be given in secrecy, before small companies in private houses, or in taverns located three or four miles out of town. No actor or spectator was safe, especially during the early days of the Puritan rule. Least of all was there any inspiration for dramatists. In 1660 the Stuart dynasty was restored to the throne of England. Charles II, the king, had been in France during the greater part of the Protectorate, together with many of the royalist party, all of whom were familiar with Paris and its fashions. Thus it was natural, upon the return of the court, that French influence should be felt, particularly in the theater. In August, 1660, Charles issued patents for two companies of players, and performances immediately began. Certain writers, in the field before the civil war, survived the period of theatrical eclipse, and now had their chance. Among these were Thomas Killigrew and William Davenant, who were quickly provided with fine playhouses.

Appearance of Women on the English Stage

It will be remembered that great indignation was aroused among the English by the appearance of French actresses in 1629. London must have learned to accept this innovation, however, for in one of the semi-private entertainments given during the Protectorate at Rutland House, the actress Mrs. Coleman took the principal part. The Siege of Rhodes, a huge spectacle designed by Davenant in 1656 (arranged in part with a view of evading the restrictions against theatrical plays) is generally noted as marking the entrance of women upon the English stage. It is also remembered for its use of movable machinery, which was something of an innovation. The panorama of The Siege offered five changes of scene, presenting"the fleet of Solyman the Magnificent, his army, the Island of Rhodes, and the varieties attending the siege of the city."

Disappearance Of National Types

By the time the theaters were reopened in England, Corneille and Racine in France had established the neo-classic standard for tragedy, and Molière was in the full tide of his success. These playwrights, with Quinault and others, for a time supplied the English with plots. The first French opera, Cadmus and Hermione, by Lully and Quinault, performed in Paris in 1673, crossed the channel almost immediately, influencing Dryden in his attempts at opera. The romantic, semi-historical romances of Madame Scudéry and the Countess de la Fayette afforded a second supply of story material, while Spanish plays and tales opened up still another. Sometimes the plots of Calderón or Lope de Vega came to the English at second-hand through French versions. Whatever the case, it was now evident that the national type of play had ceased to be written. From this time on every European nation was influence by, and exerted an influence upon, the drama of every other nation. Characters, situations, plots, themes--these things traveled from country to country, always modifying and sometimes supplanting the home product.

Persistence of Elizabethan Plays

With this influx of foreign drama, there was still a steady production of the masterpieces of the Elizabethan and Jacobean periods. The diarist Samuel Pepys, an ardent lover of the theater, relates that during the first three years after the opening of the playhouses he saw Othello, Henry IV, A Midsummer Night's Dream, two plays by Ben Jonson, and others by Beaumont, Fletcher, Middleton, Shirley, and

Massinger. It must have been about this time that the practice of"improving" Shakespeare was begun, and his plays were often altered so as to be almost beyond recognition. From the time of the Restoration actors and managers, also dramatists, were good royalists; and new pieces, or refurbished old ones, were likely to acquire a political slant. The Puritans were satirized, the monarch and his wishes were flattered, and the royal order thoroughly supported by the people of the stage.

Richard Boyle, Earl of Orrery (1621-1679), seems to have the doubtful glory of re-introducing the use of rhymed verse. Boyle was a statesman, as well as a soldier and a dramatist. During the ten years or so following the Restoration, he wrote at least four tragedies on historical or legendary subjects, using the ten-syllabled rhymed couplet which (at the moment) he borrowed from France. It runs like this:

"Reason's a staff for age, when nature's gone;
But youth is strong enough to walk alone."

No more stilted sort of verse could well be contrived for dialogue. Monotonous as well as prosy, it was well suited to Orrery's plots. He took a semi-historical story, filled it with bombastic sentiments and strutting figures, producing what was known as"heroic drama." Dryden, who identified himself with this type of play, described it as concerned not with probabilities but with love and valor. A good heroic play is exciting, with perpetual bustle and commotion. The characters are extricated out of their amazing situations only by violence. Deaths are numerous. The more remote and unfamiliar the setting the better; and the speech should be suited to the action: hence the"heroic couplet." Pepys saw Guzman, by Orrery, and with his engaging frankness said it was as mean a thing as had been seen on the stage for a great while.

Parody of Heroic Drama

Other writers, Davenant, Etherege, and Sir Robert Howard, had also produced specimens of heroic plays, and by the time The Conquest of Granada reached the stage these clever gentlemen had grown tired of the species. Compared to Dryden they were nobodies in the literary world; but among them they contrived a hilarious burlesque called The Rehearsal, in which these showy but shallow productions were smartly ridiculed. Dryden is represented as Bayes (in reference to his position as poet laureate), and his peculiarities of speech and plot are amusingly derided. Though The Rehearsal was condemned as"scurrilous and ill-bred," yet it served a useful turn in puncturing an empty and overblown style.

Nature Of Restoration Comedy

In almost every important respect, Restoration drama was far inferior to the Elizabethan. Where the earlier playwrights created powerful and original characters, the Restoration writers were content to portray repeatedly a few artificial types; where the former were imaginative, the latter were clever and ingenious. The Elizabethan dramatists were steeped in poetry, the later ones in the sophistication of the fashionable world. The drama of Wycherley and Congreve was the reflection of a small section of life, and it was like life in the same sense that the mirage is like the oasis. It had polish, an edge, a perfection in its own field; but both its perfection and its naughtiness now seem unreal.

The heroes of the Restoration comedies were lively gentlemen of the city, profligates and loose livers, with a strong tendency to make love to their neighbors'wives. Husbands and fathers were dull, stupid creatures. The heroines, for the most part, were lovely and pert, too frail for any purpose beyond the glittering tinsel in which they were clothed. Their companions were busybodies and gossips, amorous widows or jealous wives. The intrigues which occupy them are not, on the whole, of so low a nature as those depicted in the Italian court comedies; but still they are sufficiently coarse. Over all the action is the gloss of superficial good breeding and social ease. Only rarely do these creatures betray the traits of sympathy, faithfulness, kindness, honesty, or loyalty. They follow a life of pleasure, bored, but yawning behind a delicate fan or a kerchief of lace. Millamant and Mirabell, in Congreve's Way of the World, are among the most charming of these Watteau figures.

Everywhere in the Restoration plays are traces of European influence. The Plain Dealer of Wycherley was an English version of The Misanthrope of Molière; and there are many admirable qualities in the French play which are lacking in the English. The Double Dealer recalls scenes from The Learned Ladies (Les femmes savantes); and Mr. Bluffe, in The Old Bachelor, is none other than our old friend Miles Gloriosus, who has traveled through Latin, Italian and French comedy. The national taste was coming into harmony, to a considerable extent, with the standards of Europe. Eccentricities were curbed; ideas, characters, and story material were interchanged. The plays, however, were not often mere imitations; in the majority of them there is original observation and independence of thought. It was this drama that kept the doors of the theater open and the love of the theater alive in the face of great public opposition.

Women Playwrights

Soon after the Restoration women began to appear as writers of drama. Mrs. Aphra Behn (1640-1689) was one of the first and most industrious of English women playwrights. Her family name was Amis (some writers say Johnson). As the wife of a wealthy Dutch merchant she lived for some time in Surinam (British Guiana). Her novel, Oroonooko, furnished Southerne with the plot for a play of the same name. After the death of her husband, Mrs. Behn was for a time employed by the British government in a political capacity. She was the author of eighteen plays, most of them highly successful and fully as indecent as any by Wycherley or Vanbrugh. Mrs. Manly and Mrs. Susannah Centlivre, both of whom lived until well into the eighteenth century, also achieved success as playwrights. The adaptations from the French, made by Mrs. Centlivre, were very popular and kep the stage for nearly a century.

Collier's Attack On The Stage

Although the Puritans had lost their dominance as a political power, yet they had not lost courage in abusing the stage. The most violent attack was made by the clergyman Jeremy Collier in 1698, in a pamphlet called A Short View of the Immorality and Profaneness of the English Stage, in which he denounced not only Congreve and Vanbrugh, but Shakespeare and most of the Elizabethans. Three points especially drew forth his denunciations: the so-called lewdness of the plays, the frequent references to the Bible and biblical characters, and the criticism, slander and abuse flung from the stage upon the clergy. He would not have any Desdemona, however chaste, show her love before the footlights; he would allow no reference in a comedy to anything connected with the Church or religion; and especially would he prohibit any portrayal of the clergy. Next to the men in holy orders, Collier had a tender heart for the nobility. He said in effect that if any ridicule or satire were to be indulged in, it should be against persons of low quality. To call a duke a rascal on the stage was far worse than to apply such an epithet to plain Hodge, almost as libellous as to represent a clergyman as a hypocrite. Collier made the curiously stupid error of accusing the playwrights of glorifying all the sins, passions, or peculiarities which they portrayed in their characters. He had no understanding of the point of view of the literary artist, nor any desire to understand it.

Collier's attack, unjust as it was, and foolish as certain phases of it appear today, yet it made an impression. The king, James II, was so wrought up over it that he issued a solemn proclamation"against vice and profaneness." Congreve and Vanbrugh, together with other writers, were persecuted, and fines were imposed on some of the most popular actors and actresses. Dryden, Congreve and Vanbrugh made an attempt at a justification of the stage, but it did little good. D'Urfey, Dennis, and others entered the controversy, which raged for many years. The public buzzed with the scandal set forth in The Short View, but did not stay away altogether from the playhouses. The poets answered the attack not by reformation, but by new plays in which the laughter, the satire, and the ridicule were turned upon their enemies.

Chapter 6

Complete Text

Dedication

To the Right Honourable, Thomas, Earl of Danby, Viscount Latimer, and Baron Osborne of Kiveton, in Yorkshire; Lord High Treasurer of England, one of His Majesty's Most Honourable Privy Council, and Knight of the Most Noble Order of the Garter.

My Lord,

The gratitude of poets is so troublesome a virtue to great men, that you are often in danger of your own benefits: for you are threatened with some epistle, and not suffered to do good in quiet, or to compound for their silence whom you have obliged. Yet, I confess, I neither am or ought to be surprised at this indulgence; for your lordship has the same right to favour poetry, which the great and noble have ever had-

Carmen amat, quisquis carmine digna gerit.

There is somewhat of a tie in nature betwixt those who are born for worthy actions, and those who can transmit them to posterity; and though ours be much the inferior part, it comes at least within the verge of alliance; nor are we unprofitable members of the commonwealth, when we animate others to those virtues, which we copy and describe from you.

It is indeed their interest, who endeavour the subversion of governments, to discourage poets and historians; for the best which can happen to them, is to be forgotten. But such who, under kings, are the fathers of their country, and by a just and prudent ordering of affairs preserve it, have the same reason to cherish the chroniclers of their actions, as they have to lay up in safety the deeds and evidences of their estates; for such records are their undoubted titles to the love and reverence of after ages. Your lordship's administration has already taken up a considerable part of the English annals; and many of its most happy years are owing to it. His Majesty, the most knowing judge of men, and the best master, has acknowledged the ease and benefit he receives in the incomes of his treasury, which you found not only disordered, but exhausted. All things were in the confusion of a chaos, without form or method, if not reduced beyond it, even to annihilation; so that you had not only to separate the jarring elements, but (if that boldness of expression might be allowed me) to create them. Your enemies had so embroiled the management of your office, that they looked on your advancement as the instrument of your ruin. And as if the clogging of the revenue, and the confusion of accounts, which you found in your entrance, were not sufficient, they added their own weight of malice to the public calamity, by forestalling the credit which should cure it. Your friends on the other side were only capable of pitying, but not of aiding you; no further help or counsel was remaining to you, but what was founded on yourself; and that indeed was your security; for your diligence, your constancy, and your prudence, wrought most surely within, when they were not disturbed by any outward motion. The highest virtue is best to be trusted with itself; for assistance only can be given by a genius superior to that which it assists; and it is the noblest kind of debt, when we are only obliged to God and nature.

This then, my lord, is your just commendation, and that you have wrought out yourself a way to glory, by those very means that were designed for your destruction: You have not only restored but advanced the revenues of your master, without grievance to the subject; and, as if that were little yet, the debts of the exchequer, which lay heaviest both on the crown, and on private persons, have by your conduct been established in a certainty of satisfaction. An action so much the more great and honourable, because the case was without the ordinary relief of laws; above the hopes of the afflicted and beyond the narrowness of the treasury to redress, had it been managed by a less able hand. It is certainly the happiest, and most unenvied part of all your fortune, to do good to many, while you do injury to none; to receive at once the prayers of the subject, and the praises of the prince; and, by the care of your conduct, to give him means of exerting the chiefest (if any be the chiefest) of his royal virtues, his distributive justice to the deserving, and his bounty and compassion to the wanting. The disposition of princes towards their people cannot be better discovered than in the choice of their ministers; who, like the animal spirits betwixt the soul and body, participate somewhat of both natures, and make the communication which is betwixt them.

A king, who is just and moderate in his nature, who rules according to the laws, whom God has made happy by forming the temper of his soul to the constitution of his government, and who makes us happy, by assuming over us no other sovereignty than that wherein our welfare and liberty consists; a prince, I say, of so excellent a character, and so suitable to the wishes of all good men, could not better have conveyed himself into his people's apprehensions, than in your lordship's person; who so lively express the same virtues, that you seem not so much a copy, as an emanation of him. Moderation is doubtless an establishment of greatness; but there is a steadiness of temper which is likewise requisite in a minister of state; so equal a mixture of both virtues, that he may stand like an isthmus betwixt the two encroaching seas of arbitrary power, and lawless anarchy.

The undertaking would be difficult to any but an extraordinary genius, to stand at the line, and to divide the limits; to pay what is due to the great representative of the nation, and neither to enhance, nor to yield up, the undoubted prerogatives of the crown. These, my lord, are the proper virtues of a noble Englishman, as indeed they are properly English virtues; no people in the world being capable of using them, but we who have the happiness to be born under so equal, and so well-poised a government;-a government which has all the advantages of liberty beyond a commonwealth, and all the marks of kingly sovereignty, without the danger of a tyranny. Both my nature, as I am an Englishman, and my reason, as I am a man, have bred in me a loathing to that specious name of a republic; that mock appearance of a liberty, where all who have not part in the government, are slaves; and slaves they are of a viler note, than such as are subjects to an absolute dominion. For no Christian monarchy is so absolute, but it is circumscribed with laws; but when the executive power is in the law-makers, there is no further check upon them; and the people must suffer without a remedy, because they are oppressed by their representatives. If I must serve, the number of my masters, who were born my equals, would but add to the ignominy of my bondage. The nature of our government, above all others, is exactly suited both to the situation of our country, and the temper of the natives; an island being more proper for commerce and for defence, than for extending its dominions on the Continent; for what the valour of its inhabitants might gain, by reason of its remoteness, and the casualties of the seas, it could not so easily preserve: And, therefore, neither the arbitrary power of One, in a monarchy, nor of Many, in a commonwealth, could make us greater than we are. It is true, that vaster and more frequent taxes might be gathered, when the consent of the people was not asked or needed; but this were only by conquering abroad, to be poor at home; and the examples of our neighbours teach us, that they are not always the happiest subjects, whose kings extend their dominions farthest.

Since therefore we cannot win by an offensive war, at least, a land war, the model of our government seems naturally contrived for the defensive part; and the consent of a people is easily obtained to contribute to that power which must protect it. Felices nimium, bona si sua norint, Angligenae! And yet there are not wanting malcontents among us, who, surfeiting themselves on too much happiness, would persuade the people that they might be happier by a change. It was indeed the policy of their old forefather, when himself was fallen from the station of glory, to seduce mankind into the same rebellion with him, by telling him he might yet be freer than he was; that is more free than his nature would allow, or, if I may so say, than God could make him. We have already all the liberty which freeborn subjects can enjoy, and all beyond it is but licence. But if it be liberty of conscience which they pretend, the moderation of our church is such, that its practice extends not to the severity of persecution; and its discipline is withal so easy, that it allows more freedom to dissenters than any of the sects would allow to it. In the meantime, what right can be pretended by these men to attempt innovation in church or state? Who made them the trustees, or to speak a little nearer their own language, the keepers of the liberty of England? If their call be extraordinary, let them convince us by working miracles; for ordinary vocation they can have none, to disturb the government under which they were born, and which protects them. He who has often changed his party, and always has made his interest the rule of it, gives little evidence of his sincerity for the public good; it is manifest he changes but for himself, and takes the people for tools to work his fortune. Yet the experience of all ages might let him know, that they who trouble the waters first, have seldom the benefit of the fishing; as they who began the late rebellion enjoyed not the fruit of their undertaking, but were crushed themselves by the usurpation of their own instrument. Neither is it enough for them to answer, that they only intend a reformation of the government, but not the subversion of it: on such pretence all insurrections have been founded; it is striking at the root of power, which is obedience.

Every remonstrance of private men has the seed of treason in it; and discourses, which are couched in ambiguous terms, are therefore the more dangerous, because they do all the mischief of open sedition, yet are safe from the punishment of the laws. These, my lord, are considerations, which I should not pass so lightly over, had I room to manage them as they deserve; for no man can be so inconsiderable in a nation, as not to have a share in the welfare of it; and if he be a true Englishman, he must at the same time be fired with indignation, and revenge himself as he can on the disturbers of his country. And to whom could I more fitly apply myself than to your lordship, who have not only an inborn, but an hereditary loyalty? The memorable constancy and sufferings of your father, almost to the ruin of his estate, for the royal cause, were an earnest of that which such a parent and such an institution would produce in the person of a son. But so unhappy an occasion of manifesting your own zeal, in suffering for his present majesty, the providence of God, and the prudence of your administration, will, I hope, prevent; that, as your father's fortune waited on the unhappiness of his sovereign, so your own may participate of the better fate which attends his son. The relation which you have by alliance to the noble family of your lady, serves to confirm to you both this happy augury. For what can deserve a greater place in the English chronicle, than the loyalty and courage, the actions and death, of the general of an army, fighting for his prince and country? The honour and gallantry of the Earl of Lindsey is so illustrious a subject, that it is fit to adorn an heroic poem; for he was the protomartyr of the cause, and the type of his unfortunate royal master.

Yet after all, my lord, if I may speak my thoughts, you are happy rather to us than to yourself; for the multiplicity, the cares, and the vexations of your employment, have betrayed you from yourself, and given you up into the possession of the public. You are robbed of your privacy and friends, and scarce any hour of your life you can call your own. Those, who envy your fortune, if they wanted not good-nature, might more justly pity it; and when they see you watched by a crowd of suitors, whose importunity it is impossible to avoid, would conclude, with reason, that you have lost much more in true content, than you have gained by dignity; and that a private gentleman is better attended by a single servant, than your lordship with so clamorous a train. Pardon me, my lord, if I speak like a philosopher on this subject; the fortune which makes a man uneasy, cannot make him happy; and a wise man must think himself uneasy, when few of his actions are in his choice.

This last consideration has brought me to another, and a very seasonable one for your relief; which is, that while I pity your want of leisure, I have impertinently detained you so long a time. I have put off my own business, which was my dedication, till it is so late, that I am now ashamed to begin it; and therefore I will say nothing of the poem, which I present to you, because I know not if you are like to have an hour, which, with a good conscience, you may throw away in perusing it; and for the author, I have only to beg the continuance of your protection to him.

Preface

The death of Antony and Cleopatra is a subject which has been treatedby the greatest wits of our nation, after Shakespeare; and by all sovariously, that their example has given me the confidence to trymyself in this bow of Ulysses amongst the crowd of suitors, and,withal, to take my own measures, in aiming at the mark. I doubt notbut the same motive has prevailed with all of us in this attempt;I mean the excellency of the moral: For the chief personsrepresented were famous patterns of unlawful love; and their endaccordingly was unfortunate. All reasonable men have long sinceconcluded, that the hero of the poem ought not to be a character ofperfect virtue, for then he could not, without injustice, be madeunhappy; nor yet altogether wicked, because he could not then bepitied. I have therefore steered the middle course; and have drawnthe character of Antony as favourably as Plutarch, Appian, and DionCassius would give me leave; the like I have observed in Cleopatra.That which is wanting to work up the pity to a greater height, wasnot afforded me by the story; for the crimes of love, which they bothcommitted, were not occasioned by any necessity, or fatal ignorance,but were wholly voluntary; since our passions are, or ought to be,within our power.

The fabric of the play is regular enough, as tothe inferior parts of it; and the unities of time, place, and action,more exactly observed, than perhaps the English theatre requires.Particularly, the action is so much one, that it is the only one ofthe kind without episode, or underplot; every scene in the tragedyconducing to the main design, and every act concluding with a turnof it. The greatest error in the contrivance seems to be in theperson of Octavia; for, though I might use the privilege of a poet,to introduce her into Alexandria, yet I had not enough considered,that the compassion she moved to herself and children was destructiveto that which I reserved for Antony and Cleopatra; whose mutual lovebeing founded upon vice, must lessen the favour of the audience tothem, when virtue and innocence were oppressed by it. And, thoughI justified Antony in some measure, by making Octavia's departure toproceed wholly from herself; yet the force of the first machine stillremained; and the dividing of pity, like the cutting of a river intomany channels, abated the strength of the natural stream. But thisis an objection which none of my critics have urged against me; andtherefore I might have let it pass, if I could have resolved to havebeen partial to myself. The faults my enemies have found are rathercavils concerning little and not essential decencies; which a masterof the ceremonies may decide betwixt us. The French poets,I confess, are strict observers of these punctilios:

They would not,for example, have suffered Cleopatra and Octavia to have met; or,if they had met, there must have only passed betwixt them some coldcivilities, but no eagerness of repartee, for fear of offendingagainst the greatness of their characters, and the modesty of theirsex. This objection I foresaw, and at the same time contemned; forI judged it both natural and probable, that Octavia, proud of hernew-gained conquest, would search out Cleopatra to triumph over her;and that Cleopatra, thus attacked, was not of a spirit to shun theencounter: And it is not unlikely, that two exasperated rivalsshould use such satire as I have put into their mouths; for, afterall, though the one were a Roman, and the other a queen, they wereboth women. It is true, some actions, though natural, are not fit tobe represented; and broad obscenities in words ought in good mannersto be avoided: expressions therefore are a modest clothing of ourthoughts, as breeches and petticoats are of our bodies. If I havekept myself within the bounds of modesty, all beyond, it is butnicety and affectation; which is no more but modesty depraved intoa vice. They betray themselves who are too quick of apprehension in such cases, and leave all reasonable men to imagine worse of them, than of the poet. Honest Montaigne goes yet further: Nous ne sommes que ceremonie;la ceremonie nous emporte, et laissons la substance des choses. Nousnous tenons aux branches, et abandonnons le tronc et le corps. Nousavons appris aux dames de rougir, oyans seulement nommer ce qu'ellesne craignent aucunement a faire: Nous n'osons appeller a droit nosmembres, et ne craignons pas de les employer a toute sorte dedebauche. La ceremonie nous defend d'exprimer par paroles les choseslicites et naturelles, et nous l'en croyons; la raison nous defend den'en faire point d'illicites et mauvaises, et personne ne l'en croit.My comfort is, that by this opinion my enemies are but suckingcritics, who would fain be nibbling ere their teeth are come.Yet, in this nicety of manners does the excellency of French poetryconsist.

Their heroes are the most civil people breathing; but theirgood breeding seldom extends to a word of sense; all their wit is intheir ceremony; they want the genius which animates our stage; andtherefore it is but necessary, when they cannot please, that theyshould take care not to offend. But as the civilest man in thecompany is commonly the dullest, so these authors, while they areafraid to make you laugh or cry, out of pure good manners make yousleep. They are so careful not to exasperate a critic, that theynever leave him any work; so busy with the broom, and make so cleana riddance that there is little left either for censure or forpraise: For no part of a poem is worth our discommending, where thewhole is insipid; as when we have once tasted of palled wine, we staynot to examine it glass by glass. But while they affect to shine intrifles, they are often careless in essentials. Thus, theirHippolytus is so scrupulous in point of decency, that he will ratherexpose himself to death, than accuse his stepmother to his father;and my critics I am sure will commend him for it. But we of grosserapprehensions are apt to think that this excess of generosity is notpracticable, but with fools and madmen.

This was good manners witha vengeance; and the

audience is like to be much concerned at themisfortunes of this admirable hero. But take Hippolytus out of hispoetic fit, and I suppose he would think it a wiser part to set thesaddle on the right horse, and choose rather to live with thereputation of a plain-spoken, honest man, than to die with the infamyof an incestuous villain. In the meantime we may take notice, thatwhere the poet ought to have preserved the character as it wasdelivered to us by antiquity, when he should have given us thepicture of a rough young man, of the Amazonian strain, a jollyhuntsman, and both by his profession and his early rising a mortalenemy to love, he has chosen to give him the turn of gallantry, senthim to travel from Athens to Paris, taught him to make love, andtransformed the Hippolytus of Euripides into Monsieur Hippolyte.I should not have troubled myself thus far with French poets, butthat I find our Chedreux critics wholly form their judgments by them.But for my part, I desire to be tried by the laws of my own country;for it seems unjust to me, that the French should prescribe here,till they have conquered. Our little sonneteers, who follow them,have too narrow souls to judge of poetry. Poets themselves are themost proper, though I conclude not the only critics.

But till somegenius, as universal as Aristotle, shall arise, one who can penetrateinto all arts and sciences, without the practice of them, I shallthink it reasonable, that the judgment of an artificer in his own artshould be preferable to the opinion of another man; at least where heis not bribed by interest, or prejudiced by malice. And this,I suppose, is manifest by plain inductions: For, first, the crowdcannot be presumed to have more than a gross instinct of what pleasesor displeases them: Every man will grant me this; but then, by aparticular kindness to himself, he draws his own stake first, andwill be distinguished from the multitude, of which other men maythink him one. But, if I come closer to those who are allowed forwitty men, either by the advantage of their quality, or by commonfame, and affirm that neither are they qualified to decidesovereignly concerning poetry, I shall yet have a strong party of myopinion; for most of them severally will exclude the rest, eitherfrom the number of witty men, or at least of able judges. But hereagain they are all indulgent to themselves; and every one whobelieves himself a wit, that is, every man, will pretend at the sametime to a right of judging. But to press it yet further, there aremany witty men, but few poets; neither have all poets a taste oftragedy. And this is the rock on which they are daily splitting.Poetry, which is a picture of nature, must generally please; but itis not to be understood that all parts of it must please every man;therefore is not tragedy to be judged by a witty man, whose taste isonly confined to comedy. Nor is every man, who loves tragedy, asufficient judge of it; he must understand the excellences of it too,or he will only prove a blind admirer, not a critic. From hence itcomes that so many satires on poets, and censures of their writings,fly abroad.

Men of pleasant conversation (at least esteemed so),and endued with a trifling kind of fancy, perhaps helped out withsome smattering of Latin, are ambitious to distinguish themselvesfrom the herd of gentlemen, by their poetry--Rarus enim ferme sensus communis in illa Fortuna.And is not this a wretched affectation, not to be contented with whatfortune has done for them, and sit down quietly with their estates,but they must call their wits in question, and needlessly exposetheir nakedness to public view? Not considering that they are not toexpect the same approbation from sobre men, which they have foundfrom their flatterers after the third bottle.

If a little glitteringin discourse has passed them on us for witty men, where was thenecessity of undeceiving the world? Would a man who has an ill titleto an estate, but yet is in possession of it; would he bring it ofhis own accord, to be tried at Westminster? We who write, if we wantthe talent, yet have the excuse that we do it for a poor subsistence;but what can be urged in their defence, who, not having the vocationof poverty to scribble, out of mere wantonness take pains to makethemselves ridiculous? Horace was certainly in the right, where hesaid,"That no man is satisfied with his own condition." A poet isnot pleased, because he is not rich; and the rich are discontented,because the poets will not admit them of their number. Thus the caseis hard with writers: If they succeed not, they must starve; and ifthey do, some malicious satire is prepared to level them, for daringto please without their leave. But while they are so eager todestroy the fame of others, their ambition is manifest in theirconcernment; some poem of their own is to be produced, and the slavesare to be laid flat with their faces on the ground, that the monarchmay appear in the greater majesty.Dionysius and Nero had the same longings, but with all their powerthey could never bring their business well about.'Tis true, theyproclaimed themselves poets by sound of trumpet; and poets they were,upon pain of death to any man who durst call them otherwise. Theaudience had a fine time on't, you may imagine; they sat in a bodilyfear, and looked as demurely as they could: for it was a hangingmatter to laugh unseasonably; and the tyrants were suspicious, asthey had reason, that their subjects had them in the wind; so, everyman, in his own defence, set as good a face upon the business as hecould.

It was known beforehand that the monarchs were to be crownedlaureates; but when the show was over, and an honest man was sufferedto depart quietly, he took out his laughter which he had stifled,with a firm resolution never more to see an emperor's play, though hehad been ten years a-making it. In the meantime the true poets werethey who made the best markets: for they had wit enough to yield theprize with a good grace, and not contend with him who had thirtylegions. They were sure to be rewarded, if they confessed themselvesbad writers, and that was somewhat better than to be martyrs fortheir reputation. Lucan's example was enough to teach them manners;and after he was put to death, for overcoming Nero, the emperorcarried it without dispute for the best poet in his dominions.No man was ambitious of that grinning honour; for if he heard themalicious trumpeter proclaiming his name before his betters, he knewthere was but one way with him. Maecenas took another course, and weknow he was more than a great man, for he was witty too: But findinghimself far gone in poetry, which Seneca assures us was not histalent, he thought it his best way to be well with Virgil and withHorace; that at least he might be a poet at the second hand; and wesee how happily it has succeeded with him; for his own bad poetry isforgotten, and their panegyrics of him still remain. But they whoshould be our patrons are for no such expensive ways to fame; theyhave much of the poetry of Maecenas, but little of his liberality.They are for prosecuting Horace and Virgil, in the persons of theirsuccessors; for such is every man who has any part of their soul andfire, though in a less degree. Some of their little zanies yet gofurther; for they are persecutors even of Horace himself, as far asthey are able, by their ignorant and vile imitations of him; bymaking an unjust use of his authority, and turning his artilleryagainst his friends.

But how would he disdain to be copied by suchhands! I dare answer for him, he would be more uneasy in theircompany, than he was with Crispinus, their forefather, in the HolyWay; and would no more have allowed them a place amongst the critics,than he would Demetrius the mimic, and Tigellius the buffoon;

Demetri, teque, Tigelli,Discipulorum inter jubeo plorare cathedras.With what scorn would he look down on such miserable translators,who make doggerel of his Latin, mistake his meaning, misapply hiscensures, and often contradict their own? He is fixed as a landmarkto set out the bounds of poetry

Saxum antiquum, ingens,--Limes agro positus, litem ut discerneret arvis.But other arms than theirs, and other sinews are required, to raisethe weight of such an author; and when they would toss him againstenemies--Genua labant, gelidus concrevit frigore sanguis.Tum lapis ipse viri, vacuum per inane volatus,Nec spatium evasit totum, nec pertulit ictum.For my part, I would wish no other revenge, either for myself,or the rest of the poets, from this rhyming judge of the twelve-pennygallery, this legitimate son of Sternhold, than that he wouldsubscribe his name to his censure, or (not to tax him beyond hislearning) set his mark: For, should he own himself publicly, andcome from behind the lion's skin, they whom he condemns would bethankful to him, they whom he praises would choose to be condemned;and the magistrates, whom he has elected, would modestly withdrawfrom their employment, to avoid the scandal of his nomination.The sharpness of his satire, next to himself, falls most heavily on his friends, and they ought never to forgive him for commending them perpetually the wrong way, and sometimes by contraries. If he have a friend, whose hastiness in writing is his greatest fault, Horace would have taught him to have minced the matter, and to have called it readiness of thought, and a flowing fancy; for friendship will allow a man to christen an imperfection by the name of some neighbour virtue--Vellem in amicitia sic erraremus; et isti Errori nomen virtus posuisset honestum. But he would never allowed him to have called a slow man hasty, or a hasty writer a slow drudge, as Juvenal explains it--

Canibus pigris, scabieque vestusta
Laevibus, et siccae lambentibus ora lucernae,
Nomen erit, Pardus, Tigris, Leo; si quid adhuc est
Quod fremit in terris violentius.

Yet Lucretius laughs at a foolish lover, even for excusing the imperfections of his mistress--

Nigra melichroos est, immunda et foetida <akosmos>
Balba loqui non quit, traylizei; muta pudens est, etc.

But to drive it ad Aethiopem cygnum is not to be endured. I leave him to interpret this by the benefit of his French version on the other side, and without further considering him, than I have the rest of my illiterate censors, whom I have disdained to answer, because they are not qualified for judges. It remains that I acquiant the reader, that I have endeavoured in this play to follow the practice of the ancients, who, as Mr. Rymer has judiciously observed, are and ought to be our masters. Horace likewise gives it for a rule in his art of poetry--

Vos exemplaria Graeca Nocturna versate manu, versate diurna. Yet, though their models are regular, they are too little for English tragedy; which requires to be built in a larger compass. I could give an instance in the Oedipus Tyrannus, which was the masterpiece of Sophocles; but I reserve it for a more fit occasion, which I hope to have hereafter. In my style, I have professed to imitate the divine Shakespeare; which that I might perform more freely, I have disencumbered myself from rhyme. Not that I condemn my former way, but that this is more proper to my present purpose. I hope I need not to explain myself, that I have not copied my author servilely: Words and phrases must of necessity receive a change in succeeding ages; but it is almost a miracle that much of his language remains so pure; and that he who began dramatic poetry amongst us, untaught by any, and as Ben Jonson tells us, without learning, should by the force of his own genius perform so much, that in a manner he has left no praise for any who come after him. The occasion is fair, and the subject would be pleasant to handle the difference of styles betwixt him and Fletcher, and wherein, and how far they are both to be imitated. But since I must not be over-confident of my own performance after him, it will be prudence in me to be silent. Yet, I hope, I may affirm, and without vanity, that, by imitating him, I have excelled myself throughout the play; and particularly, that I prefer the scene betwixt Antony and Ventidius in the first act, to anything which I have written in this kind.

PROLOGUE

What flocks of critics hover here to-day,
As vultures wait on armies for their prey,
All gaping for the carcase of a play!
With croaking notes they bode some dire event,
And follow dying poets by the scent.
Ours gives himself for gone; y'have watched your time:
He fights this day unarmed,--without his rhyme;--
And brings a tale which often has been told;
As sad as Dido's; and almost as old.
His hero, whom you wits his bully call,
Bates of his mettle, and scarce rants at all;
He's somewhat lewd; but a well-meaning mind;
Weeps much; fights little; but is wond'rous kind.
In short, a pattern, and companion fit,
For all the keeping Tonies of the pit.
I could name more: a wife, and mistress too;
Both (to be plain) too good for most of you:
The wife well-natured, and the mistress true.
Now, poets, if your fame has been his care,

Allow him all the candour you can spare.
A brave man scorns to quarrel once a day;
Like Hectors in at every petty fray.
Let those find fault whose wit's so very small,
They've need to show that they can think at all;
Errors, like straws, upon the surface flow;
He who would search for pearls, must dive below.
Fops may have leave to level all they can;
As pigmies would be glad to lop a man.
Half-wits are fleas; so little and so light,
We scarce could know they live, but that they bite.
But, as the rich, when tired with daily feasts,
For change, become their next poor tenant's guests;
Drink hearty draughts of ale from plain brown bowls,
And snatch the homely rasher from the coals:
So you, retiring from much better cheer,
For once, may venture to do penance here.
And since that plenteous autumn now is past,
Whose grapes and peaches have indulged your taste,
Take in good part, from our poor poet's board,
Such rivelled fruits as winter can afford.

ALL FOR LOVE

or

THE WORLD WELL LOST

A TRAGEDY

DRAMATIS PERSONAE

MARK ANTONY.
VENTIDIUS, his General.
DOLABELLA, his Friend.
ALEXAS, the Queen's Eunuch.
SERAPION, Priest of Isis.
MYRIS, another Priest.
Servants to Antony.
CLEOPATRA, Queen of Egypt.
OCTAVIA, Antony's Wife.
CHARMION, Cleopatra's Maid.
IRAS, Cleopatra's Maid.
Antony's two little Daughters.

SCENE.--Alexandria.
Act I
Scene I.--The Temple of Isis
Enter SERAPION, MYRIS, Priests of Isis
SERAPION. Portents and prodigies have grown so frequent,
That they have lost their name. Our fruitful Nile
Flowed ere the wonted season, with a torrent
So unexpected, and so wondrous fierce,
That the wild deluge overtook the haste
Even of the hinds that watched it: Men and beasts
Were borne above the tops of trees, that grew
On the utmost margin of the water-mark.
Then, with so swift an ebb the flood drove backward,
It slipt from underneath the scaly herd:
Here monstrous phocae panted on the shore;
Forsaken dolphins there with their broad tails,
Lay lashing the departing waves: hard by them,
Sea horses floundering in the slimy mud,
Tossed up their heads, and dashed the ooze about them.
Enter ALEXAS behind them
MYRIS. Avert these omens, Heaven!
SERAPION. Last night, between the hours of twelve and one,
In a lone aisle of the temple while I walked,
A whirlwind rose, that, with a violent blast,
Shook all the dome: the doors around me clapt;
The iron wicket, that defends the vault,
Where the long race of Ptolemies is laid,
Burst open, and disclosed the mighty dead.
>From out each monument, in order placed,
An armed ghost starts up: the boy-king last
Reared his inglorious head. A peal of groans
Then followed, and a lamentable voice
Cried, Egypt is no more! My blood ran back,
My shaking knees against each other knocked;
On the cold pavement down I fell entranced,
And so unfinished left the horrid scene.

ALEXAS. And dreamed you this? or did invent the story,
[Showing himself.]
To frighten our Egyptian boys withal,
And train them up, betimes, in fear of priesthood?
SERAPION. My lord, I saw you not,
Nor meant my words should reach you ears; but what
I uttered was most true.
ALEXAS. A foolish dream,
Bred from the fumes of indigested feasts,
And holy luxury.
SERAPION. I know my duty:
This goes no further.
ALEXAS.'Tis not fit it should;
Nor would the times now bear it, were it true.
All southern, from yon hills, the Roman camp
Hangs o'er us black and threatening like a storm
Just breaking on our heads.
SERAPION. Our faint Egyptians pray for Antony;
But in their servile hearts they own Octavius.
MYRIS. Why then does Antony dream out his hours,
And tempts not fortune for a noble day,
Which might redeem what Actium lost?
ALEXAS. He thinks'tis past recovery.
SERAPION. Yet the foe
Seems not to press the siege.
ALEXAS. Oh, there's the wonder.
Maecenas and Agrippa, who can most
With Caesar, are his foes. His wife Octavia,
Driven from his house, solicits her revenge;
And Dolabella, who was once his friend,
Upon some private grudge, now seeks his ruin:
Yet still war seems on either side to sleep.
SERAPION.'Tis strange that Antony, for some days past,
Has not beheld the face of Cleopatra;
But here, in Isis'temple, lives retired,
And makes his heart a prey to black despair.
ALEXAS.'Tis true; and we much fear he hopes by absence
To cure his mind of love.

SERAPION. If he be vanquished,
Or make his peace, Egypt is doomed to be
A Roman province; and our plenteous harvests
Must then redeem the scarceness of their soil.
While Antony stood firm, our Alexandria
Rivalled proud Rome (dominion's other seat),
And fortune striding, like a vast Colossus,
Could fix an equal foot of empire here.
ALEXAS. Had I my wish, these tyrants of all nature,
Who lord it o'er mankind, rhould perish,--perish,
Each by the other's sword; But, since our will
Is lamely followed by our power, we must
Depend on one; with him to rise or fall.
SERAPION. How stands the queen affected?
ALEXAS. Oh, she dotes,
She dotes, Serapion, on this vanquished man,
And winds herself about his mighty ruins;
Whom would she yet forsake, yet yield him up,
This hunted prey, to his pursuer's hands,
She might preserve us all: but'tis in vain--
This changes my designs, this blasts my counsels,
And makes me use all means to keep him here.
Whom I could wish divided from her arms,
Far as the earth's deep centre. Well, you know
The state of things; no more of your ill omens
And black prognostics; labour to confirm
The people's hearts.
Enter VENTIDIUS, talking aside with a Gentleman of ANTONY'S
SERAPION. These Romans will o'erhear us.
But who's that stranger? By his warlike port,
His fierce demeanour, and erected look,
He's of no vulgar note.
ALEXAS. Oh,'tis Ventidius,
Our emperor's great lieutenant in the East,
Who first showed Rome that Parthia could be conquered.
When Antony returned from Syria last,
He left this man to guard the Roman frontiers.

SERAPION. You seem to know him well.
ALEXAS. Too well. I saw him at Cilicia first,
When Cleopatra there met Antony:
A mortal foe was to us, and Egypt.
But,--let me witness to the worth I hate,--
A braver Roman never drew a sword;
Firm to his prince, but as a friend, not slave,
He ne'er was of his pleasures; but presides
O'er all his cooler hours, and morning counsels:
In short the plainness, fierceness, rugged virtue,
Of an old true-stampt Roman lives in him.
His coming bodes I know not what of ill
To our affairs. Withdraw to mark him better;
And I'll acquaint you why I sought you here,
And what's our present work.
[They withdraw to a corner of the stage; and VENTIDIUS, with the other, comes forward to the front.]
VENTIDIUS. Not see him; say you?
I say, I must, and will.
GENTLEMAN. He has commanded,
On pain of death, none should approach his presence.
VENTIDIUS. I bring him news will raise his drooping spirits,
Give him new life.
GENTLEMAN. He sees not Cleopatra.
VENTIDIUS. Would he had never seen her!
GENTLEMAN. He eats not, drinks not, sleeps not, has no use
Of anything, but thought; or if he talks,
'Tis to himself, and then'tis perfect raving:
Then he defies the world, and bids it pass,
Sometimes he gnaws his lips, and curses loud
The boy Octavius; then he draws his mouth
Into a scornful smile, and cries,"Take all,
The world's not worth my care."
VENTIDIUS. Just, just his nature.
Virtue's his path; but sometimes'tis too narrow
For his vast soul; and then he starts out wide,

And bounds into a vice, that bears him far
>From his first course, and plunges him in ills:
But, when his danger makes him find his faults,
Quick to observe, and full of sharp remorse,
He censures eagerly his own misdeeds,
Judging himself with malice to himself,
And not forgiving what as man he did,
Because his other parts are more than man.--
He must not thus be lost.
[ALEXAS and the Priests come forward.]
ALEXAS. You have your full instructions, now advance,
Proclaim your orders loudly.
SERAPION. Romans, Egyptians, hear the queen's command.
Thus Cleopatra bids: Let labour cease;
To pomp and triumphs give this happy day,
That gave the world a lord:'tis Antony's.
Live, Antony; and Cleopatra live!
Be this the general voice sent up to heaven,
And every public place repeat this echo.
VENTIDIUS. Fine pageantry!
[Aside.]
SERAPION. Set out before your doors
The images of all your sleeping fathers,
With laurels crowned; with laurels wreath your posts,
And strew with flowers the pavement; let the priests
Do present sacrifice; pour out the wine,
And call the gods to join with you in gladness.
VENTIDIUS. Curse on the tongue that bids this general joy!
Can they be friends of Antony, who revel
When Antony's in danger? Hide, for shame,
You Romans, your great grandsires'images,
For fear their souls should animate their marbles,
To blush at their degenerate progeny.
ALEXAS. A love, which knows no bounds, to Antony,
Would mark the day with honours, when all heaven
Laboured for him, when each propitious star

Stood wakeful in his orb, to watch that hour
And shed his better influence. Her own birthday
Our queen neglected like a vulgar fate,
That passed obscurely by.
VENTIDIUS. Would it had slept,
Divided far from his; till some remote
And future age had called it out, to ruin
Some other prince, not him!
ALEXAS. Your emperor,
Though grown unkind, would be more gentle, than
To upbraid my queen for loving him too well.
VENTIDIUS. Does the mute sacrifice upbraid the priest!
He knows him not his executioner.
Oh, she has decked his ruin with her love,
Led him in golden bands to gaudy slaughter,
And made perdition pleasing: She has left him
The blank of what he was.
I tell thee, eunuch, she has quite unmanned him.
Can any Roman see, and know him now,
Thus altered from the lord of half mankind,
Unbent, unsinewed, made a woman's toy,
Shrunk from the vast extent of all his honours,
And crampt within a corner of the world?
O Antony!
Thou bravest soldier, and thou best of friends!
Bounteous as nature; next to nature's God!
Couldst thou but make new worlds, so wouldst thou give them,
As bounty were thy being! rough in battle,
As the first Romans when they went to war;
Yet after victory more pitiful
Than all their praying virgins left at home!
ALEXAS. Would you could add, to those more shining virtues,
His truth to her who loves him.
VENTIDIUS. Would I could not!
But wherefore waste I precious hours with thee!
Thou art her darling mischief, her chief engine,

Antony's other fate. Go, tell thy queen,
Ventidius is arrived, to end her charms.
Let your Egyptian timbrels play alone,
Nor mix effeminate sounds with Roman trumpets,
You dare not fight for Antony; go pray
And keep your cowards'holiday in temples.
[Exeunt ALEXAS, SERAPION.]
Re-enter the Gentleman of M. ANTONY
2 Gent. The emperor approaches, and commands,
On pain of death, that none presume to stay.
1 Gent. I dare not disobey him.
[Going out with the other.]
VENTIDIUS. Well, I dare.
But I'll observe him first unseen, and find
Which way his humour drives: The rest I'll venture.
[Withdraws.]
Enter ANTONY, walking with a disturbed motion before he speaks
ANTONY. They tell me,'tis my birthday, and I'll keep it
With double pomp of sadness.
'Tis what the day deserves, which gave me breath.
Why was I raised the meteor of the world,
Hung in the skies, and blazing as I travelled,
'Till all my fires were spent; and then cast downward,
To be trod out by Caesar?
VENTIDIUS. [aside.] On my soul,
'Tis mournful, wondrous mournful!
ANTONY. Count thy gains.
Now, Antony, wouldst thou be born for this?
Glutton of fortune, thy devouring youth
Has starved thy wanting age.
VENTIDIUS. How sorrow shakes him!
[Aside.]
So, now the tempest tears him up by the roots,
And on the ground extends the noble ruin.
[ANTONY having thrown himself down.]
Lie there, thou shadow of an emperor;
The place thou pressest on thy mother earth

Is all thy empire now: now it contains thee;
Some few days hence, and then'twill be too large,
When thou'rt contracted in thy narrow urn,
Shrunk to a few ashes; then Octavia
(For Cleopatra will not live to see it),
Octavia then will have thee all her own,
And bear thee in her widowed hand to Caesar;
Caesar will weep, the crocodile will weep,
To see his rival of the universe
Lie still and peaceful there. I'll think no more on't.
ANTONY. Give me some music, look that it be sad.
I'll soothe my melancholy, till I swell,
And burst myself with sighing.--
[Soft music.]
'Tis somewhat to my humour; stay, I fancy
I'm now turned wild, a commoner of nature;
Of all forsaken, and forsaking all;
Live in a shady forest's sylvan scene,
Stretched at my length beneath some blasted oak,
I lean my head upon the mossy bark,
And look just of a piece as I grew from it;
My uncombed locks, matted like mistletoe,
Hang o'er my hoary face; a murm'ring brook
Runs at my foot.
VENTIDIUS. Methinks I fancy
Myself there too.
ANTONY. The herd come jumping by me,
And fearless, quench their thirst, while I look on,
And take me for their fellow-citizen.
More of this image, more; it lulls my thoughts.
[Soft music again.]
VENTIDIUS. I must disturb him; I can hold no longer.
[Stands before him.]
ANTONY. [starting up]. Art thou Ventidius?
VENTIDIUS. Are you Antony?
I'm liker what I was, than you to him
I left you last.
ANTONY. I'm angry.

VENTIDIUS. So am I.
ANTONY. I would be private: leave me.
VENTIDIUS. Sir, I love you,
And therefore will not leave you.
ANTONY. Will not leave me!
Where have you learnt that answer? Who am I?
VENTIDIUS. My emperor; the man I love next Heaven:
If I said more, I think'twere scare a sin:
You're all that's good, and god-like.
ANTONY. All that's wretched.
You will not leave me then?
VENTIDIUS.'Twas too presuming
To say I would not; but I dare not leave you:
And,'tis unkind in you to chide me hence
So soon, when I so far have come to see you.
ANTONY. Now thou hast seen me, art thou satisfied?
For, if a friend, thou hast beheld enough;
And, if a foe, too much.
VENTIDIUS. Look, emperor, this is no common dew.
[Weeping.]
I have not wept this forty years; but now
My mother comes afresh into my eyes;
I cannot help her softness.
ANTONY. By heavens, he weeps! poor good old man, he weeps!
The big round drops course one another down
The furrows of his cheeks.--Stop them, Ventidius,
Or I shall blush to death, they set my shame,
That caused them, full before me.
VENTIDIUS. I'll do my best.
ANTONY. Sure there's contagion in the tears of friends:
See, I have caught it too. Believe me,'tis not
For my own griefs, but thine.--Nay, father!
VENTIDIUS. Emperor.
ANTONY. Emperor! Why, that's the style of victory;
The conqu'ring soldier, red with unfelt wounds,
Salutes his general so; but never more
Shall that sound reach my ears.

VENTIDIUS. I warrant you.
ANTONY. Actium, Actium! Oh!--
VENTIDIUS. It sits too near you.
ANTONY. Here, here it lies a lump of lead by day,
And, in my short, distracted, nightly slumbers,
The hag that rides my dreams.--
VENTIDIUS. Out with it; give it vent.
ANTONY. Urge not my shame.
I lost a battle,--
VENTIDIUS. So has Julius done.
ANTONY. Thou favour'st me, and speak'st not half thou think'st;
For Julius fought it out, and lost it fairly.
But Antony--
VENTIDIUS. Nay, stop not.
ANTONY. Antony--
Well, thou wilt have it,--like a coward, fled,
Fled while his soldiers fought; fled first, Ventidius.
Thou long'st to curse me, and I give thee leave.
I know thou cam'st prepared to rail.
VENTIDIUS. I did.
ANTONY. I'll help thee.--I have been a man, Ventidius.
VENTIDIUS. Yes, and a brave one! but--
ANTONY. I know thy meaning.
But I have lost my reason, have disgraced
The name of soldier, with inglorious ease.
In the full vintage of my flowing honours,
Sat still, and saw it prest by other hands.
Fortune came smiling to my youth, and wooed it,
And purple greatness met my ripened years.
When first I came to empire, I was borne
On tides of people, crowding to my triumphs;
The wish of nations, and the willing world
Received me as its pledge of future peace;
I was so great, so happy, so beloved,
Fate could not ruin me; till I took pains,
And worked against my fortune, child her from me,
And returned her loose; yet still she came again.

My careless days, and my luxurious nights,
At length have wearied her, and now she's gone,
Gone, gone, divorced for ever. Help me, soldier,
To curse this madman, this industrious fool,
Who laboured to be wretched: Pr'ythee, curse me.
VENTIDIUS. No.
ANTONY. Why?
VENTIDIUS. You are too sensible already
Of what you've done, too conscious of your failings;
And, like a scorpion, whipt by others first
To fury, sting yourself in mad revenge.
I would bring balm, and pour it in your wounds,
Cure your distempered mind, and heal your fortunes.
ANTONY. I know thou would'st.
VENTIDIUS. I will.
ANTONY. Ha, ha, ha, ha!
VENTIDIUS. You laugh.
ANTONY. I do, to see officious love.
Give cordials to the dead.
VENTIDIUS. You would be lost, then?
ANTONY. I am.
VENTIDIUS. I say you are not. Try your fortune.
ANTONY. I have, to the utmost. Dost thou think me desperate,
Without just cause? No, when I found all lost
Beyond repair, I hid me from the world,
And learnt to scorn it here; which now I do
So heartily, I think it is not worth
The cost of keeping.
VENTIDIUS. Caesar thinks not so;
He'll thank you for the gift he could not take.
You would be killed like Tully, would you? do,
Hold out your throat to Caesar, and die tamely.
ANTONY. No, I can kill myself; and so resolve.
VENTIDIUS. I can die with you too, when time shall serve;
But fortune calls upon us now to live,
To fight, to conquer.
ANTONY. Sure thou dream'st, Ventidius.

VENTIDIUS. No;'tis you dream; you sleep away your hours
In desperate sloth, miscalled philosophy.
Up, up, for honour's sake; twelve legions wait you,
And long to call you chief: By painful journeys
I led them, patient both of heat and hunger,
Down form the Parthian marches to the Nile.
'Twill do you good to see their sunburnt faces,
Their scarred cheeks, and chopt hands: there's virtue in them.
They'll sell those mangled limbs at dearer rates
Than yon trim bands can buy.
ANTONY. Where left you them?
VENTIDIUS. I said in Lower Syria.
ANTONY. Bring them hither;
There may be life in these.
VENTIDIUS. They will not come.
ANTONY. Why didst thou mock my hopes with promised aids,
To double my despair? They're mutinous.
VENTIDIUS. Most firm and loyal.
ANTONY. Yet they will not march
To succour me. O trifler!
VENTIDIUS. They petition
You would make haste to head them.
ANTONY. I'm besieged.
VENTIDIUS. There's but one way shut up: How came I hither?
ANTONY. I will not stir.
VENTIDIUS. They would perhaps desire
A better reason.
ANTONY. I have never used
My soldiers to demand a reason of
My actions. Why did they refuse to march?
VENTIDIUS. They said they would not fight for Cleopatra.
ANTONY. What was't they said?
VENTIDIUS. They said they would not fight for

Cleopatra.
Why should they fight indeed, to make her conquer,
And make you more a slave? to gain you kingdoms,
Which, for a kiss, at your next midnight feast,
You'll sell to her? Then she new-names her jewels,
And calls this diamond such or such a tax;
Each pendant in her ear shall be a province.
ANTONY. Ventidius, I allow your tongue free licence
On all my other faults; but, on your life,
No word of Cleopatra: she deserves
More worlds than I can lose.
VENTIDIUS. Behold, you Powers,
To whom you have intrusted humankind!
See Europe, Afric, Asia, put in balance,
And all weighed down by one light, worthless woman!
I think the gods are Antonies, and give,
Like prodigals, this nether world away
To none but wasteful hands.
ANTONY. You grow presumptuous.
VENTIDIUS. I take the privilege of plain love to speak.
ANTONY. Plain love! plain arrogance, plain insolence!
Thy men are cowards; thou, an envious traitor;
Who, under seeming honesty, hast vented
The burden of thy rank, o'erflowing gall.
O that thou wert my equal; great in arms
As the first Caesar was, that I might kill thee
Without a stain to honour!
VENTIDIUS. You may kill me;
You have done more already,--called me traitor.
ANTONY. Art thou not one?
VENTIDIUS. For showing you yourself,
Which none else durst have done? but had I been
That name, which I disdain to speak again,
I needed not have sought your abject fortunes,
Come to partake your fate, to die with you.
What hindered me to have led my conquering eagles
To fill Octavius'bands? I could have been
A traitor then, a glorious, happy traitor,

And not have been so called.
ANTONY. Forgive me, soldier;
I've been too passionate.
VENTIDIUS. You thought me false;
Thought my old age betrayed you: Kill me, sir,
Pray, kill me; yet you need not, your unkindness
Has left your sword no work.
ANTONY. I did not think so;
I said it in my rage: Pr'ythee, forgive me.
Why didst thou tempt my anger, by discovery
Of what I would not hear?
VENTIDIUS. No prince but you
Could merit that sincerity I used,
Nor durst another man have ventured it;
But you, ere love misled your wandering eyes,
Were sure the chief and best of human race,
Framed in the very pride and boast of nature;
So perfect, that the gods, who formed you, wondered
At their own skill, and cried--A lucky hit
Has mended our design. Their envy hindered,
Else you had been immortal, and a pattern,
When Heaven would work for ostentation's sake
To copy out again.
ANTONY. But Cleopatra--
Go on; for I can bear it now.
VENTIDIUS. No more.
ANTONY. Thou dar'st not trust my passion, but thou may'st;
Thou only lov'st, the rest have flattered me.
VENTIDIUS. Heaven's blessing on your heart for that kind word!
May I believe you love me? Speak again.
ANTONY. Indeed I do. Speak this, and this, and this. [Hugging him.]
Thy praises were unjust; but, I'll deserve them,
And yet mend all. Do with me what thou wilt;
Lead me to victory! thou know'st the way.
VENTIDIUS. And, will you leave this--

ANTONY. Pr'ythee, do not curse her,
And I will leave her; though, Heaven knows, I love
Beyond life, conquest, empire, all, but honour;
But I will leave her.
VENTIDIUS. That's my royal master;
And, shall we fight?
ANTONY. I warrant thee, old soldier.
Thou shalt behold me once again in iron;
And at the head of our old troops, that beat
The Parthians, cry aloud--Come, follow me!
VENTIDIUS. Oh, now I hear my emperor! in that word
Octavius fell. Gods, let me see that day,
And, if I have ten years behind, take all:
I'll thank you for the exchange.
ANTONY. O Cleopatra!
VENTIDIUS. Again?
ANTONY. I've done: In that last sigh she went.
Caesar shall know what'tis to force a lover
>From all he holds most dear.
VENTIDIUS. Methinks, you breathe
Another soul: Your looks are more divine;
You speak a hero, and you move a god.
ANTONY. Oh, thou hast fired me; my soul's up in arms,
And mans each part about me: Once again,
That noble eagerness of fight has seized me;
That eagerness with which I darted upward
To Cassius'camp: In vain the steepy hill
Opposed my way; in vain a war of spears
Sung round my head, and planted on my shield;
I won the trenches, while my foremost men
Lagged on the plain below.
VENTIDIUS. Ye gods, ye gods,
For such another honour!
ANTONY. Come on, my soldier!
Our hearts and arms are still the same: I long
Once more to meet our foes; that thou and I,
Like Time and Death, marching before our troops,
May taste fate to them; mow them out a passage,

And, entering where the foremost squadrons yield,
Begin the noble harvest of the field.
[Exeunt.]
Act II
Scene I
Enter CLEOPATRA, IRAS, and ALEXAS
CLEOPATRA. What shall I do, or whither shall I turn?
Ventidius has o'ercome, and he will go.
ALEXAS. He goes to fight for you.
CLEOPATRA. Then he would see me, ere he went to fight:
Flatter me not: If once he goes, he's lost,
And all my hopes destroyed.
ALEXAS. Does this weak passion
Become a mighty queen?
CLEOPATRA. I am no queen:
Is this to be a queen, to be besieged
By yon insulting Roman, and to wait
Each hour the victor's chain? These ills are small:
For Antony is lost, and I can mourn
For nothing else but him. Now come, Octavius,
I have no more to lose! prepare thy bands;
I'm fit to be a captive: Antony
Has taught my mind the fortune of a slave.
IRAS. Call reason to assist you.
CLEOPATRA. I have none,
And none would have: My love's a noble madness,
Which shows the cause deserved it. Moderate sorrow
Fits vulgar love, and for a vulgar man:
But I have loved with such transcendent passion,
I soared, at first, quite out of reason's view,
And now am lost above it. No, I'm proud
'Tis thus: Would Antony could see me now
Think you he would not sigh, though he must leave me?
Sure he would sigh; for he is noble-natured,
And bears a tender heart: I know him well.
Ah, no, I know him not; I knew him once,
But now'tis past.
IRAS. Let it be past with you:

Forget him, madam.
CLEOPATRA. Never, never, Iras.
He once was mine; and once, though now'tis gone,
Leaves a faint image of possession still.
ALEXAS. Think him inconstant, cruel, and ungrateful.
CLEOPATRA. I cannot: If I could, those thoughts were vain.
Faithless, ungrateful, cruel, though he be,
I still must love him.
Enter CHARMION
Now, what news, my Charmion?
Will he be kind? and will he not forsake me?
Am I to live, or die?--nay, do I live?
Or am I dead? for when he gave his answer,
Fate took the word, and then I lived or died.
CHARMION. I found him, madam--
CLEOPATRA. A long speech preparing?
If thou bring'st comfort, haste, and give it me,
For never was more need.
IRAS. I know he loves you.
CLEOPATRA. Had he been kind, her eyes had told me so,
Before her tongue could speak it: Now she studies,
To soften what he said; but give me death,
Just as he sent it, Charmion, undisguised,
And in the words he spoke.
CHARMION. I found him, then,
Encompassed round, I think, with iron statues;
So mute, so motionless his soldiers stood,
While awfully he cast his eyes about,
And every leader's hopes or fears surveyed:
Methought he looked resolved, and yet not pleased.
When he beheld me struggling in the crowd,
He blushed, and bade make way.
ALEXAS. There's comfort yet.
CHARMION. Ventidius fixed his eyes upon my passage
Severely, as he meant to frown me back,
And sullenly gave place: I told my message,

Just as you gave it, broken and disordered;
I numbered in it all your sighs and tears,
And while I moved your pitiful request,
That you but only begged a last farewell,
He fetched an inward groan; and every time
I named you, sighed, as if his heart were breaking,
But, shunned my eyes, and guiltily looked down:
He seemed not now that awful Antony,
Who shook and armed assembly with his nod;
But, making show as he would rub his eyes,
Disguised and blotted out a falling tear.
CLEOPATRA. Did he then weep? And was I worth a tear?
If what thou hast to say be not as pleasing,
Tell me no more, but let me die contented.
CHARMION. He bid me say,--He knew himself so well,
He could deny you nothing, if he saw you;
And therefore--
CLEOPATRA. Thou wouldst say, he would not see me?
CHARMION. And therefore begged you not to use a power,
Which he could ill resist; yet he should ever
Respect you, as he ought.
CLEOPATRA. Is that a word
For Antony to use to Cleopatra?
O that faint word, RESPECT! how I disdain it!
Disdain myself, for loving after it!
He should have kept that word for cold Octavia.
Respect is for a wife: Am I that thing,
That dull, insipid lump, without desires,
And without power to give them?
ALEXAS. You misjudge;
You see through love, and that deludes your sight;
As, what is straight, seems crooked through the water:
But I, who bear my reason undisturbed,
Can see this Antony, this dreaded man,
A fearful slave, who fain would run away,
And shuns his master's eyes: If you pursue him,
My life on't, he still drags a chain along.

That needs must clog his flight.
CLEOPATRA. Could I believe thee!--
ALEXAS. By every circumstance I know he loves.
True, he's hard prest, by interest and by honour;
Yet he but doubts, and parleys, and casts out
Many a long look for succour.
CLEOPATRA. He sends word,
He fears to see my face.
ALEXAS. And would you more?
He shows his weakness who declines the combat,
And you must urge your fortune. Could he speak
More plainly? To my ears, the message sounds--
Come to my rescue, Cleopatra, come;
Come, free me from Ventidius; from my tyrant:
See me, and give me a pretence to leave him!--
I hear his trumpets. This way he must pass.
Please you, retire a while; I'll work him first,
That he may bend more easy.
CLEOPATRA. You shall rule me;
But all, I fear, in vain.
[Exit with CHARMION and IRAS.]
ALEXAS. I fear so too;
Though I concealed my thoughts, to make her bold;
But'tis our utmost means, and fate befriend it!
[Withdraws.]
Enter Lictors with Fasces; one bearing the Eagle; then enter ANTONY with VENTIDIUS, followed by other Commanders
ANTONY. Octavius is the minion of blind chance,
But holds from virtue nothing.
VENTIDIUS. Has he courage?
ANTONY. But just enough to season him from coward.
Oh,'tis the coldest youth upon a charge,
The most deliberate fighter! if he ventures
(As in Illyria once, they say, he did,
To storm a town),'tis when he cannot choose;
When all the world have fixt their eyes upon him;
And then he lives on that for seven years after;

But, at a close revenge he never fails.
VENTIDIUS. I heard you challenged him.
ANTONY. I did, Ventidius.
What think'st thou was his answer?'Twas so tame!--
He said, he had more ways than one to die;
I had not.
VENTIDIUS. Poor!
ANTONY. He has more ways than one;
But he would choose them all before that one.
VENTIDIUS. He first would choose an ague, or a fever.
ANTONY. No; it must be an ague, not a fever;
He Has not warmth enough to die by that.
VENTIDIUS. Or old age and a bed.
ANTONY. Ay, there's his choice,
He would live, like a lamp, to the last wink,
And crawl the utmost verge of life.
O Hercules! Why should a man like this,
Who dares not trust his fate for one great action,
Be all the care of Heaven? Why should he lord it
O'er fourscore thousand men, of whom each one
Is braver than himself?
VENTIDIUS. You conquered for him:
Philippi knows it; there you shared with him
That empire, which your sword made all your own.
ANTONY. Fool that I was, upon my eagle's wings
I bore this wren, till I was tired with soaring,
And now he mounts above me.
Good heavens, is this,--is this the man who braves me?
Who bids my age make way? Drives me before him,
To the world's ridge, and sweeps me off like rubbish?
VENTIDIUS. Sir, we lose time; the troops are mounted all.
ANTONY. Then give the word to march:
I long to leave this prison of a town,
To join thy legions; and, in open field,
Once more to show my face. Lead, my deliverer.
Enter ALEXAS
ALEXAS. Great emperor,

In mighty arms renowned above mankind,
But, in soft pity to the opprest, a god;
This message sends the mournful Cleopatra
To her departing lord.
VENTIDIUS. Smooth sycophant!
ALEXAS. A thousand wishes, and ten thousand prayers,
Millions of blessings wait you to the wars;
Millions of sighs and tears she sends you too,
And would have sent
As many dear embraces to your arms,
As many parting kisses to your lips;
But those, she fears, have wearied you already.
VENTIDIUS. [aside.] False crocodile!
ALEXAS. And yet she begs not now, you would not leave her;
That were a wish too mighty for her hopes,
Too presuming
For her low fortune, and your ebbing love;
That were a wish for her more prosperous days,
Her blooming beauty, and your growing kindness.
ANTONY. [aside.] Well, I must man it out:--What would the queen?
ALEXAS. First, to these noble warriors, who attend
Your daring courage in the chase of fame,--
Too daring, and too dangerous for her quiet,--
She humbly recommends all she holds dear,
All her own cares and fears,--the care of you.
VENTIDIUS. Yes, witness Actium.
ANTONY. Let him speak, Ventidius.
ALEXAS. You, when his matchless valour bears him forward,
With ardour too heroic, on his foes,
Fall down, as she would do, before his feet;
Lie in his way, and stop the paths of death:
Tell him, this god is not invulnerable;
That absent Cleopatra bleeds in him;
And, that you may remember her petition,
She begs you wear these trifles, as a pawn,

Which, at your wished return, she will redeem
[Gives jewels to the Commanders.]
With all the wealth of Egypt:
This to the great Ventidius she presents,
Whom she can never count her enemy,
Because he loves her lord.
VENTIDIUS. Tell her, I'll none on't;
I'm not ashamed of honest poverty;
Not all the diamonds of the east can bribe
Ventidius from his faith. I hope to see
These and the rest of all her sparkling store,
Where they shall more deservingly be placed.
ANTONY. And who must wear them then?
VENTIDIUS. The wronged Octavia.
ANTONY. You might have spared that word.
VENTIDIUS. And he that bribe.
ANTONY. But have I no remembrance?
ALEXAS. Yes, a dear one;
Your slave the queen--
ANTONY. My mistress.
ALEXAS. Then your mistress;
Your mistress would, she says, have sent her soul,
But that you had long since; she humbly begs
This ruby bracelet, set with bleeding hearts,
The emblems of her own, may bind your arm.
[Presenting a bracelet.]
VENTIDIUS. Now, my best lord,--in honour's name, I ask you,
For manhood's sake, and for your own dear safety,--
Touch not these poisoned gifts,
Infected by the sender; touch them not;
Myriads of bluest plagues lie underneath them,
And more than aconite has dipt the silk.
ANTONY. Nay, now you grow too cynical, Ventidius:
A lady's favours may be worn with honour.
What, to refuse her bracelet! On my soul,
When I lie pensive in my tent alone,
'Twill pass the wakeful hours of winter nights,

To tell these pretty beads upon my arm,
To count for every one a soft embrace,
A melting kiss at such and such a time:
And now and then the fury of her love,
When----And what harm's in this?
ALEXAS. None, none, my lord,
But what's to her, that now'tis past for ever.
ANTONY. [going to tie it.]
We soldiers are so awkward--help me tie it.
ALEXAS. In faith, my lord, we courtiers too are awkward
In these affairs: so are all men indeed:
Even I, who am not one. But shall I speak?
ANTONY. Yes, freely.
ALEXAS. Then, my lord, fair hands alone
Are fit to tie it; she, who sent it can.
VENTIDIUS. Hell, death! this eunuch pander ruins you.
You will not see her?
[ALEXAS whispers an ATTENDANT, who goes out.]
ANTONY. But to take my leave.
VENTIDIUS. Then I have washed an Aethiop. You're undone;
Y'are in the toils; y'are taken; y'are destroyed:
Her eyes do Caesar's work.
ANTONY. You fear too soon.
I'm constant to myself: I know my strength;
And yet she shall not think me barbarous neither,
Born in the depths of Afric: I am a Roman,
Bred in the rules of soft humanity.
A guest, and kindly used, should bid farewell.
VENTIDIUS. You do not know
How weak you are to her, how much an infant:
You are not proof against a smile, or glance:
A sigh will quite disarm you.
ANTONY. See, she comes!
Now you shall find your error.--Gods, I thank you:
I formed the danger greater than it was,
And now'tis near,'tis lessened.
VENTIDIUS. Mark the end yet.

Enter CLEOPATRA, CHARMION, and IRAS

ANTONY. Well, madam, we are met.

CLEOPATRA. Is this a meeting?
Then, we must part?

ANTONY. We must.

CLEOPATRA. Who says we must?

ANTONY. Our own hard fates.

CLEOPATRA. We make those fates ourselves.

ANTONY. Yes, we have made them; we have loved each other,
Into our mutual ruin.

CLEOPATRA. The gods have seen my joys with envious eyes;
I have no friends in heaven; and all the world,
As'twere the business of mankind to part us,
Is armed against my love: even you yourself
Join with the rest; you, you are armed against me.

ANTONY. I will be justified in all I do
To late posterity, and therefore hear me.
If I mix a lie
With any truth, reproach me freely with it;
Else, favour me with silence.

CLEOPATRA. You command me,
And I am dumb.

VENTIDIUS. I like this well; he shows authority.

ANTONY. That I derive my ruin
>From you alone----

CLEOPATRA. O heavens! I ruin you!

ANTONY. You promised me your silence, and you break it
Ere I have scarce begun.

CLEOPATRA. Well, I obey you.

ANTONY. When I beheld you first, it was in Egypt.
Ere Caesar saw your eyes, you gave me love,
And were too young to know it; that I settled
Your father in his throne, was for your sake;
I left the acknowledgment for time to ripen.
Caesar stept in, and, with a greedy hand,

Plucked the green fruit, ere the first blush of red,
Yet cleaving to the bough. He was my lord,
And was, beside, too great for me to rival;
But, I deserved you first, though he enjoyed you.
When, after, I beheld you in Cilicia,
An enemy to Rome, I pardoned you.
CLEOPATRA. I cleared myself----
ANTONY. Again you break your promise.
I loved you still, and took your weak excuses,
Took you into my bosom, stained by Caesar,
And not half mine: I went to Egypt with you,
And hid me from the business of the world,
Shut out inquiring nations from my sight,
To give whole years to you.
VENTIDIUS. Yes, to your shame be't spoken.
[Aside.]
ANTONY. How I loved.
Witness, ye days and nights, and all ye hours,
That danced away with down upon your feet,
As all your business were to count my passion!
One day passed by, and nothing saw but love;
Another came, and still'twas only love:
The suns were wearied out with looking on,
And I untired with loving.
I saw you every day, and all the day;
And every day was still but as the first,
So eager was I still to see you more.
VENTIDIUS.'Tis all too true.
ANTONY. Fulvia, my wife, grew jealous,
(As she indeed had reason) raised a war
In Italy, to call me back.
VENTIDIUS. But yet
You went not.
ANTONY. While within your arms I lay,
The world fell mouldering from my hands each hour,
And left me scarce a grasp--I thank your love for't.
VENTIDIUS. Well pushed: that last was home.
CLEOPATRA. Yet may I speak?

ANTONY. If I have urged a falsehood, yes; else, not.
Your silence says, I have not. Fulvia died,
(Pardon, you gods, with my unkindness died);
To set the world at peace, I took Octavia,
This Caesar's sister; in her pride of youth,
And flower of beauty, did I wed that lady,
Whom blushing I must praise, because I left her.
You called; my love obeyed the fatal summons:
This raised the Roman arms; the cause was yours.
I would have fought by land, where I was stronger;
You hindered it: yet, when I fought at sea,
Forsook me fighting; and (O stain to honour!
O lasting shame!) I knew not that I fled;
But fled to follow you.
VENTIDIUS. What haste she made to hoist her purple sails!
And, to appear magnificent in flight,
Drew half our strength away.
ANTONY. All this you caused.
And, would you multiply more ruins on me?
This honest man, my best, my only friend,
Has gathered up the shipwreck of my fortunes;
Twelve legions I have left, my last recruits.
And you have watched the news, and bring your eyes
To seize them too. If you have aught to answer,
Now speak, you have free leave.
ALEXAS. [aside.] She stands confounded:
Despair is in her eyes.
VENTIDIUS. Now lay a sigh in the way to stop his passage:
Prepare a tear, and bid it for his legions;
'Tis like they shall be sold.
CLEOPATRA. How shall I plead my cause, when you, my judge,
Already have condemned me? Shall I bring
The love you bore me for my advocate?
That now is turned against me, that destroys me;
For love, once past, is, at the best, forgotten;

But oftener sours to hate:'twill please my lord
To ruin me, and therefore I'll be guilty.
But, could I once have thought it would have pleased you,
That you would pry, with narrow searching eyes,
Into my faults, severe to my destruction,
And watching all advantages with care,
That serve to make me wretched? Speak, my lord,
For I end here. Though I deserved this usage,
Was it like you to give it?
ANTONY. Oh, you wrong me,
To think I sought this parting, or desired
To accuse you more than what will clear myself,
And justify this breach.
CLEOPATRA. Thus low I thank you;
And, since my innocence will not offend,
I shall not blush to own it.
VENTIDIUS. After this,
I think she'll blush at nothing.
CLEOPATRA. You seem grieved
(And therein you are kind) that Caesar first
Enjoyed my love, though you deserved it better:
I grieve for that, my lord, much more than you;
For, had I first been yours, it would have saved
My second choice: I never had been his,
And ne'er had been but yours. But Caesar first,
You say, possessed my love. Not so, my lord:
He first possessed my person; you, my love:
Caesar loved me; but I loved Antony.
If I endured him after,'twas because
I judged it due to the first name of men;
And, half constrained, I gave, as to a tyrant,
What he would take by force.
VENTIDIUS. O Syren! Syren!
Yet grant that all the love she boasts were true,
Has she not ruined you? I still urge that,
The fatal consequence.
CLEOPATRA. The consequence indeed--
For I dare challenge him, my greatest foe,

To say it was designed:'tis true, I loved you,
And kept you far from an uneasy wife,--
Such Fulvia was.
Yes, but he'll say, you left Octavia for me;--
And, can you blame me to receive that love,
Which quitted such desert, for worthless me?
How often have I wished some other Caesar,
Great as the first, and as the second young,
Would court my love, to be refused for you!
VENTIDIUS. Words, words; but Actium, sir; remember Actium.
CLEOPATRA. Even there, I dare his malice. True, I counselled
To fight at sea; but I betrayed you not.
I fled, but not to the enemy.'Twas fear;
Would I had been a man, not to have feared!
For none would then have envied me your friendship,
Who envy me your love.
ANTONY. We are both unhappy:
If nothing else, yet our ill fortune parts us.
Speak; would you have me perish by my stay?
CLEOPATRA. If, as a friend, you ask my judgment, go;
If, as a lover, stay. If you must perish--
'Tis a hard word--but stay.
VENTIDIUS. See now the effects of her so boasted love!
She strives to drag you down to ruin with her;
But, could she'scape without you, oh, how soon
Would she let go her hold, and haste to shore,
And never look behind!
CLEOPATRA. Then judge my love by this.
[Giving ANTONY a writing.]
Could I have borne
A life or death, a happiness or woe,
>From yours divided, this had given me means.
ANTONY. By Hercules, the writing of Octavius!
I know it well:'tis that proscribing hand,
Young as it was, that led the way to mine,
And left me but the second place in murder.--

See, see, Ventidius! here he offers Egypt,
And joins all Syria to it, as a present;
So, in requital, she forsake my fortunes,
And join her arms with his.
CLEOPATRA. And yet you leave me!
You leave me, Antony; and yet I love you,
Indeed I do: I have refused a kingdom;
That is a trifle;
For I could part with life, with anything,
But only you. Oh, let me die but with you!
Is that a hard request?
ANTONY. Next living with you,
'Tis all that Heaven can give.
ALEXAS. He melts; we conquer.
[Aside.]
CLEOPATRA. No; you shall go: your interest calls you hence;
Yes; your dear interest pulls too strong, for these
Weak arms to hold you here.
[Takes his hand.]
Go; leave me, soldier
(For you're no more a lover): leave me dying:
Push me, all pale and panting, from your bosom,
And, when your march begins, let one run after,
Breathless almost for joy, and cry--She's dead.
The soldiers shout; you then, perhaps, may sigh,
And muster all your Roman gravity:
Ventidius chides; and straight your brow clears up,
As I had never been.
ANTONY. Gods,'tis too much; too much for man to bear.
CLEOPATRA. What is't for me then,
A weak, forsaken woman, and a lover?--
Here let me breathe my last: envy me not
This minute in your arms: I'll die apace,
As fast as e'er I can, and end your trouble.
ANTONY. Die! rather let me perish; loosened nature
Leap from its hinges, sink the props of heaven,
And fall the skies, to crush the nether world!

My eyes, my soul, my all!
[Embraces her.]
VENTIDIUS. And what's this toy,
In balance with your fortune, honour, fame?
ANTONY. What is't, Ventidius?--it outweighs them all;
Why, we have more than conquered Caesar now:
My queen's not only innocent, but loves me.
This, this is she, who drags me down to ruin!
"But, could she'scape without me, with what haste
Would she let slip her hold, and make to shore,
And never look behind!"
Down on thy knees, blasphemer as thou art,
And ask forgiveness of wronged innocence.
VENTIDIUS. I'll rather die, than take it. Will you go?
ANTONY. Go! whither? Go from all that's excellent?
Faith, honour, virtue, all good things forbid,
That I should go from her, who sets my love
Above the price of kingdoms! Give, you gods,
Give to your boy, your Caesar,
This rattle of a globe to play withal,
This gewgaw world, and put him cheaply off:
I'll not be pleased with less than Cleopatra.
CLEOPATRA. She's wholly yours. My heart's so full of joy,
That I shall do some wild extravagance
Of love, in public; and the foolish world,
Which knows not tenderness, will think me mad.
VENTIDIUS. O women! women! women! all the gods
Have not such power of doing good to man,
As you of doing harm.
[Exit.]
ANTONY. Our men are armed:--
Unbar the gate that looks to Caesar's camp:
I would revenge the treachery he meant me;
And long security makes conquest easy.
I'm eager to return before I go;
For, all the pleasures I have known beat thick
On my remembrance.--How I long for night!

That both the sweets of mutual love may try,
And triumph once o'er Caesar ere we die.
[Exeunt.]

Act III

Scene I

At one door enter CLEOPATRA, CHARMION, IRAS, and ALEXAS, a Train of EGYPTIANS: at the other ANTONY and ROMANS.
The entrance on both sides is prepared by music; the trumpets first sounding on Antony's part: then answered by timbrels, etc., on CLEOPATRA'S. CHARMION and IRAS hold a laurel wreath betwixt them. A Dance of EGYPTIANS.
After the ceremony, CLEOPATRA crowns ANTONY.

ANTONY. I thought how those white arms would fold me in,
And strain me close, and melt me into love;
So pleased with that sweet image, I sprung forwards,
And added all my strength to every blow.
CLEOPATRA. Come to me, come, my soldier, to my arms!
You've been too long away from my embraces;
But, when I have you fast, and all my own,
With broken murmurs, and with amorous sighs,
I'll say, you were unkind, and punish you,
And mark you red with many an eager kiss.
ANTONY. My brighter Venus!
CLEOPATRA. O my greater Mars!
ANTONY. Thou join'st us well, my love!
Suppose me come from the Phlegraean plains,
Where gasping giants lay, cleft by my sword,
And mountain-tops paired off each other blow,
To bury those I slew. Receive me, goddess!
Let Caesar spread his subtle nets; like Vulcan,
In thy embraces I would be beheld
By heaven and earth at once;
And make their envy what they meant their sport

Let those, who took us, blush; I would love on,
With awful state, regardless of their frowns,
As their superior gods.
There's no satiety of love in thee:
Enjoyed, thou still art new; perpetual spring
Is in thy arms; the ripened fruit but falls,
And blossoms rise to fill its empty place;
And I grow rich by giving.
Enter VENTIDIUS, and stands apart
ALEXAS. Oh, now the danger's past, your general comes!
He joins not in your joys, nor minds your triumphs;
But, with contracted brows, looks frowning on,
As envying your success.
ANTONY. Now, on my soul, he loves me; truly loves me:
He never flattered me in any vice,
But awes me with his virtue: even this minute,
Methinks, he has a right of chiding me.
Lead to the temple: I'll avoid his presence;
It checks too strong upon me.
[Exeunt the rest.]
[As ANTONY is going, VENTIDIUS pulls him by the robe.
VENTIDIUS. Emperor!
ANTONY.'Tis the old argument; I pr'ythee, spare me.
[Looking back.]
VENTIDIUS. But this one hearing, emperor.
ANTONY. Let go
My robe; or, by my father Hercules--
VENTIDIUS. By Hercules'father, that's yet greater,
I bring you somewhat you would wish to know.
ANTONY. Thou see'st we are observed; attend me here,
And I'll return.
[Exit.]
VENTIDIUS. I am waning in his favour, yet I love him;
I love this man, who runs to meet his ruin;
And sure the gods, like me, are fond of him:
His virtues lie so mingled with his crimes,
As would confound their choice to punish one,
And not reward the other.

Enter ANTONY
ANTONY. We can conquer,
You see, without your aid.
We have dislodged their troops;
They look on us at distance, and, like curs
Scaped from the lion's paws, they bay far off,
And lick their wounds, and faintly threaten war.
Five thousand Romans, with their faces upward,
Lie breathless on the plain.
VENTIDIUS.'Tis well; and he,
Who lost them, could have spared ten thousand more.
Yet if, by this advantage, you could gain
An easier peace, while Caesar doubts the chance
Of arms--
ANTONY. Oh, think not on't, Ventidius!
The boy pursues my ruin, he'll no peace;
His malice is considerable in advantage.
Oh, he's the coolest murderer! so staunch,
He kills, and keeps his temper.
VENTIDIUS. Have you no friend
In all his army, who has power to move him?
Maecenas, or Agrippa, might do much.
ANTONY. They're both too deep in Caesar's interests.
We'll work it out by dint of sword, or perish.
VENTIDIUS. Fain I would find some other.
ANTONY. Thank thy love.
Some four or five such victories as this
Will save thy further pains.
VENTIDIUS. Expect no more; Caesar is on his guard:
I know, sir, you have conquered against odds;
But still you draw supplies from one poor town,
And of Egyptians: he has all the world,
And, at his beck, nations come pouring in,
To fill the gaps you make. Pray, think again.
ANTONY. Why dost thou drive me from myself, to search
For foreign aids?--to hunt my memory,
And range all o'er a waste and barren place,
To find a friend? The wretched have no friends.

Yet I had one, the bravest youth of Rome,
Whom Caesar loves beyond the love of women:
He could resolve his mind, as fire does wax,
>From that hard rugged image melt him down,
And mould him in what softer form he pleased.
VENTIDIUS. Him would I see; that man, of all the world;
Just such a one we want.
ANTONY. He loved me too;
I was his soul; he lived not but in me:
We were so closed within each other's breasts,
The rivets were not found, that joined us first.
That does not reach us yet: we were so mixt,
As meeting streams, both to ourselves were lost;
We were one mass; we could not give or take,
But from the same; for he was I, I he.
VENTIDIUS. He moves as I would wish him.
[Aside.]
ANTONY. After this,
I need not tell his name;--'twas Dolabella.
VENTIDIUS. He's now in Caesar's camp.
ANTONY. No matter where,
Since he's no longer mine. He took unkindly,
That I forbade him Cleopatra's sight,
Because I feared he loved her: he confessed,
He had a warmth, which, for my sake, he stifled;
For'twere impossible that two, so one,
Should not have loved the same. When he departed,
He took no leave; and that confirmed my thoughts.
VENTIDIUS. It argues, that he loved you more than her,
Else he had stayed; but he perceived you jealous,
And would not grieve his friend: I know he loves you.
ANTONY. I should have seen him, then, ere now.
VENTIDIUS. Perhaps
He has thus long been labouring for your peace.
ANTONY. Would he were here!
VENTIDIUS. Would you believe he loved you?
I read your answer in your eyes, you would.
Not to conceal it longer, he has sent

A messenger from Caesar's camp, with letters.
ANTONY. Let him appear.
VENTIDIUS. I'll bring him instantly.
[Exit VENTIDIUS, and re-enters immediately with DOLABELLA.]
ANTONY.'Tis he himself! himself, by holy friendship!
[Runs to embrace him.]
Art thou returned at last, my better half?
Come, give me all myself!
Let me not live,
If the young bridegroom, longing for his night,
Was ever half so fond.
DOLABELLA. I must be silent, for my soul is busy
About a nobler work; she's new come home,
Like a long-absent man, and wanders o'er
Each room, a stranger to her own, to look
If all be safe.
ANTONY. Thou hast what's left of me;
For I am now so sunk from what I was,
Thou find'st me at my lowest water-mark.
The rivers that ran in, and raised my fortunes,
Are all dried up, or take another course:
What I have left is from my native spring;
I've still a heart that swells, in scorn of fate,
And lifts me to my banks.
DOLABELLA. Still you are lord of all the world to me.
ANTONY. Why, then I yet am so; for thou art all.
If I had any joy when thou wert absent,
I grudged it to myself; methought I robbed
Thee of thy part. But, O my Dolabella!
Thou has beheld me other than I am.
Hast thou not seen my morning chambers filled
With sceptred slaves, who waited to salute me?
With eastern monarchs, who forgot the sun,
To worship my uprising?--menial kings
Ran coursing up and down my palace-yard,
Stood silent in my presence, watched my eyes,
And, at my least command, all started out,

Like racers to the goal.
DOLABELLA. Slaves to your fortune.
ANTONY. Fortune is Caesar's now; and what am I?
VENTIDIUS. What you have made yourself; I will not flatter.
ANTONY. Is this friendly done?
DOLABELLA. Yes; when his end is so, I must join with him;
Indeed I must, and yet you must not chide;
Why am I else your friend?
ANTONY. Take heed, young man,
How thou upbraid'st my love: The queen has eyes,
And thou too hast a soul. Canst thou remember,
When, swelled with hatred, thou beheld'st her first,
As accessary to thy brother's death?
DOLABELLA. Spare my remembrance;'twas a guilty day,
And still the blush hangs here.
ANTONY. To clear herself,
For sending him no aid, she came from Egypt.
Her galley down the silver Cydnus rowed,
The tackling silk, the streamers waved with gold;
The gentle winds were lodged in purple sails:
Her nymphs, like Nereids, round her couch were placed;
Where she, another sea-born Venus, lay.
DOLABELLA. No more; I would not hear it.
ANTONY. Oh, you must!
She lay, and leant her cheek upon her hand,
And cast a look so languishingly sweet,
As if, secure of all beholders'hearts,
Neglecting, she could take them: boys, like Cupids,
Stood fanning, with their painted wings, the winds.
That played about her face. But if she smiled
A darting glory seemed to blaze abroad,
That men's desiring eyes were never wearied,
But hung upon the object: To soft flutes
The silver oars kept time; and while they played,
The hearing gave new pleasure to the sight;
And both to thought.'Twas heaven, or somewhat more;

For she so charmed all hearts, that gazing crowds
Stood panting on the shore, and wanted breath
To give their welcome voice.
Then, Dolabella, where was then thy soul?
Was not thy fury quite disarmed with wonder?
Didst thou not shrink behind me from those eyes
And whisper in my ear--Oh, tell her not
That I accused her with my brother's death?
DOLABELLA. And should my weakness be a plea for yours?
Mine was an age when love might be excused,
When kindly warmth, and when my springing youth
Made it a debt to nature. Yours--
VENTIDIUS. Speak boldly.
Yours, he would say, in your declining age,
When no more heat was left but what you forced,
When all the sap was needful for the trunk,
When it went down, then you constrained the course,
And robbed from nature, to supply desire;
In you (I would not use so harsh a word)
'Tis but plain dotage.
ANTONY. Ha!
DOLABELLA.'Twas urged too home.--
But yet the loss was private, that I made;
'Twas but myself I lost: I lost no legions;
I had no world to lose, no people's love.
ANTONY. This from a friend?
DOLABELLA. Yes, Antony, a true one;
A friend so tender, that each word I speak
Stabs my own heart, before it reach your ear.
Oh, judge me not less kind, because I chide!
To Caesar I excuse you.
ANTONY. O ye gods!
Have I then lived to be excused to Caesar?
DOLABELLA. As to your equal.
ANTONY. Well, he's but my equal:
While I wear this he never shall be more.
DOLABELLA. I bring conditions from him.

ANTONY. Are they noble?
Methinks thou shouldst not bring them else; yet he
Is full of deep dissembling; knows no honour
Divided from his interest. Fate mistook him;
For nature meant him for an usurer:
He's fit indeed to buy, not conquer kingdoms.
VENTIDIUS. Then, granting this,
What power was theirs, who wrought so hard a temper
To honourable terms?
ANTONY. I was my Dolabella, or some god.
DOLABELLA. Nor I, nor yet Maecenas, nor Agrippa:
They were your enemies; and I, a friend,
Too weak alone; yet'twas a Roman's deed.
ANTONY.'Twas like a Roman done: show me that man,
Who has preserved my life, my love, my honour;
Let me but see his face.
VENTIDIUS. That task is mine,
And, Heaven, thou know'st how pleasing.
[Exit VENTIDIUS.]
DOLABELLA. You'll remember
To whom you stand obliged?
ANTONY. When I forget it
Be thou unkind, and that's my greatest curse.
My queen shall thank him too,
DOLABELLA. I fear she will not.
ANTONY. But she shall do it: The queen, my Dolabella!
Hast thou not still some grudgings of thy fever?
DOLABELLA. I would not see her lost.
ANTONY. When I forsake her,
Leave me my better stars! for she has truth
Beyond her beauty. Caesar tempted her,
At no less price than kingdoms, to betray me;
But she resisted all: and yet thou chidest me
For loving her too well. Could I do so?
DOLABELLA. Yes; there's my reason.
Re-enter VENTIDIUS, with OCTAVIA,
leading ANTONY'S two little DAUGHTERS
ANTONY. Where?--Octavia there!

[Starting back.]
VENTIDIUS: What, is she poison to you?--a disease?
Look on her, view her well, and those she brings:
Are they all strangers to your eyes? has nature
No secret call, no whisper they are yours?
DOLABELLA. For shame, my lord, if not for love, receive them
With kinder eyes. If you confess a man,
Meet them, embrace them, bid them welcome to you.
Your arms should open, even without your knowledge,
To clasp them in; your feet should turn to wings,
To bear you to them; and your eyes dart out
And aim a kiss, ere you could reach the lips.
ANTONY. I stood amazed, to think how they came hither.
VENTIDIUS. I sent for them; I brought them in unknown
To Cleopatra's guards.
DOLABELLA. Yet, are you cold?
OCTAVIA. Thus long I have attended for my welcome;
Which, as a stranger, sure I might expect.
Who am I?
ANTONY. Caesar's sister.
OCTAVIA. That's unkind.
Had I been nothing more than Caesar's sister,
Know, I had still remained in Caesar's camp:
But your Octavia, your much injured wife,
Though banished from your bed, driven from your house,
In spite of Caesar's sister, still is yours.
'Tis true, I have a heart disdains your coldness,
And prompts me not to seek what you should offer;
But a wife's virtue still surmounts that pride.
I come to claim you as my own; to show
My duty first; to ask, nay beg, your kindness:
Your hand, my lord;'tis mine, and I will have it.
[Taking his hand.]
VENTIDIUS. Do, take it; thou deserv'st it.
DOLABELLA. On my soul,
And so she does: she's neither too submissive,
Nor yet too haughty; but so just a mean

Shows, as it ought, a wife and Roman too.
ANTONY. I fear, Octavia, you have begged my life.
OCTAVIA. Begged it, my lord?
ANTONY. Yes, begged it, my ambassadress;
Poorly and basely begged it of your brother.
OCTAVIA. Poorly and basely I could never beg:
Nor could my brother grant.
ANTONY. Shall I, who, to my kneeling slave, could say,
Rise up, and be a king; shall I fall down
And cry,--Forgive me, Caesar! Shall I set
A man, my equal, in the place of Jove,
As he could give me being? No; that word,
Forgive, would choke me up,
And die upon my tongue.
DOLABELLA. You shall not need it.
ANTONY. I will not need it. Come, you've all betrayed me,--
My friend too!--to receive some vile conditions.
My wife has bought me, with her prayers and tears;
And now I must become her branded slave.
In every peevish mood, she will upbraid
The life she gave: if I but look awry,
She cries--I'll tell my brother.
OCTAVIA. My hard fortune
Subjects me still to your unkind mistakes.
But the conditions I have brought are such,
Your need not blush to take: I love your honour,
Because'tis mine; it never shall be said,
Octavia's husband was her brother's slave.
Sir, you are free; free, even from her you loathe;
For, though my brother bargains for your love,
Makes me the price and cement of your peace,
I have a soul like yours; I cannot take
Your love as alms, nor beg what I deserve.
I'll tell my brother we are reconciled;
He shall draw back his troops, and you shall march
To rule the East: I may be dropt at Athens;
No matter where. I never will complain,

But only keep the barren name of wife,
And rid you of the trouble.
VENTIDIUS. Was ever such a strife of sullen honour! [Apart]
Both scorn to be obliged.
DOLABELLA. Oh, she has touched him in the tenderest part;[Apart]
See how he reddens with despite and shame,
To be outdone in generosity!
VENTIDIUS. See how he winks! how he dries up a tear, [Apart]
That fain would fall!
ANTONY. Octavia, I have heard you, and must praise
The greatness of your soul;
But cannot yield to what you have proposed:
For I can ne'er be conquered but by love;
And you do all for duty. You would free me,
And would be dropt at Athens; was't not so?
OCTAVIA. It was, my lord.
ANTONY. Then I must be obliged
To one whc loves me not; who, to herself,
May call me thankless and ungrateful man:--
I'll not endure it; no.
VENTIDIUS. I am glad it pinches there. [Aside.]
OCTAVIA. Would you triumph o'er poor Octavia's virtue?
That pride was all I had to bear me up;
That you might think you owed me for your life,
And owed it to my duty, not my love.
I have been injured, and my haughty soul
Could brook but ill the man who slights my bed.
ANTONY. Therefore you love me not.
OCTAVIA. Therefore, my lord,
I should not love you.
ANTONY. Therefore you would leave me?
OCTAVIA. And therefore I should leave you--if I could.
DOLABELLA. Her soul's too great, after such injuries,

To say she loves; and yet she lets you see it.
Her modesty and silence plead her cause.
ANTONY. O Dolabella, which way shall I turn?
I find a secret yielding in my soul;
But Cleopatra, who would die with me,
Must she be left? Pity pleads for Octavia;
But does it not plead more for Cleopatra?
VENTIDIUS. Justice and pity both plead for Octavia;
For Cleopatra, neither.
One would be ruined with you; but she first
Had ruined you: The other, you have ruined,
And yet she would preserve you.
In everything their merits are unequal.
ANTONY. O my distracted soul!
OCTAVIA. Sweet Heaven compose it!--
Come, come, my lord, if I can pardon you,
Methinks you should accept it. Look on these;
Are they not yours? or stand they thus neglected,
As they are mine? Go to him, children, go;
Kneel to him, take him by the hand, speak to him;
For you may speak, and he may own you too,
Without a blush; and so he cannot all
His children: go, I say, and pull him to me,
And pull him to yourselves, from that bad woman.
You, Agrippina, hang upon his arms;
And you, Antonia, clasp about his waist:
If he will shake you off, if he will dash you
Against the pavement, you must bear it, children;
For you are mine, and I was born to suffer.
[Here the CHILDREN go to him, etc.]
VENTIDIUS. Was ever sight so moving?--Emperor!
DOLABELLA. Friend!
OCTAVIA. Husband!
BOTH CHILDREN. Father!
ANTONY. I am vanquished: take me,
Octavia; take me, children; share me all.
[Embracing them.]
I've been a thriftless debtor to your loves,

And run out much, in riot, from your stock;
But all shall be amended.
OCTAVIA. O blest hour!
DOLABELLA. O happy change!
VENTIDIUS. My joy stops at my tongue;
But it has found two channels here for one,
And bubbles out above.
ANTONY. [to OCTAVIA]
This is thy triumph; lead me where thou wilt;
Even to thy brother's camp.
OCTAVIA. All there are yours.
Enter ALEXAS hastily
ALEXAS. The queen, my mistress, sir, and yours--
ANTONY.'Tis past.--
Octavia, you shall stay this night: To-morrow,
Caesar and we are one.
[Exit leading OCTAVIA; DOLABELLA and the CHILDREN follow.]
VENTIDIUS. There's news for you; run, my officious eunuch,
Be sure to be the first; haste forward:
Haste, my dear eunuch, haste.
[Exit.]
ALEXAS. This downright fighting fool, this thick-skulled hero,
This blunt, unthinking instrument of death,
With plain dull virtue has outgone my wit.
Pleasure forsook my earliest infancy;
The luxury of others robbed my cradle,
And ravished thence the promise of a man.
Cast out from nature, disinherited
Of what her meanest children claim by kind,
Yet greatness kept me from contempt: that's gone.
Had Cleopatra followed my advice,
Then he had been betrayed who now forsakes.
She dies for love; but she has known its joys:
Gods, is this just, that I, who know no joys,
Must die, because she loves?

Enter CLEOPATRA, CHARMION, IRAS, and Train
O madam, I have seen what blasts my eyes!
Octavia's here.
CLEOPATRA. Peace with that raven's note.
I know it too; and now am in
The pangs of death.
ALEXAS. You are no more a queen;
Egypt is lost.
CLEOPATRA. What tell'st thou me of Egypt?
My life, my soul is lost! Octavia has him!--
O fatal name to Cleopatra's love!
My kisses, my embraces now are hers;
While I--But thou hast seen my rival; speak,
Does she deserve this blessing? Is she fair?
Bright as a goddess? and is all perfection
Confined to her? It is. Poor I was made
Of that coarse matter, which, when she was finished,
The gods threw by for rubbish.
ALEXAS. She is indeed a very miracle.
CLEOPATRA. Death to my hopes, a miracle!
ALEXAS. A miracle;
[Bowing.]
I mean of goodness; for in beauty, madam,
You make all wonders cease.
CLEOPATRA. I was too rash:
Take this in part of recompense. But, oh!
[Giving a ring.]
I fear thou flatterest me.
CHARMION. She comes! she's here!
IRAS. Fly, madam, Caesar's sister!
CLEOPATRA. Were she the sister of the thunderer Jove,
And bore her brother's lightning in her eyes,
Thus would I face my rival.
[Meets OCTAVIA with VENTIDIUS. OCTAVIA bears up to her. Their Trains come up on either side.]
OCTAVIA. I need not ask if you are Cleopatra;
Your haughty carriage--
CLEOPATRA. Shows I am a queen:

Nor need I ask you, who you are.
OCTAVIA. A Roman:
A name, that makes and can unmake a queen.
CLEOPATRA. Your lord, the man who serves me, is a Roman.
OCTAVIA. He was a Roman, till he lost that name,
To be a slave in Egypt; but I come
To free him thence.
CLEOPATRA. Peace, peace, my lover's Juno.
When he grew weary of that household clog,
He chose my easier bonds.
OCTAVIA. I wonder not
Your bonds are easy: you have long been practised
In that lascivious art: He's not the first
For whom you spread your snares: Let Caesar witness.
CLEOPATRA. I loved not Caesar;'twas but gratitude
I paid his love: The worst your malice can,
Is but to say the greatest of mankind
Has been my slave. The next, but far above him
In my esteem, is he whom law calls yours,
But whom his love made mine.
OCTAVIA. I would view nearer.
[Coming up close to her.]
That face, which has so long usurped my right,
To find the inevitable charms, that catch
Mankind so sure, that ruined my dear lord.
CLEOPATRA. Oh, you do well to search; for had you known
But half these charms, you had not lost his heart.
OCTAVIA. Far be their knowledge from a Roman lady,
Far from a modest wife! Shame of our sex,
Dost thou not blush to own those black endearments,
That make sin pleasing?
CLEOPATRA. You may blush, who want them.
If bounteous nature, if indulgent Heaven
Have given me charms to please the bravest man,
Should I not thank them? Should I be ashamed,
And not be proud? I am, that he has loved me;

And, when I love not him, Heaven change this face
For one like that.
OCTAVIA. Thou lov'st him not so well.
CLEOPATRA. I love him better, and deserve him more.
OCTAVIA. You do not; cannot: You have been his ruin.
Who made him cheap at Rome, but Cleopatra?
Who made him scorned abroad, but Cleopatra?
At Actium, who betrayed him? Cleopatra.
Who made his children orphans, and poor me
A wretched widow? only Cleopatra.
CLEOPATRA. Yet she, who loves him best, is Cleopatra.
If you have suffered, I have suffered more.
You bear the specious title of a wife,
To gild your cause, and draw the pitying world
To favour it: the world condemns poor me.
For I have lost my honour, lost my fame,
And stained the glory of my royal house,
And all to bear the branded name of mistress.
There wants but life, and that too I would lose
For him I love.
OCTAVIA. Be't so, then; take thy wish.
[Exit with her Train.]
CLEOPATRA. And'tis my wish,
Now he is lost for whom alone I lived.
My sight grows dim, and every object dances,
And swims before me, in the maze of death.
My spirits, while they were opposed, kept up;
They could not sink beneath a rival's scorn!
But now she's gone, they faint.
ALEXAS. Mine have had leisure
To recollect their strength, and furnish counsel,
To ruin her, who else must ruin you.
CLEOPATRA. Vain promiser!
Lead me, my Charmion; nay, your hand too, Iras.
My grief has weight enough to sink you both.
Conduct me to some solitary chamber,
And draw the curtains round;
Then leave me to myself, to take alone

My fill of grief:
There I till death will his unkindness weep;
As harmless infants moan themselves asleep.
[Exeunt.]
Act IV
Scene I
Enter ANTONY and DOLABELLA
DOLABELLA. Why would you shift it from yourself on me?
Can you not tell her, you must part?
ANTONY. I cannot.
I could pull out an eye, and bid it go,
And t'other should not weep. O Dolabella,
How many deaths are in this word, DEPART!
I dare not trust my tongue to tell her so:
One look of hers would thaw me into tears,
And I should melt, till I were lost again.
DOLABELLA. Then let Ventidius;
He's rough by nature.
ANTONY. Oh, he'll speak too harshly;
He'll kill her with the news: Thou, only thou.
DOLABELLA. Nature has cast me in so soft a mould,
That but to hear a story, feigned for pleasure,
Of some sad lover's death, moistens my eyes,
And robs me of my manhood. I should speak
So faintly, with such fear to grieve her heart,
She'd not believe it earnest.
ANTONY. Therefore,--therefore
Thou only, thou art fit: Think thyself me;
And when thou speak'st (but let it first be long),
Take off the edge from every sharper sound,
And let our parting be as gently made,
As other loves begin: Wilt thou do this?
DOLABELLA. What you have said so sinks into my soul,
That, if I must speak, I shall speak just so.
ANTONY. I leave you then to your sad task: Farewell.
I sent her word to meet you.
[Goes to the door, and comes back.]

I forgot;
Let her be told, I'll make her peace with mine,
Her crown and dignity shall be preserved,
If I have power with Caesar.--Oh, be sure
To think on that.
DOLABELLA. Fear not, I will remember.
[ANTONY goes again to the door, and comes back.]
ANTONY. And tell her, too, how much I was constrained;
I did not this, but with extremest force.
Desire her not to hate my memory,
For I still cherish hers:--insist on that.
DOLABELLA. Trust me. I'll not forget it.
ANTONY. Then that's all.
[Goes out, and returns again.]
Wilt thou forgive my fondness this once more?
Tell her, though we shall never meet again,
If I should hear she took another love,
The news would break my heart.--Now I must go;
For every time I have returned, I feel
My soul more tender; and my next command
Would be, to bid her stay, and ruin both.
[Exit.]
DOLABELLA. Men are but children of a larger growth;
Our appetites as apt to change as theirs,
And full as craving too, and full as vain;
And yet the soul, shut up in her dark room,
Viewing so clear abroad, at home sees nothing:
But, like a mole in earth, busy and blind,
Works all her folly up, and casts it outward
To the world's open view: Thus I discovered,
And blamed the love of ruined Antony:
Yet wish that I were he, to be so ruined.
Enter VENTIDIUS above
VENTIDIUS. Alone, and talking to himself? concerned too?
Perhaps my guess is right; he loved her once,
And may pursue it still.
DOLABELLA. O friendship! friendship!

Ill canst thou answer this; and reason, worse:
Unfaithful in the attempt; hopeless to win;
And if I win, undone: mere madness all.
And yet the occasion's fair. What injury
To him, to wear the robe which he throws by!
VENTIDIUS. None, none at all. This happens as I wish,
To ruin her yet more with Antony.
Enter CLEOPATRA talking with ALEXAS;
CHARMION, IRAS on the other side.
DOLABELLA. She comes! What charms have sorrow on that face!
Sorrow seems pleased to dwell with so much sweetness;
Yet, now and then, a melancholy smile
Breaks loose, like lightning in a winter's night,
And shows a moment's day.
VENTIDIUS. If she should love him too! her eunuch there?
That porc'pisce bodes ill weather. Draw, draw nearer,
Sweet devil, that I may hear.
ALEXAS. Believe me; try
[DOLABELLA goes over to CHARMION and IRAS; seems to talk with them.]
To make him jealous; jealousy is like
A polished glass held to the lips when life's in doubt;
If there be breath,'twill catch the damp, and show it.
CLEOPATRA. I grant you, jealousy's a proof of love,
But'tis a weak and unavailing medicine;
It puts out the disease, and makes it show,
But has no power to cure.
ALEXAS.'Tis your last remedy, and strongest too:
And then this Dolabella, who so fit
To practise on? He's handsome, valiant, young,
And looks as he were laid for nature's bait,
To catch weak women's eyes.
He stands already more than half suspected
Of loving you: the least kind word or glance,
You give this youth, will kindle him with love:
Then, like a burning vessel set adrift,
You'll send him down amain before the wind,

To fire the heart of jealous Antony.
CLEOPATRA. Can I do this? Ah, no, my love's so true,
That I can neither hide it where it is,
Nor show it where it is not. Nature meant me
A wife; a silly, harmless, household dove,
Fond without art, and kind without deceit;
But Fortune, that has made a mistress of me,
Has thrust me out to the wide world, unfurnished
Of falsehood to be happy.
ALEXAS. Force yourself.
The event will be, your lover will return,
Doubly desirous to possess the good
Which once he feared to lose.
CLEOPATRA. I must attempt it;
But oh, with what regret!
[Exit ALEXAS. She comes up to DOLABELLA.]
VENTIDIUS. So, now the scene draws near; they're in my reach.
CLEOPATRA. [to DOLABELLA.]
Discoursing with my women! might not I
Share in your entertainment?
CHARMION. You have been
The subject of it, madam.
CLEOPATRA. How! and how!
IRAS. Such praises of your beauty!
CLEOPATRA. Mere poetry.
Your Roman wits, your Gallus and Tibullus,
Have taught you this from Cytheris and Delia.
DOLABELLA. Those Roman wits have never been in Egypt;
Cytheris and Delia else had been unsung:
I, who have seen--had I been born a poet,
Should choose a nobler name.
CLEOPATRA. You flatter me.
But,'tis your nation's vice: All of your country
Are flatterers, and all false. Your friend's like you.
I'm sure, he sent you not to speak these words.
DOLABELLA. No, madam; yet he sent me--

CLEOPATRA. Well, he sent you--
DOLABELLA. Of a less pleasing errand.
CLEOPATRA. How less pleasing?
Less to yourself, or me?
DOLABELLA. Madam, to both;
For you must mourn, and I must grieve to cause it.
CLEOPATRA. You, Charmion, and your fellow, stand at distance.--
Hold up, my spirits. [Aside.]--Well, now your mournful matter;
For I'm prepared, perhaps can guess it too.
DOLABELLA. I wish you would; for'tis a thankless office,
To tell ill news: And I, of all your sex,
Most fear displeasing you.
CLEOPATRA. Of all your sex,
I soonest could forgive you, if you should.
VENTIDIUS. Most delicate advances! Women! women!
Dear, damned, inconstant sex!
CLEOPATRA. In the first place,
I am to be forsaken; is't not so?
DOLABELLA. I wish I could not answer to that question.
CLEOPATRA. Then pass it o'er, because it troubles you:
I should have been more grieved another time.
Next I'm to lose my kingdom--Farewell, Egypt!
Yet, is there ary more?
DOLABELLA. Madam, I fear
Your too deep sense of grief has turned your reason.
CLEOPATRA. No, no, I'm not run mad; I can bear fortune:
And love may be expelled by other love,
As poisons are by poisons.
DOLABELLA. You o'erjoy me, madam,
To find your griefs so moderately borne.
You've heard the worst; all are not false like him.
CLEOPATRA. No; Heaven forbid they should.
DOLABELLA. Some men are constant.
CLEOPATRA. And constancy deserves reward, that's certain.
DOLABELLA. Deserves it not; but give it leave to hope.

VENTIDIUS. I'll swear, thou hast my leave. I have enough:
But how to manage this! Well, I'll consider.
[Exit.]
DOLABELLA. I came prepared
To tell you heavy news; news, which I thought
Would fright the blood from your pale cheeks to hear:
But you have met it with a cheerfulness,
That makes my task more easy; and my tongue,
Which on another's message was employed,
Would gladly speak its own.
CLEOPATRA. Hold, Dolabella.
First tell me, were you chosen by my lord?
Or sought you this employment?
DOLABELLA. He picked me out; and, as his bosom friend,
He charged me with his words.
CLEOPATRA. The message then
I know was tender, and each accent smooth,
To mollify that rugged word, DEPART.
DOLABELLA. Oh, you mistake: He chose the harshest words;
With fiery eyes, and contracted brows,
He coined his face in the severest stamp;
And fury shook his fabric, like an earthquake;
He heaved for vent, and burst like bellowing Aetna,
In sounds scarce human--"Hence away for ever,
Let her begone, the blot of my renown,
And bane of all my hopes!"
[All the time of this speech, CLEOPATRA seems more and more concerned, till she sinks quite down.]
"Let her be driven, as far as men can think,
>From man's commerce! she'll poison to the centre."
CLEOPATRA. Oh, I can bear no more!
DOLABELLA. Help, help!--O wretch! O cursed, cursed wretch!
What have I done!
CHARMION. Help, chafe her temples, Iras.
IRAS. Bend, bend her forward quickly.

CHARMION. Heaven be praised,
She comes again.
CLEOPATRA. Oh, let him not approach me.
Why have you brought me back to this loathed being;
The abode of falsehood, violated vows,
And injured love? For pity, let me go;
For, if there be a place of long repose,
I'm sure I want it. My disdainful lord
Can never break that quiet; nor awake
The sleeping soul, with hollowing in my tomb
Such words as fright her hence.--Unkind, unkind!
DOLABELLA. Believe me,'tis against myself I speak;
[Kneeling.]
That sure desires belief; I injured him:
My friend ne'er spoke those words. Oh, had you seen
How often he came back, and every time
With something more obliging and more kind,
To add to what he said; what dear farewells;
How almost vanquished by his love he parted,
And leaned to what unwillingly he left!
I, traitor as I was, for love of you
(But what can you not do, who made me false?)
I forged that lie; for whose forgiveness kneels
This self-accused, self-punished criminal.
CLEOPATRA. With how much ease believe we what we wish!
Rise, Dolabella; if you have been guilty,
I have contributed, and too much love
Has made me guilty too.
The advance of kindness, which I made, was feigned,
To call back fleeting love by jealousy;
But'twould not last. Oh, rather let me lose,
Than so ignobly trifle with his heart.
DOLABELLA. I find your breast fenced round from human reach,
Transparent as a rock of solid crystal;
Seen through, but never pierced. My friend, my friend,
What endless treasure hast thou thrown away;

And scattered, like an infant, in the ocean,
Vain sums of wealth, which none can gather thence!
CLEOPATRA. Could you not beg
An hour's admittance to his private ear?
Like one, who wanders through long barren wilds
And yet foreknows no hospitable inn
Is near to succour hunger, eats his fill,
Before his painful march;
So would I feed a while my famished eyes
Before we part; for I have far to go,
If death be far, and never must return.
VENTIDIUS with OCTAVIA, behind
VENTIDIUS. From hence you may discover--oh, sweet, sweet!
Would you indeed? The pretty hand in earnest?
DOLABELLA. I will, for this reward.
[Takes her hand.]
Draw it not back.
'Tis all I e'er will beg.
VENTIDIUS. They turn upon us.
OCTAVIA. What quick eyes has guilt!
VENTIDIUS. Seem not to have observed them, and go on.
[They enter.]
DOLABELLA. Saw you the emperor, Ventidius?
VENTIDIUS. No.
I sought him; but I heard that he was private,
None with him but Hipparchus, his freedman.
DOLABELLA. Know you his business?
VENTIDIUS. Giving him instructions,
And letters to his brother Caesar.
DOLABELLA. Well,
He must be found.
[Exeunt DOLABELLA and CLEOPATRA.]
OCTAVIA. Most glorious impudence!
VENTIDIUS. She looked, methought,
As she would say--Take your old man, Octavia;
Thank you, I'm better here.--
Well, but what use

Make we of this discovery?
OCTAVIA. Let it die.
VENTIDIUS. I pity Dolabella; but she's dangerous:
Her eyes have power beyond Thessalian charms,
To draw the moon from heaven; for eloquence,
The sea-green Syrens taught her voice their flattery;
And, while she speaks, night steals upon the day,
Unmarked of those that hear. Then she's so charming,
Age buds at sight of her, and swells to youth:
The holy priests gaze on her when she smiles;
And with heaved hands, forgetting gravity,
They bless her wanton eyes: Even I, who hate her,
With a malignant joy behold such beauty;
And, while I curse, desire it. Antony
Must needs have some remains of passion still,
Which may ferment into a worse relapse,
If now not fully cured. I know, this minute,
With Caesar he's endeavouring her peace.
OCTAVIA. You have prevailed:--But for a further purpose
[Walks off.]
I'll prove how he will relish this discovery.
What, make a strumpet's peace! it swells my heart:
It must not, shall not be.
VENTIDIUS. His guards appear.
Let me begin, and you shall second me.
Enter ANTONY
ANTONY. Octavia, I was looking you, my love:
What, are your letters ready? I have given
My last instructions.
OCTAVIA. Mine, my lord, are written.
ANTONY. Ventidius.
[Drawing him aside.]
VENTIDIUS. My lord?
ANTONY. A word in private.--
When saw you Dolabella?
VENTIDIUS. Now, my lord,
He parted hence; and Cleopatra with him.
ANTONY. Speak softly.--'Twas by my command he went,

To bear my last farewell.
VENTIDIUS. It looked indeed
[Aloud.]
Like your farewell.
ANTONY. More softly.--My farewell?
What secret meaning have you in those words
Of--My farewell? He did it by my order.
VENTIDIUS. Then he obeyed your order. I suppose
[Aloud.]
You bid him do it with all gentleness,
All kindness, and all--love.
ANTONY. How she mourned,
The poor forsaken creature!
VENTIDIUS. She took it as she ought; she bore your parting
As she did Caesar's, as she would another's,
Were a new love to come.
ANTONY. Thou dost belie her;
[Aloud.]
Most basely, and maliciously belie her.
VENTIDIUS. I thought not to displease you; I have done.
OCTAVIA. You seemed disturbed, my Lord.
[Coming up.]
ANTONY. A very trifle.
Retire, my love.
VENTIDIUS. It was indeed a trifle.
He sent--
ANTONY. No more. Look how thou disobey'st me;
[Angrily.]
Thy life shall answer it.
OCTAVIA. Then'tis no trifle.
VENTIDIUS. [to OCTAVIA.]
'Tis less; a very nothing: You too saw it,
As well as I, and therefore'tis no secret.
ANTONY. She saw it!
VENTIDIUS. Yes: She saw young Dolabella--
ANTONY. Young Dolabella!
VENTIDIUS. Young, I think him young,

And handsome too; and so do others think him.
But what of that? He went by your command,
Indeed'tis probable, with some kind message;
For she received it graciously; she smiled;
And then he grew familiar with her hand,
Squeezed it, and worried it with ravenous kisses;
She blushed, and sighed, and smiled, and blushed again;
At last she took occasion to talk softly,
And brought her cheek up close, and leaned on his;
At which, he whispered kisses back on hers;
And then she cried aloud--That constancy
Should be rewarded.
OCTAVIA. This I saw and heard.
ANTONY. What woman was it, whom you heard and saw
So playful with my friend?
Not Cleopatra?
VENTIDIUS. Even she, my lord.
ANTONY. My Cleopatra?
VENTIDIUS. Your Cleopatra;
Dolabella's Cleopatra; every man's Cleopatra.
ANTONY. Thou liest.
VENTIDIUS. I do not lie, my lord.
Is this so strange? Should mistresses be left,
And not provide against a time of change?
You know she's not much used to lonely nights.
ANTONY. I'll think no more on't.
I know'tis false, and see the plot betwixt you.--
You needed not have gone this way, Octavia.
What harms it you that Cleopatra's just?
She's mine no more. I see, and I forgive:
Urge it no further, love.
OCTAVIA. Are you concerned,
That she's found false?
ANTONY. I should be, were it so;
For, though'tis past, I would not that the world
Should tax my former choice, that I loved one
Of so light note; but I forgive you both.
VENTIDIUS. What has my age deserved, that you should

think
I would abuse your ears with perjury?
If Heaven be true, she's false.
ANTONY. Though heaven and earth
Should witness it, I'll not believe her tainted.
VENTIDIUS. I'll bring you, then, a witness
>From hell, to prove her so.--Nay, go not back;
[Seeing ALEXAS just entering, and starting back.]
For stay you must and shall.
ALEXAS. What means my lord?
VENTIDIUS. To make you do what most you hate,--speak truth.
You are of Cleopatra's private counsel,
Of her bed-counsel, her lascivious hours;
Are conscious of each nightly change she makes,
And watch her, as Chaldaeans do the moon,
Can tell what signs she passes through, what day.
ALEXAS. My noble lord!
VENTIDIUS. My most illustrious pander,
No fine set speech, no cadence, no turned periods,
But a plain homespun truth, is what I ask.
I did, myself, o'erhear your queen make love
To Dolabella. Speak; for I will know,
By your confession, what more passed betwixt them;
How near the business draws to your employment;
And when the happy hour.
ANTONY. Speak truth, Alexas; whether it offend
Or please Ventidius, care not: Justify
Thy injured queen from malice: Dare his worst.
OCTAVIA. [aside.] See how he gives him courage! how he fears
To find her false! and shuts his eyes to truth,
Willing to be misled!
ALEXAS. As far as love may plead for woman's frailty,
Urged by desert and greatness of the lover,
So far, divine Octavia, may my queen
Stand even excused to you for loving him
Who is your lord: so far, from brave Ventidius,

May her past actions hope a fair report.
ANTONY.'Tis well, and truly spoken: mark, Ventidius.
ALEXAS. To you, most noble emperor, her strong passion
Stands not excused, but wholly justified.
Her beauty's charms alone, without her crown,
>From Ind and Meroe drew the distant vows
Of sighing kings; and at her feet were laid
The sceptres of the earth, exposed on heaps,
To choose where she would reign:
She thought a Roman only could deserve her,
And, of all Romans, only Antony;
And, to be less than wife to you, disdained
Their lawful passion.
ANTONY.'Tis but truth.
ALEXAS. And yet, though love, and your unmatched desert,
Have drawn her from the due regard of honour,
At last Heaven opened her unwilling eyes
To see the wrongs she offered fair Octavia,
Whose holy bed she lawlessly usurped.
The sad effects of this improsperous war
Confirmed those pious thoughts.
VENTIDIUS. [aside.] Oh, wheel you there?
Observe him now; the man begins to mend,
And talk substantial reason.--Fear not, eunuch;
The emperor has given thee leave to speak.
ALEXAS. Else had I never dared to offend his ears
With what the last necessity has urged
On my forsaken mistress; yet I must not
Presume to say, her heart is wholly altered.
ANTONY. No, dare not for thy life, I charge thee dare not
Pronounce that fatal word!
OCTAVIA. Must I bear this? Good Heaven, afford me patience.
[Aside.]
VENTIDIUS. On, sweet eunuch; my dear half-man, proceed.
ALEXAS. Yet Dolabella

Has loved her long; he, next my god-like lord,
Deserves her best; and should she meet his passion,
Rejected, as she is, by him she loved----
ANTONY. Hence from my sight! for I can bear no more:
Let furies drag thee quick to hell; let all
The longer damned have rest; each torturing hand
Do thou employ, till Cleopatra comes;
Then join thou too, and help to torture her!
[Exit ALEXAS, thrust out by ANTONY.]
OCTAVIA.'Tis not well.
Indeed, my lord,'tis much unkind to me,
To show this passion, this extreme concernment,
For an abandoned, faithless prostitute.
ANTONY. Octavia, leave me; I am much disordered:
Leave me, I say.
OCTAVIA. My lord!
ANTONY. I bid you leave me.
VENTIDIUS. Obey him, madam: best withdraw a while,
And see how this will work.
OCTAVIA. Wherein have I offended you, my lord,
That I am bid to leave you? Am I false,
Or infamous? Am I a Cleopatra?
Were I she,
Base as she is, you would not bid me leave you;
But hang upon my neck, take slight excuses,
And fawn upon my falsehood.
ANTONY.'Tis too much.
Too much, Octavia; I am pressed with sorrows
Too heavy to be borne; and you add more:
I would retire, and recollect what's left
Of man within, to aid me.
OCTAVIA. You would mourn,
In private, for your love, who has betrayed you.
You did but half return to me: your kindness
Lingered behind with her, I hear, my lord,
You make conditions for her,
And would include her treaty. Wondrous proofs
Of love to me!

ANTONY. Are you my friend, Ventidius?
Or are you turned a Dolabella too,
And let this fury loose?
VENTIDIUS. Oh, be advised,
Sweet madam, and retire.
OCTAVIA. Yes, I will go; but never to return.
You shall no more be haunted with this Fury.
My lord, my lord, love will not always last,
When urged with long unkindness and disdain:
Take her again, whom you prefer to me;
She stays but to be called. Poor cozened man!
Let a feigned parting give her back your heart,
Which a feigned love first got; for injured me,
Though my just sense of wrongs forbid my stay,
My duty shall be yours.
To the dear pledges of our former love
My tenderness and care shall be transferred,
And they shall cheer, by turns, my widowed nights:
So, take my last farewell; for I despair
To have you whole, and scorn to take you half.
[Exit.]
VENTIDIUS. I combat Heaven, which blasts my best designs;
My last attempt must be to win her back;
But oh! I fear in vain.
[Exit.]
ANTONY. Why was I framed with this plain, honest heart,
Which knows not to disguise its griefs and weakness,
But bears its workings outward to the world?
I should have kept the mighty anguish in,
And forced a smile at Cleopatra's falsehood:
Octavia had believed it, and had stayed.
But I am made a shallow-forded stream,
Seen to the bottom: all my clearness scorned,
And all my faults exposed.--See where he comes,
Enter DOLLABELLA
Who has profaned the sacred name of friend,
And worn it into vileness!

With how secure a brow, and specious form,
He gilds the secret villain! Sure that face
Was meant for honesty; but Heaven mismatched it,
And furnished treason out with nature's pomp,
To make its work more easy.
DOLABELLA. O my friend!
ANTONY. Well, Dolabella, you performed my message?
DOLABELLA. I did, unwillingly.
ANTONY. Unwillingly?
Was it so hard for you to bear our parting?
You should have wished it.
DOLABELLA. Why?
ANTONY. Because you love me.
And she received my message with as true,
With as unfeigned a sorrow as you brought it?
DOLABELLA. She loves you, even to madness.
ANTONY. Oh, I know it.
You, Dolabella, do not better know
How much she loves me. And should I
Forsake this beauty? This all-perfect creature?
DOLABELLA. I could not, were she mine.
ANTONY. And yet you first
Persuaded me: How come you altered since?
DOLABELLA. I said at first I was not fit to go:
I could not hear her sighs, and see her tears,
But pity must prevail: And so, perhaps,
It may again with you; for I have promised,
That she should take her last farewell: And, see,
She comes to claim my word.
Enter CLEOPATRA
ANTONY. False Dolabella!
DOLABELLA. What's false, my lord?
ANTONY. Why, Dolabella's false,
And Cleopatra's false; both false and faithless.
Draw near, you well-joined wickedness, you serpents,
Whom I have in my kindly bosom warmed,
Till I am stung to death.
DOLABELLA. My lord, have I

Deserved to be thus used?
CLEOPATRA. Can Heaven prepare
A newer torment? Can it find a curse
Beyond our separation?
ANTONY. Yes, if fate
Be just, much greater: Heaven should be ingenious
In punishing such crimes. The rolling stone,
And gnawing vulture, were slight pains, invented
When Jove was young, and no examples known
Of mighty ills; but you have ripened sin,
To such a monstrous growth,'twill pose the gods
To find an equal torture. Two, two such!--
Oh, there's no further name,--two such! to me,
To me, who locked my soul within your breasts,
Had no desires, no joys, no life, but you;
When half the globe was mine, I gave it you
In dowry with my heart; I had no use,
No fruit of all, but you: A friend and mistress
Was what the world could give. O Cleopatra!
O Dolabella! how could you betray
This tender heart, which with an infant fondness
Lay lulled betwixt your bosoms, and there slept,
Secure of injured faith?
DOLABELLA. If she has wronged you,
Heaven, hell, and you revenge it.
ANTONY. If she has wronged me!
Thou wouldst evade thy part of guilt; but swear
Thou lov'st not her.
DOLABELLA. Not so as I love you.
ANTONY. Not so? Swear, swear, I say, thou dost not love her.
DOLABELLA. No more than friendship will allow.
ANTONY. No more?
Friendship allows thee nothing: Thou art perjured--
And yet thou didst not swear thou lov'st her not;
But not so much, no more. O trifling hypocrite,
Who dar'st not own to her, thou dost not love,
Nor own to me, thou dost! Ventidius heard it;

Octavia saw it.
CLEOPATRA. They are enemies.
ANTONY. Alexas is not so: He, he confessed it;
He, who, next hell, best knew it, he avowed it.
Why do I seek a proof beyond yourself?
[To DOLABELLA.]
You, whom I sent to bear my last farewell,
Returned, to plead her stay.
DOLABELLA. What shall I answer?
If to have loved be guilt, then I have sinned;
But if to have repented of that love
Can wash away my crime, I have repented.
Yet, if I have offended past forgiveness,
Let not her suffer: She is innocent.
CLEOPATRA. Ah, what will not a woman do, who loves?
What means will she refuse, to keep that heart,
Where all her joys are placed?'Twas I encouraged,
'Twas I blew up the fire that scorched his soul,
To make you jealous, and by that regain you.
But all in vain; I could not counterfeit:
In spite of all the dams my love broke o'er,
And drowned by heart again: fate took the occasion;
And thus one minute's feigning has destroyed
My whole life's truth.
ANTONY. Thin cobweb arts of falsehood;
Seen, and broke through at first.
DOLABELLA. Forgive your mistress.
CLEOPATRA. Forgive your friend.
ANTONY. You have convinced yourselves.
You plead each other's cause: What witness have you,
That you but meant to raise my jealousy?
CLEOPATRA. Ourselves, and Heaven.
ANTONY. Guilt witnesses for guilt. Hence, love and friendship!
You have no longer place in human breasts,
These two have driven you out: Avoid my sight!
I would not kill the man whom I have loved,
And cannot hurt the woman; but avoid me:

I do not know how long I can be tame;
For, if I stay one minute more, to think
How I am wronged, my justice and revenge
Will cry so loud within me, that my pity
Will not be heard for either.
DOLABELLA. Heaven has but
Our sorrow for our sins; and then delights
To pardon erring man: Sweet mercy seems
Its darling attribute, which limits justice;
As if there were degrees in infinite,
And infinite would rather want perfection
Than punish to extent.
ANTONY. I can forgive
A foe; but not a mistress and a friend.
Treason is there in its most horrid shape,
Where trust is greatest; and the soul resigned,
Is stabbed by its own guards: I'll hear no more;
Hence from my sight for ever!
CLEOPATRA. How? for ever!
I cannot go one moment from your sight,
And must I go for ever?
My joys, my only joys, are centred here:
What place have I to go to? My own kingdom?
That I have lost for you: Or to the Romans?
They hate me for your sake: Or must I wander
The wide world o'er, a helpless, banished woman,
Banished for love of you; banished from you?
Ay, there's the banishment! Oh, hear me; hear me,
With strictest justice: For I beg no favour;
And if I have offended you, then kill me,
But do not banish me.
ANTONY. I must not hear you.
I have a fool within me takes your part;
But honour stops my ears.
CLEOPATRA. For pity hear me!
Would you cast off a slave who followed you?
Who crouched beneath your spurn?--He has no pity!
See, if he gives one tear to my departure;

One look, one kind farewell: O iron heart!
Let all the gods look down, and judge betwixt us,
If he did ever love!
ANTONY. No more: Alexas!
DOLABELLA. A perjured villain!
ANTONY. [to CLEOPATRA.] Your Alexas; yours.
CLEOPATRA. Oh,'twas his plot; his ruinous design,
To engage you in my love by jealousy.
Hear him; confront him with me; let him speak.
ANTONY. I have; I have.
CLEOPATRA. And if he clear me not--
ANTONY. Your creature! one, who hangs upon your smiles!
Watches your eye, to say or to unsay,
Whate'er you please! I am not to be moved.
CLEOPATRA. Then must we part? Farewell, my cruel lord!
The appearance is against me; and I go,
Unjustified, for ever from your sight.
How I have loved, you know; how yet I love,
My only comfort is, I know myself:
I love you more, even now you are unkind,
Then when you loved me most; so well, so truly
I'll never strive against it; but die pleased,
To think you once were mine.
ANTONY. Good heaven, they weep at parting!
Must I weep too? that calls them innocent.
I must not weep; and yet I must, to think
That I must not forgive.--
Live, but live wretched;'tis but just you should,
Who made me so: Live from each other's sight:
Let me not hear you meet. Set all the earth,
And all the seas, betwixt your sundered loves:
View nothing common but the sun and skies.
Now, all take several ways;
And each your own sad fate, with mine, deplore;
That you were false, and I could trust no more.
[Exeunt severally.]

Act V
Scene I
Enter CLEOPATRA, CHARMION, and IRAS
CHARMION. Be juster, Heaven; such virtue punished thus,
Will make us think that chance rules all above,
And shuffles, with a random hand, the lots,
Which man is forced to draw.
CLEOPATRA. I could tear out these eyes, that gained his heart,
And had not power to keep it. O the curse
Of doting on, even when I find it dotage!
Bear witness, gods, you heard him bid me go;
You, whom he mocked with imprecating vows
Of promised faith!--I'll die; I will not bear it.
You may hold me--
[She pulls out her dagger, and they hold her.]
But I can keep my breath; I can die inward,
And choke this love.
Enter ALEXAS
IRAS. Help, O Alexas, help!
The queen grows desperate; her soul struggles in her
With all the agonies of love and rage,
And strives to force its passage.
CLEOPATRA. Let me go.
Art thou there, traitor!--O,
O for a little breath, to vent my rage,
Give, give me way, and let me loose upon him.
ALEXAS. Yes, I deserve it, for my ill-timed truth.
Was it for me to prop
The ruins of a falling majesty?
To place myself beneath the mighty flaw,
Thus to be crushed, and pounded into atoms,
By its o'erwhelming weight?'Tis too presuming
For subjects to preserve that wilful power,
Which courts its own destruction.
CLEOPATRA. I would reason
More calmly with you. Did not you o'errule,

And force my plain, direct, and open love,
Into these crooked paths of jealousy?
Now, what's the event? Octavia is removed;
But Cleopatra's banished. Thou, thou villain,
Hast pushed my boat to open sea; to prove,
At my sad cost, if thou canst steer it back.
It cannot be; I'm lost too far; I'm ruined:
Hence, thou impostor, traitor, monster, devil!--
I can no more: Thou, and my griefs, have sunk
Me down so low, that I want voice to curse thee.
ALEXAS. Suppose some shipwrecked seaman near the shore,
Dropping and faint, with climbing up the cliff,
If, from above, some charitable hand
Pull him to safety, hazarding himself,
To draw the other's weight; would he look back,
And curse him for his pains? The case is yours;
But one step more, and you have gained the height.
CLEOPATRA. Sunk, never more to rise.
ALEXAS. Octavia's gone, and Dolabella banished.
Believe me, madam, Antony is yours.
His heart was never lost, but started off
To jealousy, love's last retreat and covert;
Where it lies hid in shades, watchful in silence,
And listening for the sound that calls it back.
Some other, any man ('tis so advanced),
May perfect this unfinished work, which I
(Unhappy only to myself) have left
So easy to his hand.
CLEOPATRA. Look well thou do't; else--
ALEXAS. Else, what your silence threatens.--Antony
Is mounted up the Pharos; from whose turret,
He stands surveying our Egyptian galleys,
Engaged with Caesar's fleet. Now death or conquest!
If the first happen, fate acquits my promise;
If we o'ercome, the conqueror is yours.
[A distant shout within.]
CHARMION. Have comfort, madam: Did you mark that

shout?
[Second shout nearer.]
IRAS. Hark! they redouble it.
ALEXAS.'Tis from the port.
The loudness shows it near: Good news, kind heavens!
CLEOPATRA. Osiris make it so!
Enter SERAPION
SERAPION. Where, where's the queen?
ALEXAS. How frightfully the holy coward stares
As if not yet recovered of the assault,
When all his gods, and, what's more dear to him,
His offerings, were at stake.
SERAPION. O horror, horror!
Egypt has been; our latest hour has come:
The queen of nations, from her ancient seat,
Is sunk for ever in the dark abyss:
Time has unrolled her glories to the last,
And now closed up the volume.
CLEOPATRA. Be more plain:
Say, whence thou comest; though fate is in thy face,
Which from the haggard eyes looks wildly out,
And threatens ere thou speakest.
SERAPION. I came from Pharos;
>From viewing (spare me, and imagine it)
Our land's last hope, your navy--
CLEOPATRA. Vanquished?
SERAPION. No:
They fought not.
CLEOPATRA. Then they fled.
SERAPION. Nor that. I saw,
With Antony, your well-appointed fleet
Row out; and thrice he waved his hand on high,
And thrice with cheerful cries they shouted back:
'Twas then false Fortune, like a fawning strumpet,
About to leave the bankrupt prodigal,
With a dissembled smile would kiss at parting,
And flatter to the last; the well-timed oars,
Now dipt from every bank, now smoothly run

To meet the foe; and soon indeed they met,
But not as foes. In few, we saw their caps
On either side thrown up; the Egyptian galleys,
Received like friends, passed through, and fell behind
The Roman rear: And now, they all come forward,
And ride within the port.
CLEOPATRA. Enough, Serapion:
I've heard my doom.--This needed not, you gods:
When I lost Antony, your work was done;
'Tis but superfluous malice.--Where's my lord?
How bears he this last blow?
SERAPION. His fury cannot be expressed by words:
Thrice he attempted headlong to have fallen
Full on his foes, and aimed at Caesar's galley:
Withheld, he raves on you; cries,--He's betrayed.
Should he now find you--
ALEXAS. Shun him; seek your safety,
Till you can clear your innocence.
CLEOPATRA. I'll stay.
ALEXAS. You must not; haste you to your monument,
While I make speed to Caesar.
CLEOPATRA. Caesar! No,
I have no business with him.
ALEXAS. I can work him
To spare your life, and let this madman perish.
CLEOPATRA. Base fawning wretch! wouldst thou betray him too?
Hence from my sight! I will not hear a traitor;
'Twas thy design brought all this ruin on us.--
Serapion, thou art honest; counsel me:
But haste, each moment's precious.
SERAPION. Retire; you must not yet see Antony.
He who began this mischief,
'Tis just he tempt the danger; let him clear you:
And, since he offered you his servile tongue,
To gain a poor precarious life from Caesar,
Let him expose that fawning eloquence,
And speak to Antony.

ALEXAS. O heavens! I dare not;
I meet my certain death.
CLEOPATRA. Slave, thou deservest it.--
Not that I fear my lord, will I avoid him;
I know him noble: when he banished me,
And thought me false, he scorned to take my life;
But I'll be justified, and then die with him.
ALEXAS. O pity me, and let me follow you.
CLEOPATRA. To death, if thou stir hence. Speak, if thou canst,
Now for thy life, which basely thou wouldst save;
While mine I prize at--this! Come, good Serapion.
[Exeunt CLEOPATRA, SERAPION, CHARMION, and IRAS.]
ALEXAS. O that I less could fear to lose this being,
Which, like a snowball in my coward hand,
The more'tis grasped, the faster melts away.
Poor reason! what a wretched aid art thou!
For still, in spite of thee,
These two long lovers, soul and body, dread
Their final separation. Let me think:
What can I say, to save myself from death?
No matter what becomes of Cleopatra.
ANTONY. Which way? where?
[Within.]
VENTIDIUS. This leads to the monument.
[Within.]
ALEXAS. Ah me! I hear him; yet I'm unprepared:
My gift of lying's gone;
And this court-devil, which I so oft have raised,
Forsakes me at my need. I dare not stay;
Yet cannot far go hence.
[Exit.]
Enter ANTONY and VENTIDIUS
ANTONY. O happy Caesar! thou hast men to lead:
Think not'tis thou hast conquered Antony;
But Rome has conquered Egypt. I'm betrayed.
VENTIDIUS. Curse on this treacherous train!

Their soil and heaven infect them all with baseness:
And their young souls come tainted to the world
With the first breath they draw.
ANTONY. The original villain sure no god created;
He was a bastard of the sun, by Nile,
Aped into man; with all his mother's mud
Crusted about his soul.
VENTIDIUS. The nation is
One universal traitor; and their queen
The very spirit and extract of them all.
ANTONY. Is there yet left
A possibility of aid from valour?
Is there one god unsworn to my destruction?
The least unmortgaged hope? for, if there be,
Methinks I cannot fall beneath the fate
Of such a boy as Caesar.
The world's one half is yet in Antony;
And from each limb of it, that's hewed away,
The soul comes back to me.
VENTIDIUS. There yet remain
Three legions in the town. The last assault
Lopt off the rest; if death be your design,--
As I must wish it now,--these are sufficient
To make a heap about us of dead foes,
An honest pile for burial.
ANTONY. They are enough.
We'll not divide our stars; but, side by side,
Fight emulous, and with malicious eyes
Survey each other's acts: So every death
Thou giv'st, I'll take on me, as a just debt,
And pay thee back a soul.
VENTIDIUS. Now you shall see I love you. Not a word
Of chiding more. By my few hours of life,
I am so pleased with this brave Roman fate,
That I would not be Caesar, to outlive you.
When we put off this flesh, and mount together,
I shall be shown to all the ethereal crowd,--
Lo, this is he who died with Antony!

ANTONY. Who knows, but we may pierce through all their troops,
And reach my veterans yet?'tis worth the'tempting,
To o'erleap this gulf of fate,
And leave our wandering destinies behind.
Enter ALEXAS, trembling
VENTIDIUS. See, see, that villain!
See Cleopatra stamped upon that face,
With all her cunning, all her arts of falsehood!
How she looks out through those dissembling eyes!
How he sets his countenance for deceit,
And promises a lie, before he speaks!
Let me despatch him first.
[Drawing.]
ALEXAS. O spare me, spare me!
ANTONY. Hold; he's not worth your killing.--On thy life,
Which thou may'st keep, because I scorn to take it,
No syllable to justify thy queen;
Save thy base tongue its office.
ALEXAS. Sir, she is gone.
Where she shall never be molested more
By love, or you.
ANTONY. Fled to her Dolabella!
Die, traitor! I revoke my promise! die!
[Going to kill him.]
ALEXAS. O hold! she is not fled.
ANTONY. She is: my eyes
Are open to her falsehood; my whole life
Has been a golden dream of love and friendship;
But, now I wake, I'm like a merchant, roused
>From soft repose, to see his vessel sinking,
And all his wealth cast over. Ungrateful woman!
Who followed me, but as the swallow summer,
Hatching her young ones in my kindly beams,
Singing her flatteries to my morning wake:
But, now my winter comes, she spreads her wings,
And seeks the spring of Caesar.
ALEXAS. Think not so;

Her fortunes have, in all things, mixed with yours.
Had she betrayed her naval force to Rome,
How easily might she have gone to Caesar,
Secure by such a bribe!
VENTIDIUS. She sent it first,
To be more welcome after.
ANTONY.'Tis too plain;
Else would she have appeared, to clear herself.
ALEXAS. Too fatally she has: she could not bear
To be accused by you; but shut herself
Within her monument; looked down and sighed;
While, from her unchanged face, the silent tears
Dropt, as they had not leave, but stole their parting.
Some indistinguished words she only murmured;
At last, she raised her eyes; and, with such looks
As dying Lucrece cast--
ANTONY. My heart forebodes--
VENTIDIUS. All for the best:--Go on.
ALEXAS. She snatched her poniard,
And, ere we could prevent the fatal blow,
Plunged it within her breast; then turned to me:
Go, bear my lord, said she, my last farewell;
And ask him, if he yet suspect my faith.
More she was saying, but death rushed betwixt.
She half pronounced your name with her last breath,
And buried half within her.
VENTIDIUS. Heaven be praised!
ANTONY. Then art thou innocent, my poor dear love,
And art thou dead?
O those two words! their sound should be divided:
Hadst thou been false, and died; or hadst thou lived,
And hadst been true--But innocence and death!
This shows not well above. Then what am I,
The murderer of this truth, this innocence!
Thoughts cannot form themselves in words so horrid
As can express my guilt!
VENTIDIUS. Is't come to this? The gods have been too gracious;

And thus you thank them for it!
ANTONY. [to ALEXAS.] Why stayest thou here?
Is it for thee to spy upon my soul,
And see its inward mourning? Get thee hence;
Thou art not worthy to behold, what now
Becomes a Roman emperor to perform.
ALEXAS. He loves her still:
His grief betrays it. Good! the joy to find
She's yet alive, completes the reconcilement.
I've saved myself, and her. But, oh! the Romans!
Fate comes too fast upon my wit,
Hunts me too hard, and meets me at each double.
[Aside.]
[Exit.]
VENTIDIUS. Would she had died a little sooner, though!
Before Octavia went, you might have treated:
Now'twill look tame, and would not be received.
Come, rouse yourself, and let's die warm together.
ANTONY. I will not fight: there's no more work for war.
The business of my angry hours is done.
VENTIDIUS. Caesar is at your gates.
ANTONY. Why, let him enter;
He's welcome now.
VENTIDIUS. What lethargy has crept into your soul?
ANTONY.'Tis but a scorn of life, and just desire
To free myself from bondage.
VENTIDIUS. Do it bravely.
ANTONY. I will; but not by fighting. O Ventidius!
What should I fight for now?--my queen is dead.
I was but great for her; my power, my empire,
Were but my merchandise to buy her love;
And conquered kings, my factors. Now she's dead,
Let Caesar take the world,--
An empty circle, since the jewel's gone
Which made it worth my strife: my being's nauseous;
For all the bribes of life are gone away.
VENTIDIUS. Would you be taken?
ANTONY. Yes, I would be taken;

But, as a Roman ought,--dead, my Ventidius:
For I'll convey my soul from Caesar's reach,
And lay down life myself.'Tis time the world
Should have a lord, and know whom to obey.
We two have kept its homage in suspense,
And bent the globe, on whose each side we trod,
Till it was dented inwards. Let him walk
Alone upon't: I'm weary of my part.
My torch is out; and the world stands before me,
Like a black desert at the approach of night:
I'll lay me down, and stray no farther on.
VENTIDIUS. I could be grieved,
But that I'll not outlive you: choose your death;
For, I have seen him in such various shapes,
I care not which I take: I'm only troubled,
The life I bear is worn to such a rag,
'Tis scarce worth giving. I could wish, indeed,
We threw it from us with a better grace;
That, like two lions taken in the toils,
We might at last thrust out our paws, and wound
The hunters that inclose us.
ANTONY. I have thought on it.
Ventidius, you must live.
VENTIDIUS. I must not, sir.
ANTONY. Wilt thou not live, to speak some good of me?
To stand by my fair fame, and guard the approaches
>From the ill tongues of men?
VENTIDIUS. Who shall guard mine,
For living after you?
ANTONY. Say, I command it.
VENTIDIUS. If we die well, our deaths will speak themselves
And need no living witness.
ANTONY. Thou hast loved me,
And fain I would reward thee. I must die;
Kill me, and take the merit of my death,
To make thee friends with Caesar.
VENTIDIUS. Thank your kindness.

You said I loved you; and in recompense,
You bid me turn a traitor: Did I think
You would have used me thus?--that I should die
With a hard thought of you?
ANTONY. Forgive me, Roman.
Since I have heard of Cleopatra's death,
My reason bears no rule upon my tongue,
But lets my thoughts break all at random out.
I've thought better; do not deny me twice.
VENTIDIUS. By Heaven I will not.
Let it not be to outlive you.
ANTONY. Kill me first,
And then die thou; for'tis but just thou serve
Thy friend, before thyself.
VENTIDIUS. Give me your hand.
We soon shall meet again. Now, farewell, emperor!--
[Embrace.]
Methinks that word's too cold to be my last:
Since death sweeps all distinctions, farewell, friend!
That's all--
I will not make a business of a trifle;
And yet I cannot look on you, and kill you;
Pray turn your face.
ANTONY. I do: strike home, be sure.
VENTIDIUS. Home as my sword will reach.
[Kills himself.]
ANTONY. Oh, thou mistak'st;
That wound was not of thine; give it me back:
Thou robb'st me of my death.
VENTIDIUS. I do indeed;
But think'tis the first time I e'er deceived you,
If that may plead my pardon.--And you, gods,
Forgive me, if you will; for I die perjured,
Rather than kill my friend.
[Dies.]
ANTONY. Farewell! Ever my leader, even in death!
My queen and thou have got the start of me,
And I'm the lag of honour.--Gone so soon?

Is Death no more? he used him carelessly,
With a familiar kindness: ere he knocked,
Ran to the door, and took him in his arms,
As who should say--You're welcome at all hours,
A friend need give no warning. Books had spoiled him;
For all the learned are cowards by profession.
'Tis not worth
My further thought; for death, for aught I know,
Is but to think no more. Here's to be satisfied.
[Falls on his sword.]
I've missed my heart. O unperforming hand!
Thou never couldst have erred in a worse time.
My fortune jades me to the last; and death,
Like a great man, takes state, and makes me wait
For my admittance.--
[Trampling within.]
Some, perhaps, from Caesar:
If he should find me living, and suspect
That I played booty with my life! I'll mend
My work, ere they can reach me.
[Rises upon his knees.]
Enter CLEOPATRA, CHARMION, and IRAS
CLEOPATRA. Where is my lord? where is he?
CHARMION. There he lies,
And dead Ventidius by him.
CLEOPATRA. My tears were prophets; I am come too late.
O that accursed Alexas!
[Runs to him.]
ANTONY. Art thou living?
Or am I dead before I knew, and thou
The first kind ghost that meets me?
CLEOPATRA. Help me seat him.
Send quickly, send for help!
[They place him in a chair.]
ANTONY. I am answered.
We live both. Sit thee down, my Cleopatra:
I'll make the most I can of life, to stay
A moment more with thee.

CLEOPATRA. How is it with you?
ANTONY.'Tis as with a man
Removing in a hurry; all packed up,
But one dear jewel that his haste forgot;
And he, for that, returns upon the spur:
So I come back for thee.
CLEOPATRA. Too long, ye heavens, you have been cruel to me:
Now show your mended faith, and give me back
His fleeting life!
ANTONY. It will not be, my love;
I keep my soul by force.
Say but, thou art not false.
CLEOPATRA.'Tis now too late
To say I'm true: I'll prove it, and die with you.
Unknown to me, Alexas feigned my death:
Which, when I knew, I hasted to prevent
This fatal consequence. My fleet betrayed
Both you and me.
ANTONY. And Dolabella--
CLEOPATRA. Scarce
Esteemed before he loved; but hated now.
ANTONY. Enough: my life's not long enough for more.
Thou say'st, thou wilt come after: I believe thee;
For I can now believe whate'er thou sayest,
That we may part more kindly.
CLEOPATRA. I will come:
Doubt not, my life, I'll come, and quickly too:
Caesar shall triumph o'er no part of thee.
ANTONY. But grieve not, while thou stayest,
My last disastrous times:
Think we have had a clear and glorious day
And Heaven did kindly to delay the storm,
Just till our close of evening. Ten years'love,
And not a moment lost, but all improved
To the utmost joys,--what ages have we lived?
And now to die each other's; and, so dying,
While hand in hand we walk in groves below,

Whole troops of lovers'ghosts shall flock about us,
And all the train be ours.
CLEOPATRA. Your words are like the notes of dying swans,
Too sweet to last. Were there so many hours
For your unkindness, and not one for love?
ANTONY. No, not a minute.--This one kiss--more worth
Than all I leave to Caesar.
[Dies.]
CLEOPATRA. O tell me so again,
And take ten thousand kisses for that word.
My lord, my lord! speak, if you yet have being;
Sign to me, if you cannot speak; or cast
One look! Do anything that shows you live.
IRAS. He's gone too far to hear you;
And this you see, a lump of senseless clay,
The leavings of a soul.
CHARMION. Remember, madam,
He charged you not to grieve.
CLEOPATRA. And I'll obey him.
I have not loved a Roman, not to know
What should become his wife; his wife, my Charmion!
For'tis to that high title I aspire;
And now I'll not die less. Let dull Octavia
Survive, to mourn him dead: My nobler fate
Shall knit our spousals with a tie, too strong
For Roman laws to break.
IRAS. Will you then die?
CLEOPATRA. Why shouldst thou make that question?
IRAS. Caesar is merciful.
CLEOPATRA. Let him be so
To those that want his mercy: My poor lord
Made no such covenant with him, to spare me
When he was dead. Yield me to Caesar's pride?
What! to be led in triumph through the streets,
A spectacle to base plebeian eyes;
While some dejected friend of Antony's,
Close in a corner, shakes his head, and mutters
A secret curse on her who ruined him!

I'll none of that.
CHARMION. Whatever you resolve,
I'll follow, even to death.
IRAS. I only feared
For you; but more should fear to live without you.
CLEOPATRA. Why, now,'tis as it should be. Quick, my friends,
Despatch; ere this, the town's in Caesar's hands:
My lord looks down concerned, and fears my stay,
Lest I should be surprised;
Keep him not waiting for his love too long.
You, Charmion, bring my crown and richest jewels;
With them, the wreath of victory I made
(Vain augury!) for him, who now lies dead:
You, Iras, bring the cure of all our ills.
IRAS. The aspics, madam?
CLEOPATRA. Must I bid you twice?
[Exit CHARMION and IRAS.]
'Tis sweet to die, when they would force life on me,
To rush into the dark abode of death,
And seize him first; if he be like my love,
He is not frightful, sure.
We're now alone, in secrecy and silence;
And is not this like lovers? I may kiss
These pale, cold lips; Octavia does not see me:
And, oh!'tis better far to have him thus,
Than see him in her arms.--Oh, welcome, welcome!
Enter CHARMION and IRAS
CHARMION. What must be done?
CLEOPATRA. Short ceremony, friends;
But yet it must be decent. First, this laurel
Shall crown my hero's head: he fell not basely,
Nor left his shield behind him.--Only thou
Couldst triumph o'er thyself; and thou alone
Wert worthy so to triumph.
CHARMION. To what end
These ensigns of your pomp and royalty?
CLEOPATRA. Dull, that thou art! why'tis to meet my love;

As when I saw him first, on Cydnus'bank,
All sparkling, like a goddess: so adorned,
I'll find him once again; my second spousals
Shall match my first in glory. Haste, haste, both,
And dress the bride of Antony.
CHARMION.'Tis done.
CLEOPATRA. Now seat me by my lord. I claim this place,
For I must conquer Caesar too, like him,
And win my share of the world.--Hail, you dear relics
Of my immortal love!
O let no impious hand remove you hence:
But rest for ever here! Let Egypt give
His death that peace, which it denied his life.--
Reach me the casket.
IRAS. Underneath the fruit
The aspic lies.
CLEOPATRA. Welcome, thou kind deceiver!
[Putting aside the leaves.]
Thou best of thieves: who, with an easy key,
Dost open life, and, unperceived by us,
Even steal us from ourselves; discharging so
Death's dreadful office, better than himself;
Touching our limbs so gently into slumber,
That Death stands by, deceived by his own image,
And thinks himself but sleep.
SERAPION. The queen, where is she?
[Within.]
The town is yielded, Caesar's at the gates.
Haste, bare my arm, and rouse the serpent's fury.
[Holds out her arm, and draws it back.]
Coward flesh,
Wouldst thou conspire with Caesar to betray me,
As thou wert none of mine? I'll force thee to it,
And not be sent by him,
But bring, myself, my soul to Antony.
[Turns aside, and then shows her arm bloody.]
Take hence; the work is done.
SERAPION. Break ope the door,

[Within.]
And guard the traitor well.
CHARMION. The next is ours.
IRAS. Now, Charmion, to be worthy
Of our great queen and mistress.
[They apply the aspics.]
CLEOPATRA. Already, death, I feel thee in my veins:
I go with such a will to find my lord,
That we shall quickly meet.
A heavy numbness creeps through every limb,
And now'tis at my head: My eyelids fall,
And my dear love is vanquished in a mist.
Where shall I find him, where? O turn me to him,
And lay me on his breast!--Caesar, thy worst;
Now part us, if thou canst.
[Dies.]
[IRAS sinks down at her feet, and dies;
CHARMION stands behind her chair, as dressing her head.]
Enter SERAPION, two PRIESTS, ALEXAS bound, EGYPTIANS
PRIEST. Behold, Serapion,
What havoc death has made!
SERAPION.'Twas what I feared.--
Charmion, is this well done?
CHARMION. Yes,'tis well done, and like a queen, the last
Of her great race: I follow her.
[Sinks down: dies.]
ALEXAS.'Tis true,
She has done well: Much better thus to die,
Than live to make a holiday in Rome.
SERAPION. See how the lovers sit in state together,
As they were giving laws to half mankind!
The impression of a smile, left in her face,
Shows she died pleased with him for whom she lived,
And went to charm him in another world.
Caesar's just entering: grief has now no leisure.
Secure that villain, as our pledge of safety,
To grace the imperial triumph.--Sleep, blest pair,

Secure from human chance, long ages out,
While all the storms of fate fly o'er your tomb;
And fame to late posterity shall tell,
No lovers lived so great, or died so well.
[Exeunt.]
EPILOGUE
Poets, like disputants, when reasons fail,
Have one sure refuge left--and that's to rail.
Fop, coxcomb, fool, are thundered through the pit;
And this is all their equipage of wit.
We wonder how the devil this difference grows
Betwixt our fools in verse, and yours in prose:
For,'faith, the quarrel rightly understood,
'Tis civil war with their own flesh and blood.
The threadbare author hates the gaudy coat;
And swears at the gilt coach, but swears afoot:
For'tis observed of every scribbling man,
He grows a fop as fast as e'er he can;
Prunes up, and asks his oracle, the glass,
If pink or purple best become his face.
For our poor wretch, he neither rails nor prays;
Nor likes your wit just as you like his plays;
He has not yet so much of Mr Bayes.
He does his best; and if he cannot please,
Would quietly sue out his WRIT OF EASE.
Yet, if he might his own grand jury call,
By the fair sex he begs to stand or fall.
Let Caesar's power the men's ambition move,
But grace you him who lost the world for love!
Yet if some antiquated lady say,
The last age is not copied in his play;
Heaven help the man who for that face must drudge,
Which only has the wrinkles of a judge.
Let not the young and beauteous join with those;
For should you raise such numerous hosts of foes,
Young wits and sparks he to his aid must call;
'Tis more than one man's work to please you all.

Chapter 7

Study Questions

Q. Describe how Women were Depicted in the Early Eighteenth Century plays ?

Or

Q. How the plays Depicted the Social Condition of Women in the Eighteenth Century?

The progress of humanity and the evolution of societies have been documented through oral traditions, cave paintings, textbooks and news reels. All of these forms of communication show the societies of which they tell, but only creations actually from the era they discuss can reflect an undistorted image. Literature is one of those mirrors - for it reflects not only the author's thoughts, but also the society in which the author lived.

Women's status evolution in society can be traced through literature, specifically through drama. As women began to step out from under their husbands'and fathers'thumbs, society saw an emergence of more dominating, independent female characters. The introduction of more female authors and playwrights gave rise to more dialogue from a feminine point of view and more desirable female roles. However, male writers also began developing their female characters. In addition to showing the evolution of women's role in society, drama also traced men's reactions to the female's new status. As the women gained higher status and independence, the roles for females written by several of the male playwrights became almost bipolar in relation to each other. Almost as if only together could the roles create one full character. The introduction of stronger female roles led to the extreme purification of feminine characters. The witty, self-reliant woman gained a wicked, bitter edge, and the innocent young daughter became even more devoted and tragic. While the extreme sides of the characters expanded, the middle ground between them seemed to shrink. Even in comedies, the role of the calculating woman became more wicked than humorous. As the character of the wife gained knowledge of her husband's affairs, she became the butt of more jokes and the target of humiliating acts. The biggest change comes about perhaps in the fact that the jokes were no longer at the expense of all characters, but at the expense of the newly enlightened woman.

However, the duality of the female characters, even as sexist as they were, must have heartened the actresses of the time because of the new role opportunities."No doubt the frequency of paired heroines in Restoration tragedy, passionate villainess and'Ravish'd Virgin', sexually experienced, restless intriguer and passive victim, reflects Restoration theatrical practice in providing parts for specific actresses.... But the bifurcation of Dark Lady and female saint, differentiated by the indelible stain of sexual knowledge, has deep psychological root". The root slowly sprouted and only through the passage of time did the change become apparent. Amphitryon (1690),The Beggar's Opera (1728) and The London Merchant (1731) are three plays that show the progression and evolution of the characters of the daughter, the wife and the independent, calculating woman through time.

The role of the daughter is represented in dissimilar ways with John Gay's The Beggar's Opera and George Lillo's The London Merchant. The slightly earlier play (Opera) provides Polly as the part of the young innocent daughter. Yet, she possesses a little of the individualism indicative of the independent female with her refusals to blindly obey her parents. Her persistence in marrying Macheath despité her parents wishes contradicts the image of the submissive daughter. Such an attitude, along with Polly's act of marrying for love instead of for parental approval and money demonstrates the change in women's attitudes. The knowledge of self worth and desire to make independent choices are evident in the character of Polly. However, Gay avoids attacking the females and plays more off the humour of the situation instead of the change in the traditional daughter role."'But hear, me Mother.--If you ever loved--"Those cursed play-books she reads have been her ruin. One more word, hussy, and I shall knock your brains out, if you have any"'. It is not until later in the play does Gay poke fun directly at Polly and her role as a wife.

Lillo, in contrast, makes his daughter character, Maria, every bit the innocent, submissive and tragic young girl. As if to contrast the independent thinker that was arising in women in the real world, he overemphasizes Maria's obedience to her father. When discussing marriage, Maria says her choice of husband will be the man her father considers best.

THOR. A noble birth and fortune, though they make not a bad man good, yet they are a real advantage to a worthy one, and places his virtues in the fairest light.

MA. I cannot answer for my inclinations, but they shall ever be submitted to your wisdom and authority; and, as you will not compel me to marry where I cannot love, love shall never make me act contrary to my duty.--Sir, have I your permission to retire? The daughter character of Maria is similar to that of the wife character, Alcmena, in Dryden's Amphitryon. Both are submissive, obedient and eager to please. The role of wife seems to be a mere extension onto that of a daughter. Alcmena is apparently happy as a wife and actually loves her husband (a rarity in those days)."I am the fool of love, and find within me the fondness of a bride without the fear. My whole desires and wishes are in you". While Alcmena is happy with her husband, Amphitryon, the other wife in the play, Bromia is decidedly the opposite with her husband, Sosia. He alternates between insulting her and neglecting her. However, since it is a comedy, the relationship is talked about in jest, while Sosia makes advances on Phaedra.

Sosia: I warrant I was monstrous kind to thee.

Bromia: Yes, monstrous kind indeed. You never said a truer word; for, when I came to kiss you, you pulled away your mouth and turned your cheek to me.

Sosia: Good.

Bromia: How, good! Here's fine impudence. He justifies!

Sosia: Yes, I do justify, that I turned my cheek, like a prudent person, that my breath might not offend thee; for, now I remember, I had eaten garlic.

Gay presents a similar situation with Macheath and his several wives. Polly's devotion is used as a comedic effect and he is made the comic hero at her expense. While both Polly and Lucy lay claim to Macheath, he will only recognize, as his wife, the woman who can help him the most at that time. When he is imprisoned, he refuses Polly as his wife because Lucy can help him get out of the jail. He respects neither, as his play on words in the last sentence are used to make fun of the institution of marriage that the two women hold so revered:"Be pacified, my dear Lucy--this is all a fetch of Polly's to make me desperate with you in case I get off. If I am hanged, she would fain have the credit of being thought my widow.--Really Polly, this is no time for a dispute of this sort; for whenever you are talking of marriage, I am thinking of hanging".

Polly is a tragic character in Opera, because she never moves beyond the doting wife. Lucy, on the other hand, develops into a calculating woman with her plan to poison Polly. Opera treads on the middle ground with Lucy; first making her humorous, then embittered and devious, but never evil. It is a perfect balance between the earlier character of Phaedra (Amphitryon) and the later character of Ms. Millwood (Merchant). Phaedra is used entirely for comedic effect. Her self-serving antics and devious deals make for several jokes between the characters. But, her lack of sympathy for Bromia as she makes a sexual deal with her husband is relevant. The character is not taken seriously. Mercury pokes fun at her. Sosia seems half intimidated by her. Phaedra is a woman after her own wants, using her wits and wiles to persuade. However, no one sees her as a real threat.

In Merchant, Millwood is the reason for the tragic ending. Lillo takes the image of a strong, independent woman and makes her threatening to masculinity. The tragedy comes with her victim, George Barnwell. He is the innocent youth who is overcome by the wiles of the charming older woman. Several females have played the innocent to an older man, yet the situation is more commonly found in a comedy. Merchant presents a theme that warns against such woman as Millwood."The satirist's end, then, is to release men from the power of women by attacking the entire sex. Men need to free themselves from the power of the sex [Nussbaum's emphasis]. Ideally men will learn to live without women, who only confuse them, prove them fools, and then destroy them".

Ironically, or perhaps appropriately, it is from the representation of the most threatening woman for men that we find an explanation which blames the males for the actions that they despise most in women."Woman, by whom you are, the source of joy, with cruel arts you labour to destroy; a thousand ways our ruin you pursue, yet blame in us those arts first taught by you". Millwood becomes the extreme and the vindication of the manipulating woman at the same time.

The roles of wife, daughter, and manipulator evolved through the theater world at the same time they spread through the outside world. The Beggar's Opera, Amphitryon and The London Merchant reflected the changes of the times through their similar characters. Although the first two are comedies and the latter a tragedy, all present females in certain roles. The time span between the three, especially between Opera and Amphitryon, contributes to the different representations of the same type characters because of the change in sentiment in the outside world. Lillo, perhaps, faced the varying attitudes the best with his Millwood. Her explanation of her own role, despite the character's evil nature, may have led to a less threatening view of the independent woman."The path from the whore to the fallen woman leads to greater understanding of the woman's plight, and a shift in blame from her inherent sexual characteristics to her social plight".

Q. Discuss the Type-Casting in the Restoration Theatre ?

Or

Q. Do you agree that this feature is also reflected in Dryden's plays? If yes then how? Explain

The criticism raised by Dennis is one that Dryden seems to have anticipated when he wrote the play, since he begins his Preface vindicating"the excellency of the Moral," for-as he observes-"the chief persons represented, were famous patterns of unlawful love; and their end accordingly was unfortunate" (1984). Dryden proceeds then to justify his sympathetic portrayal of the characters of Antony and Cleopatra: he could not, obviously, make them examples of perfect virtue, since that would make their final punishment unfair; but neither would he make them images of vice, because they could not in that case elicit the pity necessary to the success of the tragedy (1984. But when he comes to the character of Octavia, he acknowledges the problem that it poses in the design of his play, and seems fully aware that it might provoke a reaction like that of John Dennis:

The greatest errour in the contrivance seems to be in the person of Octavia:

For... I had not enough consider'd, that the compassion she mov'd to her self and children was destructive to that which I reserv'd for Antony and Cleopatra; whose mutual love being founded upon vice, must lessen the favour of the Audience to them, when Virtue and Innocence were oppress'd by it. The interesting thing, however, is that it apparently did not. As Dryden says:"this is an Objection which no©ne of my Critiques have urg'd against me; and therefore I might have let it pass, if I could have resolv'd to have been partial to my self" (1984. The critical silence on this point is indeed surprising, since Dryden could certainly boast a large number of enemies and detractors who were more than willing to revile him on any occasion. It seems, therefore, that he must have been wholly successful in his design and that, at least in the original production, the audience must have suspended moral judgement and given their sympathy unreservedly to the tragic lovers.

Different explanations may be offered to account for this reaction. It is true, first of all, that the libertine values of the English court in the 1670s provided a frame of reception for the play in which the behaviour of Antony and Cleopatra might appear to need little justification; as Dennis put it,"never could the Design of an Author square more exactly with the Design of White-Hall, at the time when it was written".

Indeed, the original Prologue presents a benevolent view of the adulterous Antony-"He's somewhat lewd; but a well-meaning mind"-and invites the gentlemen in the audience to identify with him:"In short, a Pattern, and Companion fit,/ For all the keeping Tonyes of the Pit" (1984. Yet the influence of courtly circles and of fashionable libertine morals is not enough to justify this suspension of judgement, since the debauchery of the court was often the object of attack in moral and satirical writings. It has also been suggested that Dryden tried to justify Antony by making his Octavia less sympathetic than his Cleopatra. Thus, for instance, Walter Scott argued that Dryden made Octavia"cold and unamiable" in order to prevent the wronged wife from drawing the audience to her side; he pointed out that the author seemed to have"studiedly lowered the character of the injured Octavia, who, in her conduct towards her husband, shews much duty and little love; and plainly intimates, that her rectitude of conduct flows from a due regard to her own reputation, rather than from attachment to Antony's person, or sympathy with his misfortunes". However, there is one factor whose importance both to the construction of the play and its reception is not often given sufficient attention: the cast.

The choice of actors was a fundamental strategy in defining the values of the play and determining the response of the audience. As I will argue here, in the case of All for Love the casting of the main female parts in the opening season was instrumental in making the audience withhold moral condemnation and pity the fate of Cleopatra; when the play was revived in 1704, however, the cast recorded on this occasion shows a completely different strategy at work, one that is clearly designed to direct sympathy towards the character of the injured wife, Octavia.

In his seminal study of the performance of Restoration drama, Peter Holland has shown the centrality of casting to the construction of the plays. Playwrights normally had a particular cast in mind as they wrote, and logically tried to adjust their characters to the talents and personalities of the actors. Holland quotes Colley Cibber's comments in the Preface to his comedy Woman's Wit (1697) as an illustration of this practice; as Cibber explains, he changed companies while he was preparing the play, which forced him to redefine his characters: Another inconvenience was, that during the time of my writing the two first Acts, I was entertain'd in the New Theatre [i.e. with Betterton at Lincoln Inn's Fields], and of course prepar'd my Characters to the taste of those Actors... In the middle of my Writing the Third Act, not liking my Station there, I return'd again to the Theatre Royal, and was then forc'd, as far as I cou'd with nature, to confine the Business of my Persons to the Capacity of different people, and not to miss the Advantage of Mr. Doggett's Excellent Action; I prepar'd a low Character, which... I knew from him cou'd not fail of Diverting.

The cast also conditioned the reception of the play, since the audience's perception of a character depended, to a large extent, on their pre-conceived image of the actor or actress who played the part. Richard Flecknoe's comedy The Damoiselles a la Mode is a good example of this close interaction between characters and actors. The play was rejected by both companies and was not acted. Flecknoe, however, had the play printed with a Preface lamenting its sad fate. This printed text includes, together with the Dramatis Personae, the cast originally intended for the performance. Flecknoe explains in a note the logic of this decision:"Together with the Persons Represented in this Comedy, I have set down the Comedians, whom I intended shou'd Represent them, that the Reader might have half the pleasure of seeing it Acted, and a lively imagination might have the pleasure of it all entire". Each actor and actress developed a particular"line" of acting and tended therefore to specialize in a certain character-type. This type depended, primarily, on their physical appearance, personality, and talent. How far an actor's physique could condition his roles is sadly illustrated in the person of Samuel Sandford. Sandford, an actor originally at the Duke's company, specialized in the tragic part of the villain, a role to which, according to Cibber, he seemed to be naturally suited by his figure:... poor Sandford was not the Stage-Villain by Choice, but from Necessity; for having a low and crooked Person, such bodily Defects were too strong to be admitted into great, or amiable Characters; so that whenever, in any new or revived Play, there was a hateful or mischievous Person, Sandford was sure to have no Competitor for it: Nor indeed (as we are not to suppose a Villain, or Traitor can be shewn for our Imitation, or not for our María José Mora Wilson suggests that the parts of Cleopatra and Octavia would have been better suited to Rebecca Marshall or Elizabeth Cox, both of whom had defected from the company a few months before the opening of All for Love.

Besides the leading ladies, he also finds Cardell Goodman "atrociously miscast" as Alexas, a role which he believes was originally designed for Edward Kynaston Abhorrence) can it be doubted, but the less comely the Actor's Person, the fitter he may be to perform them.(1968) In the case of actresses, moreover, the development of a particular"line" was also influenced by the audience's perception of her private character, as is shown, for instance, in the career of Elizabeth Currer. Mrs. Currer, who joined the Duke's company 1673, was a very popular player in the 1670s and 1680s. If Restoration actresses were often held to have loose sexual morals, Currer certainly was one to cultivate this image. In the prologues and epilogues she spoke she typically assumed a reputation for promiscuity. Thus, in the Prologue to Behn's Feign'd Curtizans (1679), she complains:"Who says this Age a Reformation wants/ When Betty Currer's Lovers all turn Saints?/In vain, alas, I flatter, swear, and vow". And in the Epilogue to Tate's The Loyal General (1679), she rebukes the poet for making her a nun: Must I be cloyster'd up? Dull Poet stay, I hate Confinement tho'but in a Play.

Doom me to a Nun's Life?--A Nun! Oh Heart!
The Name's so dreadful, that it makes me start!
No! Tell the Scribbling Fool I'm just as fit
To make a Nun as he to make a Wit. (1680: 3-8)

In line with this moral character, Mrs. Currer specialized in the roles of loose, disreputable women. She played jilts and kept mistresses, like Betty Frisque in Crowne's The Country Wit (1675), Madam Tricklove in Durfey's Squire Oldsapp (1678), Jenny Wheadle in Durfey's The Virtuous Wife (1679), or Diana in Behn's City Heiress (1682). She played the unfaithful wife Eugenia in Ravenscroft's ribald farce The London Cuckolds (1681), and the whore Aquilina in Otway's Venice Preserved (1682).

Since the actor was usually identified with a particular character-type, casting became not only a powerful tool in the definition of character, but also an effective means of establishing the expectations of the audience. Dryden was obviously well aware that his choice of actors would greatly influence the audience's perception of the characters they played and, being a resident playwright, certainly knew the possibilities of all members of the King's company well enough. The cast he employed for the opening of All for Love must, therefore, have been carefully selected to suit and substantiate his conception of the major characters. The part of Antony surely permitted no doubt: the leading actor, Charles Hart, excelled in the role of the heroic lover. However, the casting of the main female parts-Elizabeth Boutell as Cleopatra and Katherine Corey as Octavia-seems more surprising, as it did not place either actress within the character-types they usually played.

It has been suggested that the cast may have been conditioned by the straitened circumstances and internal conflicts of the King's company. A more careful analysis of this decision, however, may reveal the strategy. Milhous and Hume also point out that the choice of actresses seems incongruous, but conclude that it is appropriate to the characters as defined by Dryden (1985: 133-34). Even though she was not the first actress to play either Aspatia or St Catherine, it was Mrs. Boutell that was commonly identified with these characters. Downes lists Boutell as Aspatia in the cast he gives for The Maid's Tragedy, though she was not likely on the stage for the first Restoration production of Fletcher's play (1660) and probably began to play this character 1666. In the original production of Tyrannick Love (1669), the part of St Catherine fell to Margaret Hughes; the name of Elizabeth Boutell first appears associated with this role in the second quarto (1672) behind this choice. As he confessed in the Preface, Dryden was worried that the confrontation between Cleopatra and Octavia might inevitably result in the moral condemnation of the two lovers. He set out, therefore, to present the characters of Antony and Cleopatra in as positive a light as he could. As he introduced them to the audience in the Prologue, he emphasized the tender feelings of his hero-"[he] weeps much, fights little, but is wondrous kind" (1984: 13)-and made a daring move to elevate the moral stature of his heroine, placing her on the same level as Octavia:

I cou'd name more; a Wife, and Mistress too;
Both (to be plain) too good for most of you:

The Wife well-natur'd, and the Mistress true. (1984: 16-18) To sustain on stage this character of the"true" mistress, defined in the presentation of the play as"too good," Dryden could not have made a better choice than Elizabeth Boutell. Possibly, only an actress with the figure and stage-history of Mrs. Boutell could create a Cleopatra that would appear vulnerable enough to move the compassion of the audience, and at the same time give her the moral dignity necessary to command their admiration- even when she had to play the mistress against the injured wife. Mrs. Boutell was at this stage one of the leading actresses in the King's company. As described by Edmund Curll, she was"a very considerable Actress; she was low of Stature, had very agreeable Features, a good Complexion, but a Childish Look. Her Voice was weak, tho'very mellow; she generally acted the young, innocent Lady whom all the Heroes are mad in Love with". Mrs. Boutell, indeed, was regularly typecast as the young innocent heroine. She was the chaste Aspatia in Fletcher's The Maid's Tragedy (1666), Aurelia-a character described as"of singular beauty"-inJoyner's The Roman Empress (1670), or the saintly Queen Catherine in Dryden's TyrannickLove (1672).3 She created the roles of the naïve Margery in Wycherley's The Country

Wife(1675), the constant Fidelia in The Plain Dealer (1676), and the virtuous and gentle princessMatilda in Ravenscroft's Edgar and Alfreda (1677). Through the 1670s she was repeatedlypaired with Rebecca Marshall in a series of tragedies that proved immensely successful atthe Theatre Royal, and which included two conflicting female characters: a gentle andvirtuous heroine and a passionate villainess-"the angel and the she-devil," as ElizabethHowe terms them (1992: 152-56). In these plays Boutell always played the angel, andMarshall the she-devil. Thus, Boutell was the noble Benzayda in Dryden's Conquest ofGranada (1670 and 1671), and Marshall, the beautiful and ambitious Lyndaraxa; Boutell,the chaste Cyara in Lee's Nero (1674), and Marshall, the villainous Poppea; in Crowne'sThe Destruction of Jerusalem (1677) Boutell played the young and pious Clarona, andMarshall, the passionate Queen Berenice. A few months before the opening of All for Love,they had created these roles again in Lee's The Rival Queens (1677): Boutell was the lovingStatira-interestingly enough, the injured wife-and Marshall, the wilful Roxana.

Alexander, played by Hart, had momentarily fallen prey to the charms of Roxana and hadbroken his faith with Statira; however, when the action of the play begins, he is alreadyrepentant and begging her pardon, recognizing the superior combination of beauty andvirtue in the character played by Boutell; as Alexander says later in 4.1:"Is she not morethan mortal man can wish?/Diana's soul cast in the flesh of Venus!" (1970).This is precisely the model Dryden seems to be aiming at in his portrait of Cleopatra:in a character traditionally associated with Venus, he is trying to instill the soul of Diana.It is revealing that Dryden carefully avoids mention of the children Cleopatra had byAntony, or by Caesar. His Cleopatra appears as an almost unblemished character; she cantherefore dissociate herself from the image of the wanton seductress and claim instead thatof the true lover, placed in the position of mistress not by natural depravity, but by thedesign of Fortune:Nature meant meA Wife, a silly harmless houshold Dove,Fond without art; and kind without deceit;But Fortune... has made a Mistress of me. (1984: 4.91-

94)The casting of Boutell as Cleopatra gave substance to this image. The audience wouldnaturally associate her with the long list of virtuous heroines she had played. In her, theycould materially see the pure woman cast by accident in the role of the mistress.As Boutell's rival in the affections of the hero-and of the audience-the actressassigned the part of Octavia was Katherine Corey. The choice clearly shows that-in thisoriginal production-Octavia was designed to be no match for Cleopatra. Mrs. Corey wasa comedian, a character actress, and had scored great successes as Doll Common in TheAlchemist, Lady Would-be in Volpone (1665) or, more recently, Widow Blackacrein The Plain Dealer (1676). She also played comic parts in tragedies, like Sempronia in

Jonson's Catiline (1668). Her special"line" included" scolding wives, mothers, governesses,waiting women and bawds". As Michael Yots has observed, when sheappears on stage to claim Antony she is portrayed as the nagging wife (1977: 4). She beginsby reprimanding Antony for his lack of civility:"Thus long I have attended for mywelcome;/Which, as a stranger, sure I might expect./Who am I?" (1984: 3.253-55). She thenpresents her list of complaints, describing herself as his"much injured wife" (1984: 3.258),unjustly forsaken.When she undertook serious roles, Mrs. Corey normally acted elderly women. She wasabout fifteen years older than Elizabeth Boutell and, when both appeared together in aplay, Corey was usually cast as Boutell's mother, governess or servant; in The Rival Queens,for instance, she was Old Sysigambis, the"mother of the Royal family"-actually grandmother to Boutell's Statira. And if Boutell always played the young heroine"of singular beauty," Corey was typically given the roles of plain women, devoid of physical graces; a clear example is the character of Strega, in Duffet's The Amorous Old Woman (1674)-described in the Dramatis Personae as"an old Rich deformed Lady."

The scene is clearly modelled on a similar confrontation between Statira and Roxana in act 3 of Lee's The Rival Queens, which did not attract particular criticism. In this encounter Statira is, likeCleopatra, defeated, and reflects on her rival's beauty and seducing charms (1970); Roxana replies mocking

Statira and her"sickly virtue" (1970). Statira, played by Boutell, is incensed by Roxana's taunts and eventually casts off her meekness:"I am by love a fury made, like you" (1970); she goes as far as to threaten Roxana (1970), but does not descend to direct insult, as Roxana had done.If we keep in mind the contrasting image of these two actresses, the exchange betweenCleopatra and Octavia in act 3 of All for Love acquires new and poignant meaning. Octavia,placed by Dryden in Alexandria, has claimed and regained Antony; yet, when she meets herrival, she cannot resist the urge to look at her face and make her own assessment of thelegendary beauty of the Egyptian queen and the charms that captivated Antony.Cleopatra's words add insult to injury, and the acerbity of the dialogue escalates:CleopatraO, you do well to search; for had you knownBut half these charms, you had not lost his heart.OctaviaFar be their knowledge from a Roman Lady,Far from a modest Wife.

Shame of our Sex,Dost thou not blush, to own those black endearmentsThat make sin pleasing?CleopatraYou may blush, who want'em.If bounteous Nature, if indulgent Heav'nHave giv'n me charms to please the bravest Man;Should I not thank'em? Should I be asham'd,And not be proud? I am, that he has lov'd me;And, when I love not him, Heav'n change this FaceFor one like that. (1984: 3.438-49)It makes sense that this should be the one scene in the play that Dryden's criticsapparently objected to. Dryden's contemporaries took Cleopatra's boastingof her beauty and mocking Octavia to be below the dignity of a tragedy. Cleopatra's pridemay be dramatically justified by the fact that she is at this point vanquished, and ismustering all her spirit to face her triumphant rival. But her words may have seemedparticularly galling, since the age and plainness of the woman playing Octavia appeared tootrue in the eyes of the audience; this rendered the mockery cruel and ill-natured, verymuch out of character in a meek Boutell heroine.Bearing in mind the contrast between Boutell and Corey, and between the charactertypesthey usually played, it is not hard to see why the audience in the opening seasoncould never judge Antony's behaviour as harshly as John Dennis. The Cleopatra they sawdid not at all resemble the"loose abandon'd Prostitute" Dennis condemns; their Octavia,though virtuous, was not the"young, affectionate... charming" creature he associateswith this role. No set of three adjectives could be farther removed from their impressionof Mrs. Corey. Her Octavia could at best appear dignified, but would almost inevitablyDerek Hughes presents the parallel in more precise terms:"

Actium stands for the Third DutchWar, and the besotted hero is blind to the cunning of his mistress and inept both in his clemency andseverity" (1996). Sedley's play does not present a particularly negative view of the character ofCleopatra; rebellion, though not justified, is presented as understandable. Sedley's Antony and Cleopatra would certainly provide the most immediate point of reference-if not the only one-for the Restoration audience, and would define their view of the tragic lovers. Although Shakespeare's play may have partly inspired Dryden's portrayal of the central characters, most of the spectators in 1677 would be unfamiliar with this work. Shakespeare's tragedy was never staged during the Restoration period, and was only printed as part of the Folio editions of Shakespeare in 1663 and 1664 retain a tinge of the shrew. To the eyes of those watching the play in 1677, if any character approached the description Dennis gives for Octavia, it was precisely Cleopatra.

The strategy marked by the casting in this original production of All for Love, which firmly directs the flow of sympathy to the tragic lovers and invites the audience to suspend judgement on their actions, is one that should be read against the immediate background of the mid-1670s. The story of Antony had traditionally been used to illustrate the dangers of intemperance in great men. Plutarch, for instance, uses his parallel lives of Demetriusand Antony as examples of men who were both"insolent in prosperity, and abandonedthemselves to luxury and enjoyment". But whereas Demetrius neverallowed his pleasures to endanger his more serious pursuits, Antony neglected everythingto follow his passions; he"was often disarmed by Cleopatra, subdued by her spells, andpersuaded to drop from his hands great undertakings and necessary campaigns, only toroam about and play with her on the sea-shores by Canopus and Taphosiris". The parallel with the dissolute court of Charles II suggests itself easily, not onlyin the figure of the ruler who is more prone to indulge his pleasures than to attend affairsof state; the parallel extends to the king's relationship with his chief mistress, the FrenchLouise de Kerouaille, who was in good measure made responsible for Charles's unpopularpro-French policy. Indeed, a few months before Dryden produced All for Love, Sir CharlesSedley had used the theme of Antony and Cleopatra on the stage to present a criticalportrait of the English monarch. As N. J. Andrew pointed out, Sedley criticizes Charles II"by drawing analogies between his way of life and that of Antony, whose overriding passionfor Cleopatra leads to tyrannical misgovernment" (1975). Dryden's work has beenseen as an attempt to neutralize this image of the monarch.6 The play presents Antony asa"hero torn between his nation and a personal life vested in an alien, unpopular mistress", and endeavours to redeem his actions placing them above the judgement of ordinary men.

To set Antony's passion beyond the reach of censure, no strategy could be so effective as to present Cleopatra in the shape of Elizabeth Boutell.We do not have much information on revivals of the play between the opening seasonand the end of the century. There are records of productions in 1684, 1686 and 1694, andthe printing of new editions in 1692 and 1696 suggests that there were performances alsoin those years, but no new casts have been preserved. The quartos of 1692 and 1696, as wascommon practice, give the list of actors of the original production, which were clearly notthose acting on these occasions: Hart, for instance, had retired before the union of thetheatres in 1682, and Mrs. Boutell was away from the stage for long periods and could onlyhave been available, if at all, for the 1696 performance. The only clue we have as to the casts is in the same letter Dryden considers a possible replacement for Boutell in The Conquest ofGranada, which clearly shows that she was not available at the time. The fact that Dryden does not discuss options for Cleopatra suggests that the part had already been assigned to the rising star of the company, Mrs. Barry.John Downes sets down these two parts, together with that of Isabella in Southerne's The FatalMarriage (1694), as the roles that"gain'd her the Name of Famous Mrs. Barry." Downes praises thepower of her acting in terms similar to Cibber's:"for when ever she Acted any of those three Parts,she forc'd Tears from the Eyes of her Auditory, especially those who have any Sense of Pity for thedistress'd" of these productions is a letter written by Dryden in 1684, in which he comments on thearrangements for the revival of his play:... for the Actors in the two plays which are to be acted of mine, this winter, I had spokenwith Mr. Betterton by chance at the Coffee house the afternoon before I came away: & Ibelieve that the persons were all agreed on, to be just the same you mentioned. Only Octaviawas to be Mrs. Buttler, in case Mrs. Cooke were not on the Stage.

The interesting thing about this letter is not so much the choice of actresses beingconsidered for Octavia-both considerably younger than Mrs. Corey-but the fact thata replacement is being discussed at all. Restoration actors did not usually give up their partsand, of all three protagonists in the original run of the play, Mrs. Corey was the only onewho was still active at the time: in 1683 she played the title-character in Ravenscroft's DameDobson; in 1684, she took the part of Mrs. Trainwell in the revival of Brome's NorthernLass, and the supposed mother to Angelline in Southerne's The Disappointment. Butwhatever the circumstances that prompted Mrs. Corey's substitution, it seems clear that Dryden and Betterton were negotiating a fairly different Octavia.

A new performance is recorded in 1701, but again with no indication of the cast.However, in 1704 the play was revived at court, on the occasion of the Queen's birthday,and in this case the list of actors is preserved; it includes Betterton in the part of Antony,Elizabeth Barry as Cleopatra, and Anne Bracegirdle as Octavia. This distribution of rolesshows that the characters of Cleopatra and Octavia are being presented to the audience ina very different light. Elizabeth Barry was one of the greatest stars of the time, and wasfamous for the pathos of her performances; as Cibber says,"in the Art of exciting Pity, shehad a Power beyond all the Actresses I have yet seen" (1968). She had already achievedgreat success in the tragedies of Otway in the early 1680s, especially in the parts ofMonimia in The Orphan (1680) and Belvidera in Venice Preserved (1682). But, accordingto Cibber, it was not until the 1690s that she reached full maturity, when she was"not alittle, past her Youth" and had already lost most of her beauty-as we can conclude fromCibber's reflection"that the short Life of Beauty, is not long enough to form a completeActress" (1968).

Mrs. Barry was commonly held to be a loose and passionate woman.She had begun her stage career as the mistress of the Earl of Rochester, and was successivelyass-ociated with Etherege and Sir Henry St John; a satirical poem by Robert Gould,"ThePlay-House"(1700), draws an infamous picture of the lascivious inclinations attributedto her and sums up her character in the following words:"Messalina like, she treads theStage/And all Enjoys, but nothing can Asswage" (1709). Although she had initiallyThe quotation is slightly inaccurate. Tate's text reads:"Bold in my Virgin Innocence I'll flie/My Royal Father to Relieve, or Die" played young girls, as her reputation mounted Mrs. Barry gradually specialized in the role of the passionate woman: she was Corina, the whore in Aphra Behn's The Revenge (1680), the prostitute La Nuche in the second part of The Rover (1681), and Lady Galliard in The City Heiress (1682). In the 1690s, she also incorporated the villainess: she played Orundana in Settle's Distressed Innocence (1690), Cassandra in Dryden's Cleomenes (1692), Lady Touchwood in Congreve's The Double-Dealer (1693), and Homais in Delariviere Manley's The Royal Mischief (1696). Anne Bracegirdle cut a very different type. She was younger than Barry and was considered a great beauty. Cibber describes her as an actress with an unusual reputation for modesty in her private life: never any Woman was in such general Favour of her Spectators, which, to the last Scene of her Dramatick Life, she maintain'd by not being unguarded in her private Character. This discretion contributed, not a little, to make her the Cara, the Darling of the Theatre... And tho'she might be said to have been the Universal Passion, and under the highest Temptations; her Constancy in resisting them, serv'd but to increase the number of her Admirers. (1968)

In keeping with her personal reputation, Mrs. Bracegirdle was typecast as the young and chaste heroine. She played the virtuous Mirtilla in Durfey's Love for Money (1691), the noble Fulvia in his Richmond Heiress (1693), and created all the major roles in the comedies of Congreve: she was Araminta in The Old Bachelor (1693), Cynthia in The Double-Dealer (1693), Angelica in Love for Love (1695), and Millamant in The Way of the World (1700). Since the 1690s, she and Mrs. Barry had often appeared together in a long series of tragedies in which Barry typically acted the villainess or"darker woman," Bracegirdle the innocent heroine; it was Bracegirdle, for instance, who played Statira in the revivals of The Rival Queens, with Barry as Roxana.

That the contrasting reputations of these two actresses could impress themselves on their characters and condition the audience's response to them is suggested by an anecdote recorded by the 18th-century critic William Chetwood in 1749. According to Chetwood, when Barry played Cordelia in Tate's King Lear (1681), the line"Arm'd in my virgin innocence I'll fly" provoked the laughter of the audience, turning a scene"of Generous Pity and Compassion" ridiculous;9 but when Mrs. Bracegirdle succeeded her in that role (1706), her rendering of the same line was applauded,"more as a Reward for her reputable character than, perhaps, her Acting claim'd".

The contrast between the"lines" and the private characters of Mrs. Barry and Mrs.

Bracegirdle must obviously have influenced the audience's perception of Cleopatra andOctavia in this production. For all Barry's power to move pity and "admiration" for the"noble love of Cleopatra", she could not as easily as Boutell assume theimage of artless innocence. For the theatre-going public of the time, she was every inch theseductress. Thus, in Gildon's A Comparison between the Two Stages (1702), the speakersrefer to Mrs. Barry by the name of Cleopatra, and draw the expected parallel between theactress and the role:By that Nickname [Cleopatra], so unfortunate to poor Anthony as the other has been tomany an honest Country Gentleman, I shou'd guess whom you mean... In her time she hasbeen the very Spirit of Action every way; Nature made her for the delight of Mankind; andtill Nature began to decay in her, all the Town shar'd her Bounty. (1942)In the 1704 play, virtue and innocence would inevitably be associated with the characterplayed by Bracegirdle. Her Octavia must have perfectly fitted the image of the"young,affectionate, virtuous, charming wife" recalled by Dennis, whose wrongs could understandablyprovoke moral indignation. The audience may have been invited to admire thelove of Cleopatra and to pity her fate, but the casting of Bracegirdle as Octavia suggests thatmoral values were being clearly defined in this production, and that virtue-embodied byOctavia-was definitely shown as more attractive.

The change of perspective is clearly reflected in the prologue written by Congreve forthis performance. It states that"Virtue and Heroick Fame" are the only subjectsappropriate for the tragic muse, which will from this point on eschew all immorality:No more in mean Disguise she shall appearAnd Shapes she wou'd reform be forc'd to wearHenceforth she shall pursue a nobler Task,Shew her bright Virgin Face, and scorn the Satyr's Mask. (1928)

Whereas poets had often justified the representation of vice in their plays as necessary to satire, Congreve's prologue denounces this claim as a subterfuge adopted by playwrights to introduce ribald material in their works. It proclaims the end of this practice and hails the advent of a new era in which the stage will imitate the Court and make virtue reign supreme:

Happy her future Days! which are design'd
Alone to paint the Beauties of the Mind.
By just Originals to draw with Care,
And Copy from the Court a Faultless Fair. (1928)

Far from justifying adultery-as Dryden's original prologue largely did-this text isprimarily a celebration of virtue, and of the monarch's embodiment of this value. Like thenew cast, the new prologue reveals a change in the conception of the play, one which bringsit in line with the more sobre morals promoted by the crown after the Glorious Revolution.The different casting strategies deployed in these two productions of All for Love showthat the tragedy is built on different premises on each occasion. In the opening season, thecasting of Elizabeth Boutell in the role of Cleopatra boldly placed the adulterous mistressat the moral centre of the play, turning her into an innocent heroine, while KatherineCorey brought the injured wife close to the character of the shrew. If this first productioncould be said to condone the libertine ethos of the 1670s, when the play was revived in 1704the choice of actresses reveals a totally different strategy: the pairing of Anne Bracegirdleas Octavia with Elizabeth Barry as Cleopatra indicates that it is the forsaken wife who isnow identified as the heroine; her wrongs make the punishment that poetic justicedemands for the tragic lovers appear indeed like justice, and firmly draw the sympathies of the audience to virtue, not vice. Thus, the new cast not only redefines the characters andthe relationships between them but, in doing so, also revises the moral of the play. As thecontrast between these two productions of All for Love shows, type-casting could be used as a powerful instrument to construct meaning on the Restoration stage.

Q. Describe the Conflict Between Rectitude and Success ?

Or

Q. Interpret the role of O:tavia ir the play All for Love ?

Abstract: Since Dryden introduced the character Octavia into his play All for love, much ambiguity was aroused among the critics as well as the readers. Undoubtedly, Octavia is a virtuous character. But strangely, readers seem to hold not much sympathy for her. Being right and good is not sufficient to be a successful character. Dryden's words in his preface to All for love may give readers some explanation for the case. As the preface suggests, Dryden doesn't want the audience to hold much sympathy for her to lessen the favour of them to Antony and Cleopatra. Dryden allows a certain amount of sympathy for her, but mere enough to make her a preferable choice for Antony at the cost of the main story and of the tragedy.

John Dryden's All for love, or the world well lost (1677) is an adaptation of Shakespeare's Antony and Cleopatra. This play, though"seldom performed during Dryden's lifetime, has steadily gained in popularity". The play is inevitably compared with Shakespeare's Antony and Cleopatra. However, because of the different eras they lived in and the different styles they used in their work, this comparison is really not so meaningful. Shakespeare's play ranges over time and place."Dryden's play focuses on one spot and one day for the purpose of creating emotional intensity. His play is smaller in scope, more polished, and has a different theme". Dryden says in his preface to All for love,"The death of Antony and Cleopatra is a subject which has been treated by the greatest wits of our nation, after Shakespeare; and by all so variously, that their example has given me the confidence to try myself in this bow of Ulysses amongst the crowd of suitors, and, withal, to take my own measures, in aiming at the mark." The introduction to Dryden's All for love says about Dryden,"Here he has the daring to challenge comparison with his master" (The World Wide School). Even so, readers can still feel that his version is fresh compared with Shakespeare's. It's not mere imitation. It's more like transmutation. Dryden's view on Octavia Undoubtedly, Antony and Cleopatra's love is the most striking part in the play. But it should not be forgotten that their love is illicit. It's based upon the pain of Antony's wife Octavia.

Dryden introduced the figure of Octavia in Act III. He has some worries about the introduction of this character. He says in his preface,"The greatest error GAN Yan-ping, M.A., lecturer of College of Foreign Languages and literature, Wuhan University, visiting scholar of University of Toronto; research fields: college English teaching, English literature, literary criticism. in the contrivance seems to be in the person of Octavia: For, though I might use the privilege of a Poet, to introduce her into Alexandria, yet I had not enough consider'd, that the compassion she mov'd to her self and Children, was destructive to that which I reserv'd for Anthony and Cleopatra;

whose mutual love being founded upon vice, must lessen the favour of the Audience to them, when Virtue and Innocence were oppress'd by it." Dryden"criticizes himself for introducing Octavia, who by'the dividing of pity'between her and Cleopatra,'like the cutting of a River into many Channels, abated the strength of the natural stream.'He is even more explicit in the prologue and writes,'Both (to be plain) too good for most of you: The Wife well-natur'd, and the Mistress true'."Much of the preface appears disingenuous. Dryden worked at cross-purposes". There is indeed a certain ambiguity evident throughout Dryden's play in his simultaneous exploitation of"official'sympathy for Octavia as a lawful wife and of Cleopatra's scorn for"that thing, that dull insipid lump".

The confrontation between Cleopatra and Octavia, on one hand, shows Octavia as the victim. On the other hand, Cleopatra's words seem to be more moving and more likely to arouse readers'sympathy. Public views on Octavia. Favorable views Most of the readers and critics hold the opinion that Octavia is a virtuous character. They think she is a victim in the triangle relationship with Antony and Cleopatra and hold sympathy for her because of her beauty, tolerance, personal sacrifice, etc. The playwright and critic John Dennis wrote in a letter in 1719,"...if any person of quality or other shall turn away his Wife, his young, affectionate, virtuous, charming Wife to take to his bed a loose abandon'd prostitute, and shall in her arms exhaust his patrimony, destroy his health, emasculate his mind, and lose his reputation and all his friends, why all this is well and greatly done, his Ruine is his commendation".

Here wife refers to Octavia. Emerson (1968, p. 57) says"Octavia is so undeniably self-righteous-and it is difficult to believe that she would not have seemed so to a Restoration audience". Beautiful Everybody knows Cleopatra is beautiful and Octavia's beauty is rarely mentioned. But according to Plutarch, the Greek historian, Octavia"was renowned for her beauty and high morals. She possessed all the charms, accomplishments and virtues likely to fascinate the affections and secure a lasting influence over the mind of a husband.

Her beauty was universally allowed to be superior to that of Cleopatra..." In All for love, Octavia's beauty is not described, but from some words of the other characters, readers can get some clue about her beauty. Antony says about Octavia"in her pride of youth And flow'r of beauty did I wed that lady". When Cleopatra asks Alexas of Octavia,"Is she fair, Bright as a goddess? And is all perfection Confined to her?" Alexas answers,"She's indeed a very miracle. Suffering and tolerant It cannot be denied that Octavia is a virtuous character and her virtue can be seen in many ways. One good illustration of her morality can be seen when she pleads Antony to come back by saying to their children: You, Agrippina, hang upon his arms; And you, Antonia, clasp about his waist; If he will shake you off, if he will dash you Against the Pavement, you must bear it, children; For you are mine, and I was born to suffer Here, Antony, the Roman conqueror of worlds, is being scolded by his virtuous wife and lost his dignity and honour in front of his children.

When reading this part, we can feel deeply Octavia's suffering and bearing. This Conflict between rectitude and success: Interpretation of the character Octavia in All for love virtue of Octavia compels Antony to reconsider his love affair with Cleopatra and forces him back from her. Sacrificing Octavia is also a sacrifice for politics and an exchanged commodity between her brother and her husband. It is well known that she loved her husband very much before she was widowed. Later she married Antony for the purpose of cementing the relationship between her brother and Antony even though she finally appeared a loyal and faithful wife. But Antony sometimes mocked her status as being Caesar's sister and regarded her ambassadress from her brother. He used some sarcastic tone to indicate this fact: OCTAVIA Which, as a stranger, sure I might expect. Who am I?

ANTONY Caesar's sister.

ANTONY Yes, begged it, my ambassadress; Poorly and basely begged it of your brother.

We don't know how much she loved Antony when she first married him. But the fact we know is that she is loyal and faithful to him after they married. On several occasions she acts as a political adviser and negotiator between her husband and brother, but all is for the peace of the country and for the safety of her husband. She says,"it never shall be said, Octavia's husband was her brother's slave...I'll tell my brother we are reconciled" to comfort Antony and promised"I never will complain, But only keep the barren name of wife, And rid you of the trouble". Unfavorable views When most of the critics'opinions on Octavia are favorable ones, some different voices are also heard. Some think Octavia is too cold. She holds too much duty, not so charming as a woman. And in her quarrel with Cleopatra, she seems too aggressive. She is"short of true nobility in Shakespeare-for she turns from Antony to Caesar without hesitation and almost without regret-she becomes in Dryden a scold." Dull, not charming"Though Octavia embodies all characteristics a respectable woman has: beauty, grace, virtue, loyalty, power, wisdom, she cannot compete with sensuous, extravagant Cleopatra for Anthony's love" (Sarah). Octavia, with her sneering at erotic passion, gives just a hint as to why a man might leave her.

And Cleopatra also laughs at her for not knowing how to use a woman's charm.

CLEOPATRA

Peace, peace, my lover's Juno. When he grew weary of that household clog, He chose my easier bonds.

OCTAVIA

I wonder not Your bonds are easy: you have long been practised In that lascivious art: He's not the first For whom you spread your snares: Let Caesar witness.

CLEOPATRA

Oh, you do well to search; for had you known.
But half these charms, you had not lost his heart.

OCTAVIA

Far be their knowledge from a Roman lady, Far from a modest wife!

Octavia shows her contempt of Cleopatra's charm and calls it"lascivious art," implying that she never does such contemptible thing. Perhaps that's one of the reasons why

Antony chooses sensuous Cleopatra instead of relatively dull Octavia.

Q. What is the tragedy of Octavia?

Or

Q. How the soul and character of Octavia is damaged and why she blames Cleopatra for it?

At the first glance of the confrontation between Octavia and Cleopatra, Octavia seems to be the victim in the marriage and she blames Cleopatra violently for her behaviour. But despite that fact, Octavia's words seem to be too aggressive. Vieth points out the confrontation between Octavia and Cleopatra in Alexandria"is not, as Dryden must have realized, that it divides the audience's sympathies, or that it is unhistorical, but that it makes Octavia look like an overly aggressive middle-class housewife invading her unfaithful husband's'love nest."

Cold Reinert (1968, p. 94) thinks"Octavia is neither attractive nor evil, but neither does she represent reason-rather self-righteous marital value. More than anything else she strikes one as an unhumorous version of'the wife'of Restoration comedy,'that thing, That dull insipid lump, without desires, And without power to give them,'as Cleopatra defines her breed". Her coldness can be seen from her dialogue with Antony: Antony

Therefore you love me not.

Octavia: Therefore, my lord,

I should not love you.

Antony: Therefore you would leave me?

Octavia

And therefore I should leave you if I could.

This dialogue shows her coldness in some way no matter how much love she claims for Antony. Her decision to leave Antony seems too resolute and not regretful.

Conclusion: Octavia's nobility is historically accurate, so far as the sources can inform us. But Dryden cannot let her nobility triumph over Cleopatra (Dryden and Neoclassicism). He seems intentionally to have lowered the character of the injured Octavia. In Dryden's play, she shows much duty and little love, more reason and less passion. At the same time, the Octavia appears somewhat cold and unamiable because Dryden was aware that the justice of a wife's claim upon her husband would draw the audience to her side. When we look closely at the play, we find that it does not give a picture of"the crimes of love" (Preface to All for love) and"of unlawful lovers being punished for their voluntary transgressions. Instead, it gives us almost the opposite: a love that is inevitable, an uncontrollable force; and the lovers vindicated because of their passion. Our sympathies are drawn to the lovers and held there because their passions are not within their power. At least from this point of view Dryden builded better than he knew". So Octavia is doomed to be a victim when Dryden first introduced her into the play. Her virtue, beauty, grace and rectitude can not make her a successful character whether in her marriage to Antony or in Dryden's tragedy.

Q. Critically analyse life and works of Dryden

Or

Q. How Dryden proves to be the best playwright of the Age of Restoration?

Benvenuto Cellini tells us that when, in his boyhood, he saw a salamander come out of the fire, his grandfather forthwith gave him a sound beating, that he might the better remember so unique a prodigy. Though perhaps in this case the rod had another application than the autobiographer chooses to disclose, and was intended to fix in the pupil's mind a lesson of veracity rather than of science, the testimony to its mnemonic virtue remains. Nay, so universally was it once believed that the senses, and through them the faculties of observation and retention, were quickened by an irritation of the cuticle, that in France it was customary to whip the children annually at the boundaries of the parish, lest the true place of them might ever be lost through neglect of so inexpensive a mordant for the memory. From this practice the older school of critics would seem to have taken a hint for keeping fixed the limits of good taste, and what was somewhat vaguely called classical English. To mark these limits in poetry, they set up as Hermae the images they had made to them of

Dryden, of Pope, and later of Goldsmith. Here they solemnly castigated every new aspirant in verse, who in turn performed the same function for the next generation, thus helping to keep always sacred and immovable the ne plus ultra alike of inspiration and of the vocabulary. Though no two natures were ever much more unlike than those of Dryden and Pope, and again of Pope and Goldsmith, and no two styles, except in such externals as could be easily caught and copied, yet it was the fashion, down even to the last generation, to advise young writers to form themselves, as it was called, on these excellent models. Wordsworth himself began in this school; and though there were glimpses, here and there, of a direct study of nature, yet most of the epithets in his earlier pieces were of the traditional kind so fatal to poetry during great part of the last century; and he indulged in that alphabetic personification which enlivens all such words as Hunger, Solitude, Freedom, by the easy magic of an initial capital.

"Where the green apple shrivels on the spray,
And pines the unripened pear in summer's kindliest ray,
Even here Content has fixed her smiling reign
With Independence, child of high Disdain.
Exulting'mid the winter of the skies,
Shy as the jealous chamois, Freedom flies,
And often grasps her sword, and often eyes."

Here we have every characteristic of the artificial method, even to the triplet, which Swift hated so heartily as"a vicious way of rhyming wherewith Mr. Dryden abounded, imitated by all the bad versifiers of Charles the Second's reign." Wordsworth became, indeed, very early the leader of reform; but, like Wesley, he endeavored a reform within the Establishment. Purifying the substance, he retained the outward forms with a feeling rather than conviction that, in poetry, substance and form are but manifestations of the same inward life, the one fused into the other in the vivid heat of their common expression. Wordsworth could never wholly shake off the influence of the century into which he was born. He began by proposing a reform of the ritual, but it went no further than an attempt to get rid of the words of Latin original where the meaning was as well or better given in derivatives of the Saxon. He would have stricken out the"assemble" and left the"meet together." Like Wesley, he might be compelled by necessity to a breach of the canon; but, like him, he was never a willing schismatic, and his singing robes were the full and flowing canonicals of the church by law established. Inspiration makes short work with the usage of the best authors and ready-made elegances of diction; but where Wordsworth is not possessed by his demon, as Molière said of Corneille, he equals Thomson in verbiage, out-Miltons Milton in artifice of style, and Latinizes his diction beyond Dryden. The fact was, that he took up his early opinions on instinct, and insensibly modified them as he studied the masters of what may be called the Middle Period of English verse. As a young man, he disparaged Virgil ("We talked a great deal of nonsense in those days," he said when taken to task for it later in life); at fifty-nine he translated three books of the Aeneid, in emulation of Dryden, though falling far short of him in everything but closeness, as he seems, after a few years, to have been convinced. Keats was the first resolute and wilful heretic, the true founder of the modern school, which admits no cis-Elizabethan authority save Milton, whose own English was formed upon those earlier models.

Keats denounced the authors of that style which came in toward the close of the seventeenth century, and reigned absolute through the whole of the eighteenth, as

"A schism,
Nurtured by foppery and barbarism,
... who went about
Holding a poor decrepit standard out,
Marked with most flimsy mottoes, and in large
The name of one Boileau!"

But Keats had never then studied the writers of whom he speaks so contemptuously, though he might have profited by so doing. Boileau would at least have taught him that flimsy would have been an apter epithet for the standard than for the mottoes upon it. Dryden was the author of that schism against which Keats so vehemently asserts the claim of the orthodox teaching it had displaced. He was far more just to Boileau, of whom Keats had probably never read a word."If I would only cross the seas," he says,"I might find in France a living Horace and a Juvenal in the person of the admirable Boileau, whose numbers are excellent, whose expressions are noble, whose thoughts are just, whose language is pure, whose satire is pointed, and whose sense is just. What he borrows from the ancients he repays with usury of his own, in coin as good and almost as universally valuable."

Dryden has now been in his grave nearly a hundred and seventy years; in the second class of English poets perhaps no one stands, on the whole, so high as he; during his lifetime, in spite of jealousy, detraction, unpopular politics, and a suspicious change of faith, his pre-eminence was conceded; he was the earliest complete type of the purely literary man, in the modern sense; there is a singular unanimity in allowing him a certain claim to greatness which would be denied to men as famous and more read,--to Pope or Swift, for example; he is supposed, in some way or other, to have reformed English poetry. It is now about half a century since the only uniform edition of his works was edited by Scott. No library is complete without him, no name is more familiar than his, and yet it may be suspected that few writers are more thoroughly buried in that great cemetery of the"British Poets." If contemporary reputation be often deceitful, posthumous fame may be generally trusted, for it is a verdict made up of the suffrages of the select men in succeeding generations. This verdict has been as good as unanimous in favour of Dryden. It is, perhaps, worth while to take a fresh observation of him, to consider him neither as warning nor example, but to endeavor to make out what it is that has given so lofty and firm a position to one of the most unequal, inconsistent, and faulty writers that ever lived. He is a curious example of what we often remark of the living, but rarely of the dead,--that they get credit for what they might be quite as much as for what they are,--and posterity has applied to him one of his own rules of criticism, judging him by the best rather than the average of his achievement, a thing posterity is seldom wont to do. On the losing side in politics, it is true of his polemical writings as of Burke's,--whom in many respects he resembles, and especially in that supreme quality of a reasoner, that his mind gathers not only heat, but clearness and expansion, by its own motion,--that they have won his battle for him in the judgment of after times.

To us, looking back at him, he gradually becomes a singularly interesting and even picturesque figure. He is, in more senses than one, in language, in turn of thought, in style of mind, in the direction of his activity, the first of the moderns. He is the first literary man who was also a man of the world, as we understand the term. He succeeded Ben Jonson as the acknowledged dictator of wit and criticism, as Dr. Johnson, after nearly the same interval, succeeded him. All ages are, in some sense, ages of transition; but there are times when the transition is more marked, more rapid; and it is, perhaps, an ill fortune for a man of letters to arrive at maturity during such a period, still more to represent in himself the change that is going on, and to be an efficient cause in bringing it about. Unless, like Goethe, he is of a singularly uncontemporaneous nature, capable of being tutta in seromita, and of running parallel with his time rather than being sucked into its current, he will be thwarted in that harmonious development of native force which has so much to do with its steady and successful application. Dryden suffered, no doubt, in this way. Though in creed he seems to have drifted backward in an eddy of the general current; yet of the intellectual movement of the time, so far certainly as literature shared in it, he could say, with Aeneas, not only that he saw, but that himself was a great part of it. That movement was, on the whole, a downward one, from faith to scepticism, from enthusiasm to cynicism, from the imagination to the understanding. It was in a direction altogether away from those springs of imagination and faith at which they of the last age had slaked the thirst or renewed the vigour of their souls. Dryden himself recognized that indefinable and gregarious influence which we call nowadays the Spirit of the Age, when he said that"every Age has a kind of universal Genius." He had also a just notion of that in which he lived; for he remarks, incidentally, that"all knowing ages are naturally skeptic and not at all bigoted, which, if I am not much deceived, is the proper character of our own." It may be conceived that he was even painfully half-aware of having fallen upon a time incapable, not merely of a great poet, but perhaps of any poet at all; for nothing is so sensitive to the chill of a sceptical atmosphere as that enthusiasm which, if it be not genius, is at least the beautiful illusion that saves it from the baffling quibbles of self-consciousness. Thrice unhappy he who, horn to see things as they might be, is schooled by circumstances to see them as people say they are,--to read God in a prose translation. Such was Dryden's lot, and such, for a good part of his days, it was by his own choice. He who was of a stature to snatch the torch of life that flashes from lifted hand to hand along the generations, over the heads of inferior men, chose rather to be a link-boy to the stews.

As a writer for the stage, he deliberately adopted and repeatedly reaffirmed the maxim that

"He who lives to please, must please to live."

Without earnest convictions, no great or sound literature is conceivable. But if Dryden mostly wanted that inspiration which comes of belief in and devotion to something nobler and more abiding than the present moment and its petulant need, he had, at least, the next best thing to that,--a thorough faith in himself. He was, moreover, a man of singularly open soul, and of a temper self-confident enough to be candid even with himself. His mind was growing to the last, his judgment widening and deepening, his artistic sense refining itself more and more. He confessed his errors, and was not ashamed to retrace his steps in search of that better knowledge which the omniscience of superficial study had disparaged. Surely an intellect that is still pliable at seventy is a phenomenon as interesting as it is rare. But at whatever period of his life we look at Dryden, and whatever, for the moment, may have been his poetic creed, there was something in the nature of the man that would not be wholly subdued to what it worked in. There are continual glimpses of something in him greater than he, hints of possibilities finer than anything he has done. You feel that the whole of him was better than any random specimens, though of his best, seem to prove. Incessupatet, he has by times the large stride of the elder race, though it sinks too often into the slouch of a man who has seen better days. His grand air may, in part, spring from a habit of easy superiority to his competitors; but must also, in part, be ascribed to an innate dignity of character. That this pre-eminence should have been so generally admitted, during his life, can only be explained by a bottom of good sense, kindliness, and sound judgment, whose solid worth could afford that many a flurry of vanity, petulance, and even error should flit across the surface and be forgotten. Whatever else Dryden may have been, the last and abiding impression of him is, that he was thoroughly manly; and while it may be disputed whether he was a great poet, it may be said of him, as Wordsworth said of Burke, that"he was by far the greatest man of his age, not only abounding in knowledge himself, but feeding, in various directions, his most able contemporaries."

Dryden was born in 1631. He was accordingly six years old when Jonson died, was nearly a quarter of a century younger than Milton, and may have personally known Bishop Hall, the first English satirist, who was living till 1656. On the other side, he was older than Swift by thirty-six, than Addison by forty-one, and than Pope by fifty-seven years. Dennis says that"Dryden, for the last ten years of his life, was much acquainted with Addison, and drank with him more than he ever used to do, probably so far as to hasten his end," being commonly"an extreme sobre man." Pope tell us that, in his twelfth year, he"saw Dryden," perhaps at Will's, perhaps in the street, as Scott did Burns. Dryden himself visited Milton now and then, and was intimate with Davenant, who could tell him of Fletcher and Jonson from personal recollection. Thus he stands between the age before and that which followed him, giving a hand to each. His father was a country clergyman, of Puritan leanings, a younger son of an ancient county family. The Puritanism is thought to have come in with the poet's great-grandfather, who made in his will the somewhat singular statement that he was"assured by the Holy Ghost that he was elect of God." It would appear from this that Dryden's self-confidence was an inheritance. The solid quality of his mind showed itself early. He himself tells us that he had read Polybius"in English, with the pleasure of a boy, before he was ten years of age, and yet even then had some dark notions of the prudence with which he conducted his design." The concluding words are very characteristic, even if Dryden, as men commonly do, interpreted his boyish turn of mind by later self-knowledge. We thus get a glimpse of him browsing-for, like Johnson, Burke, and the full as distinguished from the learned men, he was always a random reader --in his father's library, and painfully culling here and there a spray of his own proper nutriment from among the stubs and thorns of Puritan divinity. After such schooling as could be had in the country, he was sent up to Westminster School, then under the headship of the celebrated Dr. Busby. Here he made his first essays in verse, translating, among other school exercises of the same kind, the third satire of Persius. In 1650 he was entered at Trinity College, Cambridge, and remained there for seven years. The only record of his college life is a discipline imposed, in 1652, for"disobedience to the Vice-Master, and contumacy in taking his punishment, inflicted by him." Whether this punishment was corporeal, as Johnson insinuates in the similar case of Milton, we are ignorant. He certainly retained no very fond recollection of his Alma Mater, for in his"Prologue to the University of Oxford," he says:--

"Oxford to him a dearer name shall be
Than his own mother university;
Thebes did his green, unknowing youth engage,
He chooses Athens in his riper age."

By the death of his father, in 1654, he came into possession of a small estate of sixty pounds a year, from which, however, a third must be deducted, for his mother's dower, till 1676. After leaving Cambridge, he became secretary to his near relative, Sir Gilbert Pickering, at that time Cromwell's chamberlain, and a member of his Upper House. In 1670 he succeeded Davenant as Poet Laureate, and Howell as Historiographer, with a yearly salary of two hundred pounds.

This place he lost at the Revolution, and had the mortification to see his old enemy and butt, Shadwell, promoted to it, as the best poet the Whig party could muster. If William was obliged to read the verses of his official minstrel, Dryden was more than avenged. From 1688 to his death, twelve years later, he earned his bread manfully by his pen, without any mean complaining, and with no allusion to his fallen fortunes that is not dignified and touching. These latter years, during which he was his own man again, were probably the happiest of his life. In 1664 or 1665 he married Lady Elizabeth Howard, daughter of the Earl of Berkshire. About a hundred pounds a year were thus added to his income. The marriage is said not to have been a happy one, and perhaps it was not, for his wife was apparently a weak-minded woman; but the inference from the internal evidence of Dryden's plays, as of Shakespeare's, is very untrustworthy, ridicule of marriage having always been a common stock in trade of the comic writers.

The earliest of his verses that have come down to us were written upon the death of Lord Hastings, and are as bad as they can be,--a kind of parody on the worst of Donne. They have every fault of his manner, without a hint of the subtle and often profound thought that more than redeems it. As the Doctor himself would have said, here is Donne outdone. The young nobleman died of the small-pox, and Dryden exclaims pathetically,--

"Was there no milder way than the small-pox,
The very filthiness of Pandora's box?"

He compares the pustules to"rosebuds stuck i'the lily skin about," and says that

"Each little pimple had a tear in it
To wail the fault its rising did commit."

But he has not done his worst yet, by a great deal. What follows is even finer:--

"No comet need foretell his change drew on,
Whose corpse might seem a constellation.
O, had he died of old, how great a strife
Had been who from his death should draw their life!
Who should, by one rich draught, become whate'er

Seneca, Cato, Numa, Caesar, were,
Learned, virtuous, pious, great, and have by this
An universal metempsychosis!
Must all these aged sires in one funeral
Expire? all die in one so young, so small?"

It is said that one of Allston's early pictures was brought to him, after he had long forgotten it, and his opinion asked as to the wisdom of the young artist's persevering in the career he had chosen. Allston advised his quitting it forthwith as hopeless. Could the same experiment have been tried with these verses upon Dryden, can any one doubt that his counsel would have been the same? It should be remembered, however, that he was barely turned eighteen when they were written, and the tendency of his style is noticeable in so early an abandonment of the participial ed in learned and aged. In the next year he appears again in some commendatory verses prefixed to the sacred epigrams of his friend, John Hoddesdon. In these he speaks of the author as a

"Young eaglet, who, thy nest thus soon forsook,
So lofty and divine a course hast took
As all admire, before the down begin
To peep, as yet, upon thy smoother chin."

Here is almost every fault, which Dryden's later nicety would have condemned. But perhaps there is no schooling so good for an author as his own youthful indiscretions. After this effort Dryden seems to have lain fallow for ten years, and then he at length reappears in thirty-seven"heroic stanzas" on the death of Cromwell. The versification is smoother, but the conceits are there again, though in a milder form. The verse is modelled after"Gondibert." A single image from nature (he was almost always happy in these) gives some hint of the maturer Dryden:--

"And wars, like mists that rise against the sun,
Made him but greater seem, not greater grow."

Two other verses,

"And the isle, when her protecting genius went,
Upon his obsequies loud sighs conferred,"

are interesting, because they show that he had been

studying the early poems of Milton. He has contrived to bury under a rubbish of verbiage one of the most purely imaginative passages ever written by the great Puritan poet.

"From haunted spring and dale,
Edged with poplar pale,
The parting genius is with sighing sent."

This is the more curious because, twenty-four years afterwards, he says, in defending rhyme:"Whatever causes he [Milton] alleges for the abolishment of rhyme, his own particular reason is plainly this, that rhyme was not his talent; he had neither the ease of doing it nor the graces of it: which is manifest in his Juvenilia,... where his rhyme is always constrained and forced, and comes hardly from him, at an age when the soul is most pliant, and the passion of love makes almost every man a rhymer, though not a poet." It was this, no doubt, that heartened Dr. Johnson to say of"Lycidas" that"the diction was harsh, the rhymes uncertain, and the numbers unpleasing." It is Dryden's excuse that his characteristic excellence is to argue persuasively and powerfully, whether in verse or prose, and that he was amply endowed with the most needful quality of an advocate,--to be always strongly and wholly of his present way of thinking, whatever it might be. Next we have, in 1660,"Astraea Redux" on the"happy restoration" of Charles II.

In this also we can forebode little of the full-grown Dryden but his defects. We see his tendency to exaggeration, and to confound physical with metaphysical, as where he says of the ships that brought home the royal brothers, that

"The joyful London meets
The princely York, himself alone a freight,
The Swiftsure groans beneath great Gloster's weight"
and speaks of the"Repeated prayer
Which stormed the skies and ravished Charles from thence."

There is also a certain everydayness, not to say vulgarity, of phrase, which Dryden never wholly refined away, and which continually tempts us to sum up at once against him as the greatest poet that ever was or could be made wholly out of prose.

"Heaven would no bargain for its blessings drive"

is an example. On the other hand, there are a few verses almost worthy of his best days, as these:--

"Some lazy ages lost in sleep and ease,
No action leave to busy chronicles;
Such whose supine felicity but makes
In story chasms, in epochas mistakes,
O'er whom Time gently shakes his wings of down,
Till with his silent sickle they are mown,"

These are all the more noteworthy, that Dryden, unless in argument, is seldom equal for six lines together. In the poem to Lord Clarendon (1662), there are four verses that have something of the"energy divine" for which Pope praised his master.

"Let envy, then, those crimes within you see
From which the happy never must be free;
Envy that does with misery reside,
The joy and the revenge of ruined pride."

In his"Aurengzebe" (1675) there is a passage, of which, as it is a good example of Dryden, I shall quote the whole, though my purpose aims mainly at the latter verses:--

"When I consider life,'t is all a cheat;
Yet, fooled with Hope, men favour the deceit,
Trust on, and think to-morrow will repay;
To-morrow's falser than the former day,
Lies worse, and, while it says we shall be blest
With some new joys, cuts off what we possest.
Strange cozenage! none would live past years again,
Yet all hope pleasure in what yet remain,
And from the dregs of life think to receive
What the first sprightly running could not give.
I'm tired of waiting for this chymic gold
Which fools us young and beggars us when old."

The"first sprightly running" of Dryden's vintage was, it must be confessed, a little muddy, if not beery; but if his own soil did not produce grapes of the choicest flavour, he knew where they were to be had; and his product, like sound wine, grew better the longer it stood upon the lees. He tells us, evidently thinking of himself, that in a poet,"from fifty to threescore, the balance generally holds even in our colder climates, for he loses not much in fancy, and judgment, which is the effect of observation, still increases. His succeeding years afford him little more than the stubble of his own harvest, yet, if his constitution be healthful, his mind may still retain a decent vigour, and the gleanings of that of Ephraim, in comparison with others, will surpass the vintage of Abiezer." Since Chaucer, none of our poets has had a constitution more healthful, and it was his old age that yielded the best of him. In him the understanding was, perhaps, in overplus for his entire good fortune as a poet, and that is a faculty among the earliest to mature.

We have seen him, at only ten years, divining the power of reason in Polybius. The same turn of mind led him later to imitate the French school of tragedy, and to admire in Ben Jonson the most correct of English poets. It was his imagination that needed quickening, and it is very curious to trace through his different prefaces the gradual opening of his eyes to the causes of the solitary pre-eminence of Shakespeare. At first he is sensible of an attraction towards him which he cannot explain, and for which he apologizes, as if it were wrong. But he feels himself drawn more and more strongly, till at last he ceases to resist altogether, and is forced to acknowledge that there is something in this one man that is not and never was anywhere else, something not to be reasoned about, ineffable, divine; if contrary to the rules, so much the worse for them. It may be conjectured that Dryden's Puritan associations may have stood in the way of his more properly poetic culture, and that his early knowledge of Shakespeare was slight. He tells us that Davenant, whom he could not have known before he himself was twenty-seven, first taught him to admire the great poet. But even after his imagination had become conscious of its prerogative, and his expression had been ennobled by frequenting this higher society, we find him continually dropping back into that sermo pedestris which seems, on the whole, to have been his more natural element. We always feel his epoch in him, that he was the lock, which let our language down from its point of highest poetry to its level of easiest and most gently flowing prose. His enthusiasm needs the contagion of other minds to arouse it; but his strong sense, his command of the happy word, his wit, which is distinguished by a certain breadth and, as it were, power of generalization, as Pope's by keenness of edge and point, were his, whether he would or no. Accordingly, his poetry is often best and his verse more flowing where (as in parts of his version of the twenty-ninth ode of the third book of Horace) he is amplifying the suggestions of another mind.

Viewed from one side, he justifies Milton's remark of him, that"he was a good rhymist, but no poet." To look at all sides, and to distrust the verdict of a single mood, is, no doubt, the duty of a critic. But how if a certain side be so often presented as to thrust forward in the memory and disturb it in the effort to recall that total impression (for the office of a critic is not, though often so misunderstood, to say guilty or not guilty of some particular fact) which is the only safe ground of judgment? It is the weight of the whole man, not of one or the other limb of him, that we want. Expende Hannibalem. Very good, but not in a scale capacious only of a single quality at a time, for it is their union, and not their addition, that assures the value of each separately.

It was not this or that which gave him his weight in council, his swiftness of decision in battle that outran the forethought of other men,--it was Hannibal. But this prosaic element in Dryden will force itself upon me. As I read him, I cannot help thinking of an ostrich, to be classed with flying things, and capable, what with leap and flap together, of leaving the earth for a longer or shorter space, but loving the open plain, where wing and foot help each other to something that is both flight and run at once. What with his haste and a certain dash, which, according to our mood, we may call florid or splendid, he seems to stand among poets where Rubens does among painters,--greater, perhaps, as a colorist than an artist, yet great here also, if we compare him with any but the first. We have arrived at Dryden's thirty-second year, and thus far have found little in him to warrant an augury that he was ever to be one of the great names in English literature, the most perfect type, that is, of his class, and that class a high one, though not the highest.

If Joseph de Maistre's axiom, Qui n'a pas vaincu à trente ans, ne vaincra jamais, were true, there would be little hope of him, for he has won no battle yet. But there is something solid and doughty in the man, that can rise from defeat, the stuff of which victories are made in due time, when we are able to choose our position better, and the sun is at our back.

Hitherto his performances have been mainly of the obbligato sort, at which few men of original force are good, least of all Dryden, who had always something of stiffness in his strength. Waller had praised the living Cromwell in perhaps the manliest verses he ever wrote,--not very manly, to be sure, but really elegant, and, on the whole, better than those in which Dryden squeezed out melodious tears. Waller, who had also made himself conspicuous as a volunteer Antony to the country squire turned Caesar,("With ermine clad and purple, let him hold A royal sceptre made of Spanish gold,") was more servile than Dryden in hailing the return of ex officio Majesty. He bewails to Charles, in snuffling heroics,

"Our sorrow and our crime
To have accepted life so long a time,
Without you here."

A weak man, put to the test by rough and angry times, as Waller was, may be pitied, but meanness is nothing but contemptible under any circumstances. If it be true that"every conqueror creates a Muse," Cromwell was unfortunate. Even Milton's sonnet, though dignified, is reserved if not distrustful. Marvell's"Horatian Ode," the most truly classic in our language, is worthy of its theme. The same poet's Elegy, in parts noble, and everywhere humanly tender, is worth more than all Carlyle's biography as a witness to the gentler qualities of the hero, and of the deep affection that stalwart nature could inspire in hearts of truly masculine temper. As it is little known, a few verses of it may be quoted to show the difference between grief that thinks of its object and grief that thinks of its rhymes:--

"Valor, religion, friendship, prudence died At once with him, and all that's good beside, And we, death's refuse, nature's dregs, confined To loathsome life, alas! are left behind.

Where we (so once we used) shall now no more, To fetch day, press about his chamber-door, No more shall hear that powerful language charm, Whose force oft spared the labour of his arm, No more shall follow where he spent the days In war or counsel, or in prayer and praise.

I saw him dead; a leaden slumber lies,
And mortal sleep, over those wakeful eyes;
Those gentle rays under the lids were fled,
Which through his looks that piercing sweetness shed;
That port, which so majestic was and strong,
Loose and deprived of vigour stretched along,
All withered, all discolored, pale, and wan,
How much another thing! no more
That Man!
O human glory! vain! O death! O wings!
O worthless world! O transitory things!
Yet dwelt that greatness in his shape decayed
That still, though dead, greater than Death he laid,
And, in his altered face, you something feign
That threatens Death he yet will live again."

Such verses might not satisfy Lindley Murray, but they are of that higher mood which satisfies the heart. These couplets, too, have an energy worthy of Milton's friend:--

"When up the armëd mountains of Dunbar
He marched, and through deep Severn, ending war."
"Thee, many ages hence, in martial verse
Shall the English soldier, ere he charge, rehearse."

On the whole, one is glad that Dryden's panegyric on the Protector was so poor. It was purely official verse-making. Had there been any feeling in it, there had been baseness in his address to Charles. As it is, we may fairly assume that he was so far sincere in both cases as to be thankful for a chance to exercise himself in rhyme, without much caring whether upon a funeral or a restoration. He might naturally enough expect that poetry would have a better chance under Charles than under Cromwell, or any successor with Commonwealth principles. Cromwell had more serious matters to think about than verses, while Charles might at least care as much about them as it was in his base good-nature to care about anything but loose women and spaniels. Dryden's sound sense, afterwards so conspicuous, shows itself even in these pieces, when we can get at it through the tangled thicket of tropical phrase. But the authentic and unmistakable Dryden first manifests himself in some verses addressed to his friend Dr. Charlton in 1663. We have first his common sense which has almost the point of wit, yet with a tang of prose:--

"The longest tyranny that ever swayed
Was that wherein our ancestors betrayed
Their freeborn reason to the Stagyrite,
And made his torch their universal light.
So truth, while only one supplied the state,
Grew scarce and dear and yet sophisticate.
Still it was bought, like emp'ric wares or charms,
Hard words sealed up with Aristotle's arms."

Then we have his graceful sweetness of fancy, where he speaks of the inhabitants of the New World:--

"Guiltless men who danced away their time,
Fresh as their groves and happy as their clime."

And, finally, there is a hint of imagination where"mighty visions of the Danish race" watch round Charles sheltered in Stonehenge after the battle of Worcester. These passages might have been written by the Dryden whom we learn to know fifteen years later. They have the advantage that he wrote them to please himself. His contemporary, Dr. Heylin, said of French cooks, that"their trade was not to feed the belly, but the palate." Dryden was a great while in learning this secret, as available in good writing as in cookery. He strove after it, but his thoroughly English nature, to the last, would too easily content itself with serving up the honest beef of his thought, without regard to daintiness of flavour in the dressing of it. Of the best English poetry, it might be said that it is understanding aërated by imagination. In Dryden the solid part too often refused to mix kindly with the leaven, either remaining lumpish or rising to a hasty puffiness. Grace and lightness were with him much more a laborious achievement than a natural gift, and it is all the more remarkable that he should so often have attained to what seems such an easy perfection in both. Always a hasty writer, he was long in forming his style, and to the last was apt to snatch the readiest word rather than wait for the fittest. He was not wholly and unconsciously poet, but a thinker who sometimes lost himself on enchanted ground and was transfigured by its touch.

This preponderance in him of the reasoning over the intuitive faculties, the one always there, the other flashing in when you least expect it, accounts for that inequality and even incongruousness in his writing which makes one revise his judgment at every tenth page. In his prose you come upon passages that persuade you he is a poet, in spite of his verses so often turning state's evidence against him as to convince you he is none. He is a prose-writer, with a kind of Aeolian attachment. For example, take this bit of prose from the dedication of his version of Virgil's Pastorals, 1694:"He found the strength of his genius betimes, and was even in his youth preluding to his Georgicks and his Aeneis.

He could not forbear to try his wings, though his pinions were not hardened to maintain a long, laborious flight; yet sometimes they bore him to a pitch as lofty as ever he was able to reach afterwards. But when he was admonished by his subject to descend, he came down gently circling in the air and singing to the ground, like a lark melodious in her mounting and continuing her song till she alights, still preparing for a higher flight at her next sally, and tuning her voice to better music." This is charming, and yet even this wants the ethereal tincture that pervades the style of Jeremy Taylor, making it, as Burke said of Sheridan's eloquence, "neither prose nor poetry, but something better than either." Let us compare Taylor's treatment of the same image:"For so have I seen a lark rising from his bed of grass and soaring upwards, singing as he rises, and hopes to get to heaven and climb above the clouds; but the poor bird was beaten back by the loud sighings of an eastern wind, and his motion made irregular and inconstant, descending more at every breath of the tempest than it could recover by the libration and frequent weighing of his wings, till the little creature was forced to sit down and pant, and stay till the storm was over, and then it made a prosperous flight, and did rise and sing as if it had learned music and motion of an angel as he passed sometimes through the air about his ministries here below." Taylor's fault is that his sentences too often smell of the library, but what an open air is here! How unpremeditated it all seems! How carelessly he knots each new thought, as it comes, to the one before it with an and, like a girl making lace! And what a slidingly musical use he makes of the sibilants with which our language is unjustly taxed by those who can only make them hiss, not sing! There are twelve of them in the first twenty words, fifteen of which are monsyllables. We notice the structure of Dryden's periods, but this grows up as we read. It gushes, like the song of the bird itself,--

"In profuse strains of unpremeditated art."

Let us now take a specimen of Dryden's bad prose from one of his poems. I open the"Annus Mirabilis" at random, and hit upon this:--

'Our little fleet was now engaged so far,
That, like the swordfish in the whale, they fought.
The combat only seemed a civil war,
Till through their bowels we our passage wrought.'

Is this Dryden, or Sternhold, or Shadwell, those Toms who made him say that"dulness was fatal to the name of Tom"? The natural history of Goldsmith in the verse of Pye! His thoughts did not"voluntary move harmonious numbers." He had his choice between prose and verse, and seems to be poetical on second thought. I do not speak without book. He was more than half conscious of it himself. In the same letter to Mrs. Steward, just cited, he says,"I am still drudging on, always a poet and never a good one"; and this from no mock-modesty, for he is always handsomely frank in telling us whatever of his own doing pleased him. This was written in the last year of his life, and at about the same time he says elsewhere:"What judgment I had increases rather than diminishes, and thoughts, such as they are, come crowding in so fast upon me that my only difficulty is to choose or to reject, to run them into verse or to give them the other harmony of prose; I have so long studied and practised both, that they are grown into a habit and become familiar to me." I think that a man who was primarily a poet would hardly have felt this equanimity of choice.

I find a confirmation of this feeling about Dryden in his early literary loves. His taste was not an instinct, but the slow result of reflection and of the manfulness with which he always acknowledged to himself his own mistakes. In this latter respect, few men deal so magnanimously with themselves as he, and accordingly few have been so happily inconsistent. Ancora imparo might have served him for a motto as well as Michael Angelo. His prefaces are a complete log of his life, and the habit of writing them was a useful one to him, for it forced him to think with a pen in his hand, which, according to Goethe,"if it do no other good, keeps the mind from staggering about." In these prefaces we see his taste gradually rising from Du Bartas to Spenser, from Cowley to Milton, from Corneille to Shakespeare."I remember when I was a boy," he says in his dedication of the"Spanish Friar," 1681,"I thought inimitable Spenser a mean poet in comparison of Sylvester's Du Bartas, and was rapt into an ecstasy when I read these lines:--

'Now when the winter's keener breath began
To crystallize the Baltic ocean,
To glaze the lakes, to bridle up the floods,
And periwig with snow the baldpate woods.'

I am much deceived if this be not abominable fustian." Swift, in his"Tale of a Tub," has a ludicrous passage in this style:"Look on this globe of earth, you will find it to be a very complete and fashionable dress. What is that which some call land, but a fine coat faced with green? or the sea, but a waistcoat of water-tabby? Proceed to the particular works of creation, you will find how curious journeyman Nature has been to trim up the vegetable beaux; observe how sparkish a periwig adorns the head of a beech, and what a fine doublet of white satin is worn by the birch." The fault is not in any inaptness of the images, nor in the mere vulgarity of the things themselves, but in that of the associations they awaken. The"prithee, undo this button" of Lear, coming where it does and expressing what it does, is one of those touches of the pathetically sublime, of which only Shakespeare ever knew the secret. Herrick, too, has a charming poem on"Julia's petticoat," the charm being that he lifts the familiar and the low to the region of sentiment. In the passage from Sylvester, it is precisely the reverse, and the wig takes as much from the sentiment as it adds to a Lord Chancellor. So Pope's proverbial verse,"True wit is Nature to advantage drest,"

unpleasantly suggests Nature under the hands of a lady's-maid. We have no word in English that will exactly define this want of propriety in diction. Vulgar is too strong, and commonplace too weak. Perhaps bourgeois comes as near as any. It is to be noticed that Dryden does not unequivocally condemn the passage he quotes, but qualifies it with an"if I am not much mistaken." Indeed, though his judgment in substantials, like that of Johnson, is always worth having, his taste, the negative half of genius, never altogether refined itself from a colloquial familiarity, which is one of the charms of his prose, and gives that air of easy strength in which his satire is unmatched. In his"Royal Martyr" (1669), the tyrant Maximin says to the gods:

"Keep you your rain and sunshine in the skies,
And I'll keep back my flame and sacrifice;
Your trade of Heaven shall soon be at a stand,
And all your goods lie dead upon your hand,"

a passage which has as many faults as only Dryden was capable of committing, even to a false idiom forced by the last rhyme. The same tyrant in dying exclaims:--

"And after thee I'll go,
Revenging still, and following e'en to th'other world my blow,
And, shoving back this earth on which I sit,
I'll mount and scatter all the gods I hit."

In the"Conquest of Grenada" (1670), we have:--

"This little loss in our vast body shews
So small, that half have never heard the news;
Fame's out of breath e'er she can fly so far
To tell'em all that you have e'er made war."
And in the same play,
"That busy thing,
The soul, is packing up, and just on wing
Like parting swallows when they seek the spring,"

where the last sweet verse curiously illustrates that inequality (poetry on a prose background) which so often puzzles us in Dryden. Infinitely worse is the speech of Almanzor to his mother's ghost:--

"I'll rush into the covert of the night
And pull thee backward by the shroud to light,
Or else I'll squeeze thee like a bladder there,
And make thee groan thyself away to air."

Q. What wonder that Dryden should have been substituted for Davenant as the butt of the"Rehearsal," and that the parody should have had such a run?

And yet it was Dryden who, in speaking of Persius, hit upon the happy phrase of"boisterous metaphors"; it was Dryden who said of Cowley, whom he elsewhere calls"the darling of my youth," that he was"sunk in reputation because he could never forgive any conceit which came in his way, but swept, like a drag-net, great and small." But the passages I have thus far cited as specimens of our poet's coarseness (for poet he surely was intus, though not always in cute) were written before he was forty, and he had an odd notion, suitable to his healthy complexion, that poets on the whole improve after that date. Man at forty, he says,"seems to be fully in his summer tropic,... and I believe that it will hold in all great poets that, though they wrote before with a certain heat of genius which inspired them, yet that heat was not perfectly digested." But artificial heat is never to be digested at all, as is plain in Dryden's case. He was a man who warmed slowly, and, in his hurry to supply the market, forced his mind. The result was the same after forty as before. In"Oedipus" (1679) we find,

"Not one bolt

Shall err from Thebes, but more be called for, more,
New-moulded thunder of a larger size!"

This play was written in conjunction with Lee, of whom Dryden relates that, when some one said to him,"It is easy enough to write like a madman," he replied,"No, it is hard to write like a madman, but easy enough to write like a fool,"-perhaps the most compendious lecture on poetry ever delivered. The splendid bit of eloquence, which has so much the sheet-iron clang of impeachment thunder (I hope that Dryden is not in the Library of Congress!) is perhaps Lee's. The following passage almost certainly is his:--

"Sure'tis the end of all things! Fate has torn The lock of Time off, and his head is now The ghastly ball of round Eternity!"

But the next, in which the soul is likened to the pocket of an indignant housemaid charged with theft, is wholly in Dryden's manner:--

"No; I dare challenge heaven to turn me outward,
And shake my soul quite empty in your sight."

In the same style, he makes his Don Sebastian (1690) say that he is as much astonished as"drowsy mortals" at the last trump,

"When, called in haste, they fumble for their limbs,"

and propose to take upon himself the whole of a crime shared with another by asking Heaven to charge the bill on him. And in"King Arthur," written ten years after the Preface from which I have quoted his confession about Dubartas, we have a passage precisely of the kind he condemned:--

"Ah for the many souls as but this morn
Were clothed with flesh and warmed with vital blood,
But naked now, or shirted but with air."

Dryden too often violated his own admirable rule, that"an author is not to write all he can, but only all he ought." In his worst images, however, there is often a vividness that half excuses them. But it is a grotesque vividness, as from the flare of a bonfire. They do not flash into sudden luster, as in the great poets, where the imaginations of poet and reader leap toward each other and meet half-way.

English prose is indebted to Dryden for having freed it from the cloister of pedantry. He, more than any other single writer, contributed, as well by precept as example, to give it suppleness of movement and the easier air of the modern world. His own style, juicy with proverbial phrases, has that familiar dignity, so hard to attain, perhaps unattainable except by one who, like Dryden, feels that his position is assured. Charles Cotton is as easy, but not so elegant; Walton as familiar, but not so flowing; Swift as idiomatic, but not so elevated; Burke more splendid, but not so equally luminous. That his style was no easy acquisition (though, of course, the aptitude was innate) he himself tells us. In his dedication of"Troilus and Cressida" (1679), where he seems to hint at the erection of an Academy, he says that"the perfect knowledge of a tongue was never attained by any single person.

The Court, the College, and the Town must all be joined in it. And as our English is a composition of the dead and living tongues, there is required a perfect knowledge, not only of the Greek and Latin, but of the Old German, French, and Italian, and to help all these, a conversation with those authors of our own who have written with the fewest faults in prose and verse. But how barbarously we yet write and speak your Lordship knows, and I am sufficiently sensible in my own English. For I am often put to a stand in considering whether what I write be the idiom of the tongue, or false grammar and nonsense couched beneath that specious name of Anglicism, and have no other way to clear my doubts but by translating my English into Latin, and thereby trying what sense the words will bear in a more stable language." Tantae molis erat. Five years later:"The proprieties and delicacies of the English are known to few; it is impossible even for a good wit to understand and practise them without the help of a liberal education, long reading and digesting of those few good authors we have amongst us, the knowledge of men and manners, the freedom of habitudes and conversation with the best company of both sexes, and, in short, without wearing off the rust which he contracted while he was laying in a stock of learning." In the passage I have italicized, it will be seen that Dryden lays some stress upon the influence of women in refining language. Swift, also, in his plan for an Academy, says:"Now, though I would by no means give the ladies the trouble of advising us in the reformation of our language, yet I cannot help thinking that, since they have been left out of all meetings except parties at play, or where worse designs are carried on, our conversation has very much degenerated." Swift affirms that the language had grown corrupt since the Restoration, and that"the Court, which used to be the standard of propriety and correctness of speech, was then, and, I think, has ever since continued, the worst school in England." He lays the blame partly on the general licentiousness, partly upon the French education of many of Charles's courtiers, and partly on the poets.

Dryden undoubtedly formed his diction by the usage of the Court. The age was a very free-and-easy, not to say a very coarse one. Its coarseness was not external, like that of Elizabeth's day, but the outward mark of an inward depravity. What Swift's notion of the refinement of women was may be judged by his anecdotes of Stella. I will not say that Dryden's prose did not gain by the conversational elasticity which his frequenting men and women of the world enabled him to give it. It is the best specimen of every-day style that we have. But the habitual dwelling of his mind in a commonplace atmosphere, and among those easy levels of sentiment which befitted Will's Coffee-house and the Bird-cage Walk, was a damage to his poetry.

Solitude is as needful to the imagination as society is wholesome for the character. He cannot always distinguish between enthusiasm and extravagance when he sees them. But apart from these influences which I have adduced in exculpation, there was certainly a vein of coarseness in him, a want of that exquisite sensitiveness which is the conscience of the artist. An old gentleman, writing to the Gentleman's Magazine in 1745, professes to remember"plain John Dryden (before he paid his court with success to the great) in one uniform clothing of Norwich drugget. I have eat tarts at the Mulberry Garden with him and Madam Reeve, when our author advanced to a sword and Chadreux wig."I always fancy

Dryden in the drugget, with wig, lace ruffles, and sword superimposed. It is the type of this curiously incongruous man.

The first poem by which Dryden won a general acknowledgment of his power was the"Annus Mirabilis," written in his thirty-seventh year. Pepys, himself not altogether a bad judge, doubtless expresses the common opinion when he says:"I am very well pleased this night with reading a poem I brought home with me last night from Westminster Hall, of Dryden's, upon the present war; a very good poem." And a very good poem, in some sort, it continues to be, in spite of its amazing blemishes. We must always bear in mind that Dryden lived in an age that supplied him with no ready-made inspiration, and that big phrases and images are apt to be pressed into the service when great ones do not volunteer. With this poem begins the long series of Dryden's prefaces, of which Swift made such excellent, though malicious, fun that I cannot forbear to quote it."

I do utterly disapprove and declare against that pernicious custom of making the preface a bill of fare to the book. For I have always looked upon it as a high point of indiscretion in monster-mongers and other retailers of strange sights to hang out a fair picture over the door, drawn after the life, with a most eloquent description underneath; this has saved me many a threepence.... Such is exactly the fate at this time of prefaces.... This expedient was admirable at first; our great Dryden has long carried it as far as it would go, and with incredible success. He has often said to me in confidence,'that the world would never have suspected him to be so great a poet, if he had not assured them so frequently, in his prefaces, that it was impossible they could either doubt or forget it.'Perhaps it may be so; however, I much fear his instructions have edified out of their place, and taught men to grow wiser in certain points where he never intended they should." The monster-mongers is a terrible thrust, when we remember some of the comedies and heroic plays which Dryden ushered in this fashion. In the dedication of the"Annus" to the city of London is one of those pithy sentences of which Dryden is ever afterwards so full, and which he lets fall with a carelessness that seems always to deepen the meaning:"

I have heard, indeed, of some virtuous persons who have ended unfortunately, but never of any virtuous nation; Providence is engaged too deeply when the cause becomes so general." In his"account" of the poem in a letter to Sir Robert Howard he says:"I have chosen to write my poem in quatrains or stanzas of four in alternate rhyme, because I have ever judged them more noble and of greater dignity, both for the sound and number, than any other verse in use amongst us.... The learned languages have certainly a great advantage of us in not being tied to the slavery of any rhyme.... But in this necessity of our rhymes, I have always found the couplet verse most easy, though not so proper for this occasion; for there the work is sooner at an end, every two lines concluding the labour of the poet."

A little further on:"They [the French] write in alexandrines, or verses of six feet, such as amongst us is the old translation of Homer by Chapman: all which, by lengthening their chain, makes the sphere of their activity the greater." I have quoted these passages because, in a small compass, they include several things characteristic of Dryden."I have ever judged," and"I have always found," are particularly so. If he took up an opinion in the morning, he would have found so many arguments for it before night that it would seem already old and familiar. So with his reproach of rhyme; a year or two before he was eagerly defending it; again a few years, and he will utterly condemn and drop it in his plays, while retaining it in his translations; afterwards his study of Milton leads him to think that blank verse would suit the epic style better, and he proposes to try it with Homer, but at last translates one book as a specimen, and behold, it is in rhyme! But the charm of this great advocate is, that, whatever side he was on, he could always find excellent reasons for it, and state them with great force, and abundance of happy illustration. He is an exception to the proverb, and is none the worse pleader than he is always pleading his own cause. The blunder about Chapman is of a kind into which his hasty temperament often betrayed him. He remembered that Chapman's"Iliad" was in a long measure, concluded without looking that it was alexandrine, and then attributes it generally to his"Homer." Chapman's"Iliad" is done in fourteen-syllable verse, and his"Odyssee" in the very metre that Dryden himself used in his own version, I remark also what he says of the couplet, that it was easy because the second verse concludes the labour of the poet.

And yet it was Dryden who found it hard for that very reason. His vehement abundance refused those narrow banks, first running over into a triplet, and, even then uncontainable, rising to an alexandrine in the concluding verse. And I have little doubt that it was the roominess, rather than the dignity, of the quatrain which led him to choose it. As apposite to this, I may quote what he elsewhere says of octosyllabic verse:"The thought can turn itself with greater ease in a larger compass. When the rhyme comes too thick upon us, it straightens the expression: we are thinking of the close, when we should be employed in adorning the thought. It makes a poet giddy with turning in a space too narrow for his imagination."

Dryden himself, as was not always the case with him, was well satisfied with his work. He calls it his best hitherto, and attributes his success to the excellence of his subject,"incomparably the best he had ever had, excepting only the Royal Family." The first part is devoted to the Dutch war; the last to the fire of London. The martial half is infinitely the better of the two. He altogether surpasses his model, Davenant. If his poem lacks the gravity of thought attained by a few stanzas of"Gondibert," it is vastly superior in life, in picturesqueness, in the energy of single lines, and, above all, in imagination. Few men have read"Gondibert," and almost every one speaks of it, as commonly of the dead, with a certain subdued respect. And it deserves respect as an honest effort to bring poetry back to its highest office in the ideal treatment of life. Davenant emulated Spenser, and if his poem had been as good as his preface, it could still be read in another spirit than that of investigation. As it is, it always reminds me of Goldsmith's famous verse. It is remote, unfriendly, solitary, and, above all, slow. Its shining passages, for there are such, remind one of distress-rockets sent up at intervals from a ship just about to founder, and sadden rather than cheer.

The first part of the"Annus Mirabilis" is by no means clear of the false taste of the time, though it has some of Dryden's manliest verses and happiest comparisons, always his two distinguishing merits. Here, as almost everywhere else in Dryden, measuring him merely as poet, we recall what he, with pathetic pride, says of himself in the prologue to"Aurengzebe":--

"Let him retire, betwixt two ages cast,
The first of this, the hindmost of the last."

What can be worse than what he says of comets?--

"Whether they unctuous exhalations are
Fired by the sun, or seeming so alone,
Or each some more remote and slippery star
Which loses footing when to mortals shown."

Or than this, of the destruction of the Dutch India ships?-

"Amidst whole heaps of spices lights a ball,
And now their odors armed against them fly;
Some preciously by shattered porcelain fall,
And some by aromatic splinters die."

Dear Dr. Johnson had his doubts about Shakespeare, but here at least was poetry! This is one of the quatrains which he pronounces"worthy of our author."

But Dryden himself has said that"a man who is resolved to praise an author with any appearance of justice must be sure to take him on the strongest siue, and where he is least liable to exceptions." This is true also of one who wishes to measure an author fairly, for the higher wisdom of criticism lies in the capacity to admire.

Leser, wie gefall ich dir?
Leser, wie gefällst du mir?

are both fair questions, the answer to the first being more often involved in that to the second than is sometimes thought. The poet in Dryden was never more fully revealed than in such verses as these:--

"And threatening France, placed like a painted Jove,
Kept idle thunder in his lifted hand";

"Silent in smoke of cannon they come on";
"And his loud guns speak thick, like angry men";
"The vigorous seaman every port-hole plies,
And adds his heart to every gun he fires";
"And, though to me unknown, they sure fought well,
Whom Rupert led, and who were British born."

This is masculine writing, and yet it must be said that there is scarcely a quatrain in which the rhyme does not trip him into a platitude, and there are too many swaggering with that expression forte d'un sentiment faible which Voltaire condemns in Çorneille,--a temptation to which Dryden always lay too invitingly open. But there are passages higher in kind than any I have cited, because they show imagination. Such are the verses in which he describes the dreams of the disheartened enemy:--

"In dreams they fearful precipices tread,
Or, shipwrecked, labour to some distant shore,
Or in dark churches walk among the dead";

and those in which he recalls glorious memories, and sees where

"The mighty ghosts of our great Harries rose,
And armëd Edwards looked with anxious eyes."

A few verses, like the pleasantly alliterative one in which he makes the spider,"from the silent ambush of his den,""feel far off the trembling of his thread," show that he was beginning to study the niceties of verse, instead of trusting wholly to what he would have called his natural fougue. On the whole, this part of the poem is very good war poetry, as war poetry goes (for there is but one first-rate poem of the kind in English,--short, national, eager as if the writer were personally engaged, with the rapid metre of a drum beating the charge,--and that is Drayton's"Battle of Agincourt"),but it shows more study of Lucan than of Virgil, and for a long time yet we shall find Dryden bewildered by bad models. He is always imitating-no, that is not the word, always emulating-somebody in his more strictly poetical attempts, for in that direction he always needed some external impulse to set his mind in motion. This is more or less true of all authors; nor does it detract from their originality, which depends wholly on their being able so far to forget themselves as to let something of themselves slip into what they write. Of absolute originality we will not speak till authors are raised by some Deucalion-and-Pyrrha process; and even then our faith would be small, for writers who have no past are pretty sure of having no future. Dryden, at any rate, always had to have his copy set him at the top of the page, and wrote ill or well accordingly. His mind (somewhat solid for a poet) warmed slowly, but, once fairly heated through, he had more of that good-luck of self-oblivion than most men. He certainly gave even a liberal interpretation to Molière's rule of taking his own property wherever he found it, though he sometimes blundered awkwardly about what was properly his; but in literature, it should be remembered, a thing always becomes his at last who says it best, and thus makes it his own.

Mr. Savage Landor once told me that he said to Wordsworth:"Mr. Wordsworth, a man may mix poetry with prose as much as he pleases, and it will only elevate and enliven; but the moment he mixes a particle of prose with his poetry, it precipitates the whole." Wordsworth, he added, never forgave him. The always hasty Dryden, as I think I have already said, was liable, like a careless apothecary's'prentice, to make the same confusion of ingredients, especially in the more mischievous way. I cannot leave the"Annus Mirabilis" without giving an example of this.

Describing the Dutch prizes, rather like an auctioneer than a poet, he says that

"Some English wool, vexed in a Belgian loom,
And into cloth of spongy softness made,
Did into France or colder Denmark doom,
To ruin with worse ware our staple trade."

One might fancy this written by the secretary of a board of trade in an unguarded moment; but we should remember that the poem is dedicated to the city of London. The depreciation of the rival fabrics is exquisite; and Dryden, the most English of our poets, would not be so thoroughly English if he had not in him some fibre of la nation boutiquière. Let us now see how he succeeds in attempting to infuse science (the most obstinately prosy material) with poetry. Speaking of"a more exact knowledge of the longitudes," as he explains in a note, he tells us that,

"Then we upon our globe's last verge shall go,
And view the ocean leaning on the sky;
From thence our rolling neighbors we shall know,
And on the lunar world securely pry."

Dr. Johnson confesses that he does not understand this. Why should he, when it is plain that Dryden was wholly in the dark himself! To understand it is none of my business, but I confess that it interests me as an Americanism. We have hitherto been credited as the inventors of the"jumping-off place" at the extreme western verge of the world. But Dryden was beforehand with us. Though he doubtless knew that the earth was a sphere (and perhaps that it was flattened at the poles), it was always a flat surface in his fancy. In his"Amphitryon," he makes Alcmena say:--

"No, I would fly thee to the ridge of earth,
And leap the precipice to'scape thy sight."

And in his"Spanish Friar," Lorenzo says to Elvira that they"will travel together to the ridge of the world, and then drop together into the next." It is idle for us poor Yankees to hope that we can invent anything. To say sooth, if Dryden had left nothing behind him but the"Annus Mirabilis," he might have served as a type of the kind of poet America would have produced by the biggest-river-and-tallest-mountain recipe,--longitude and latitude in plenty, with marks of culture scattered here and there like the carets on a proof sheet.

It is now time to say something of Dryden as a dramatist. In the thirty-two years between 1662 and 1694, he produced twenty-five plays, and assisted Lee in two. I have hinted that it took Dryden longer than most men to find the true bent of his genius. On a superficial view, he might almost seem to confirm that theory, maintained by Johnson, among others, that genius was nothing more than great intellectual power exercised persistently in some particular direction which chance decided, so that it lay in circumstance merely whether a man should turn out a Shakespeare or a Newton. But when we come to compare what he wrote, regardless of Minerva's averted face, with the spontaneous production of his happier muse, we shall be inclined to think his example one of the strongest cases against the theory in question.

He began his dramatic career, as usual, by rowing against the strong current of his nature, and pulled only the more doggedly the more he felt himself swept down the stream. His first attempt was at comedy, and, though his earliest piece of that kind (the"Wild Gallant," 1663) utterly failed, he wrote eight others afterwards. On the 23d February, 1663, Pepys writes in his diary:"To Court, and there saw the'Wild Gallant'performed by the king's house; but it was ill acted, and the play so poor a thing as I never saw in my life almost, and so little answering the name, that, from the beginning to the end, I could not, nor can at this time, tell certainly which was the Wild Gallant. The king did not seem pleased at all the whole play, nor anybody else."

After some alteration, it was revived with more success. On its publication in 1669 Dryden honestly admitted its former failure, though with a kind of salvo for his self-love."I made the town my judges, and the greater part condemned it. After which I do not think it my concernment to defend it with the ordinary zeal of a poet for his decried poem, though Corneille is more resolute in his preface before'Pertharite,'which was condemned more universally than this.... Yet it was received at Court, and was more than once the divertisement of his Majesty, by his own command." Pepys lets us amusingly behind the scenes in the matter of his Majesty's divertisement. Dryden does not seem to see that in the condemnation of something meant to amuse the public there can be no question of degree. To fail at all is to fail utterly.

"Tous les genres sont permis, hors le genre ennuyeux."

In the reading, at least, all Dryden's comic writing for the stage must be ranked with the latter class. He himself would fain make an exception of the"Spanish Friar," but I confess that I rather wonder at than envy those who can be amused by it. His comedies lack everything that a comedy should have,--lightness, quickness of transition, unexpectedness of incident, easy cleverness of dialogue, and humorous contrast of character brought out by identity of situation. The comic parts of the"Maiden Queen" seem to me Dryden's best, but the merit even of these is Shakespeare's, and there is little choice where even the best is only tolerable. The common quality, however, of all Dryden's comedies is their nastiness, the more remarkable because we have ample evidence that he was a man of modest conversation.

Pepys, who was by no means squeamish (for he found"Sir Martin Marall""the most entire piece of mirth... that certainly ever was writ... very good wit therein, not fooling"), writes in his diary of the 19th June, 1668:"My wife and Deb to the king's play-house to-day, thinking to spy me there, and saw the new play'Evening Love,'of Dryden's, which, though the world commends, she likes not." The next day he saw it himself,"and do not like it, it being very smutty, and nothing so good as the'Maiden Queen'or the'Indian Emperor'of Dryden's making. I was troubled at it." On the 22d, he adds:"Calling this day at Herringman's, he tells me Dryden do himself call it but a fifth-rate play." This was no doubt true, and yet, though Dryden in his preface to the play says,"I confess I have given [yielded] too much to the people in it, and am ashamed for them as well as for myself, that I have pleased them at so cheap a rate," he takes care to add,"not that there is anything here that I would not defend to an ill-natured judge."

The plot was from Calderon, and the author, rebutting the charge of plagiarism, tells us that the king ("without whose command they should no longer be troubled with anything of mine") had already answered for him by saying,"that he only desired that they who accused me of theft would always steal him plays like mine." Of the morals of the play he has not a word, nor do I believe that he was conscious of any harm in them till he was attacked by Collier, and then, (with some protest against what he considers the undue severity of his censor) he had the manliness to confess that he had done wrong."It becomes me not to draw my pen in the defence of a bad cause, when I have so often drawn it for a good one."And in a letter to his correspondent, Mrs. Thomas, written only a few weeks before his death, warning her against the example of Mrs. Behn, he says, with remorseful sincerity:"I confess I am the last man in the world who ought in justice to arraign her, who have been myself too much a libertine in most of my poems, which I should be well contented I had time either to purge or to see them fairly burned." Congreve was less patient, and even Dryden, in the last epilogue he ever wrote, attempts an excuse:--

"Perhaps the Parson stretched a point too far,
When with our Theatres he waged a war;
He tells you that this very moral age
Received the first infection from the Stage,
But sure a banished Court, with lewdness fraught,
The seeds of open vice returning brought.
Whitehall the naked Venus first revealed,
Who, standing, as at Cyprus, in her shrine,
The strumpet was adored with rites divine.
The poets, who must live by courts or starve,
Were proud so good a Government to serve,
And, mixing with buffoons and pimps profane,
Tainted the Stage for some small snip of gain."

Dryden least of all men should have stooped to this palliation, for he had, not without justice, said of himself"The same parts and application which have made me a poet might have raised me to any honors of the gown." Milton and Marvell neither lived by the Court, nor starved. Charles Lamb most ingeniously defends the Comedy of the Restoration as"the sanctuary and quiet Alsatia of hunted casuistry," where there was no pretence of representing a real world. But this was certainly not so. Dryden again and again boasts of the superior advantage which his age had over that of the elder dramatists, in painting polite life, and attributes it to a greater freedom of intercourse between the poets and the frequenters of the Court. We shall be less surprised at the kind of refinement upon which Dryden congratulated himself, when we learn (from the dedication of"Marriage à la Mode") that the Earl of Rochester was its exemplar:"The best comic writers of our age will join with me to acknowledge that they have copied the gallantries of courts, the delicacy of expression, and the decencies of behaviour from your Lordship."

In judging Dryden, it should be borne in mind that for some years he was under contract to deliver three plays a year, a kind of bond to which no man should subject his brain who has a decent respect for the quality of its products. We should remember, too, that in his day manners meant what we call morals, that custom always makes a larger part of virtue among average men than they are quite aware, and that the reaction from an outward conformity which had no root in inward faith may for a time have given to the frank expression of laxity an air of honesty that made it seem almost refreshing. There is no such hotbed for excess of license as excess of restraint, and the arrogant fanaticism of a single virtue is apt to make men suspicious of tyranny in all the rest. But the riot of emancipation could not last long, for the more tolerant society is of private vice, the more exacting will it be of public decorum, that excellent thing, so often the plausible substitute for things more excellent. By 1678 the public mind had so far recovered its tone that Dryden's comedy of"Limberham" was barely tolerated for three nights. I will let the man who looked at human nature from more sides, and therefore judged it more gently than any other, give the only excuse possible for Dryden:--

"Men's judgments are
A parcel of their fortunes, and things outward
Do draw the inward quality after them
To suffer all alike."

Dryden's own apology only makes matters worse for him by showing that he committed his offences with his eyes wide open, and that he wrote comedies so wholly in despite of nature as never to deviate into the comic. Failing as clown, he did not scruple to take on himself the office of Chiffinch to the palled appetite of the public."For I confess my chief endeavours are to delight the age in which I live. If the humour of this be for low comedy, small accidents, and raillery, I will force my genius to obey it, though with more reputation I could write in verse. I know I am not so fitted by nature to write comedy;

I want that gayety of humour, which is requisite to it.

My conversation is slow and dull, my humour saturnine and reserved: In short, I am none of those who endeavour to break jests in company or make repartees. So that those who decry my comedies do me no injury, except it be in point of profit: Reputation in them is the last thing to which I shall pretend." For my own part, though I have been forced to hold my nose in picking my way through these ordures of Dryden, I am free to say that I think them far less morally mischievous than that corps-de-ballet literature in which the most animal of the passions is made more temptingly naked by a veil of French gauze. Nor does Dryden's lewdness leave such a reek in the mind as the filthy cynicism of Swift, who delighted to uncover the nakedness of our common mother.

It is pleasant to follow Dryden into the more congenial region of heroic plays, though here also we find him making a false start. Anxious to please the king, and so able a reasoner as to convince even himself of the justice of whatever cause he argued, he not only wrote tragedies in the French style, but defended his practice in an essay which is by far the most delightful reproduction of the classic dialogue ever written in English. Eugenius (Lord Buckhurst), Lisideius (Sir Charles Sidley), Crites (Sir E. Howard), and Neander (Dryden) are the four partakers in the debate. The comparative merits of ancients and moderns, of the Shakespearian and contemporary drama, of rhyme and blank verse, the value of the three (supposed) Aristotelian unities, are the main topics discussed. The tone of the discussion is admirable, midway between bookishness and talk, and the fairness with which each side of the argument is treated shows the breadth of Dryden's mind perhaps better than any other one piece of his writing.

There are no men of straw set up to be knocked down again, as there commonly are in debates conducted upon this plan. The"Defence" of the Essay is to be taken as a supplement to Neander's share in it, as well as many scattered passages in subsequent prefaces and dedications. All the interlocutors agree that"the sweetness of English verse was never understood or practised by our fathers," and that"our poesy is much improved by the happiness of some writers yet living, who first taught us to mould our thoughts into easy and significant words, to retrench the superfluities of expression, and to make our rhyme so properly a part of the verse that it should never mislead the sense, but itself be led and governed by it." In another place he shows that by"living writers" he meant Waller and Denham.

"Rhyme has all the advantages of prose besides its own. But the excellence and dignity of it were never fully known till Mr. Waller taught it: he first made writing easily an art; first showed us to conclude the sense, most commonly in distiches, which in the verse before him runs on for so many lines together that the reader is out of breath to overtake it." Dryden afterwards changed his mind, and one of the excellences of his own rhymed verse is, that his sense is too ample to be concluded by the distich. Rhyme had been censured as unnatural in dialogue; but Dryden replies that it is no more so than blank verse, since no man talks any kind of verse in real life. But the argument for rhyme is of another kind."I am satisfied if it cause delight, for delight is the chief if not the only end of poesy he should have said means]; instruction can be admitted but in the second place, for poesy only instructs as it delights.... The converse, therefore, which a poet is to imitate must be heightened with all the arts and ornaments of poesy, and must be such as, strictly considered, could never be supposed spoken by any without premeditation.... Thus prose, though the rightful prince, yet is by common consent deposed as too weak for the government of serious plays, and, he failing, there now start up two competitors; one the nearer in blood, which is blank verse; the other more fit for the ends of government, which is rhyme. Blank verse is, indeed, the nearer prose, but he is blemished with the weakness of his predecessor. Rhyme (for I will deal clearly) has somewhat of the usurper in him; but he is brave and generous, and his dominion pleasing." To the objection that the difficulties of rhyme will lead to circumlocution, he answers in substance, that a good poet will know how to avoid them. It is curious how long the superstition that Waller was the refiner of English verse has prevailed since Dryden first gave it vogue. He was a very poor poet and a purely mechanical versifier. He has lived mainly on the credit of a single couplet,

"The soul's dark cottage, battered and decayed.
Lets in new light through chinks that Time hath made,"

in which the melody alone belongs to him, and the conceit, such as it is, to Samuel Daniel, who said, long before, that the body's

"Walls, grown thin, permit the mind
To look out thorough and his frailty find."

Waller has made worse nonsense of it in the transfusion. It might seem that Ben Jonson had a prophetic foreboding of him when he wrote:"Others there are that have no composition at all, but a kind of tuning and rhyming fall, in what they write. It runs and slides and only makes a sound. Women's poets they are called, as you have women's tailors.

They write a verse as smooth, as soft, as cream in which there is no torrent, nor scarce stream. You may sound these wits and find the depth of them with your middle-finger." It seems to have been taken for granted by Waller, as afterwards by Dryden, that our elder poets bestowed no thought upon their verse."Waller was smooth," but unhappily he was also flat, and his importation of the French theory of the couplet as a kind of thought-coop did nothing but mischief. He never compassed even a smoothness approaching this description of a nightingale's song by a third-rate poet of the earlier school,-

"Trails her plain ditty in one long-spun note
Through the sleek passage of her open throat,

A clear, unwrinkled song,"- one of whose beauties is its running over into the third verse. Those poets indeed

"Felt music's pulse in all her arteries;" and Dryden himself found out, when he came to try it, that blank verse was not so easy a thing as he at first conceived it, nay, that it is the most difficult of all verse, and that it must make up in harmony, by variety of pause and modulation, for what it loses in the melody of rhyme. In what makes the chief merit of his later versification, he but rediscovered the secret of his predecessors in giving to rhymed pentameters something of the freedom of blank verse, and not mistaking metre for rhythm.

Voltaire, in his Commentary on Corneille, has sufficiently lamented the awkwardness of movement imposed upon the French dramatists by the gyves of rhyme. But he considers the necessity of overcoming this obstacle, on the whole, an advantage. Difficulty is his tenth and superior muse. How did Dryden, who says nearly the same thing, succeed in his attempt at the French manner? He fell into every one of its vices, without attaining much of what constitutes its excellence. From the nature of the language, all French poetry is purely artificial, and its high polish is all that keeps out decay. The length of their dramatic verse forces the French into much tautology, into bombast in its original meaning, the stuffing out a thought with words till it fills the line. The rigid system of their rhyme, which makes it much harder to manage than in English, has accustomed them to inaccuracies of thought which would shock them in prose. For example, in the"Cinna" of Corneille, as originally written, Emilie says to Augustus,--

"Ces flammes dans nos coeurs dès longtemps étoient nées,
Et ce sont des secrets de plus de quatre années."

I say nothing of the second verse, which is purely prosaic surplusage exacted by the rhyme, nor of the jingling together of ces, dès, étoient, nées, des, and secrets, but I confess that nées does not seem to be the epithet that Corneille would have chosen for flammes, if he could have had his own way, and that flames would seem of all things the hardest to keep secret. But in revising, Corneille changed the first verse thus,-"Ces flammes dans nos coeurs sans votre ordre étoient nées.".

Can anything be more absurd than flames born to order? Yet Voltaire, on his guard against these rhyming pitfalls for the sense, does not notice this in his minute comments on this play. Of extravagant metaphor, the result of this same making sound the file-leader of sense, a single example from"Heraclius" shall suffice:--

"La vapeur de mon sang ira grossir la foudre
Que Dieu tient déja prête à le reduire en poudre."

One cannot think of a Louis Quatorze Apollo except in a

full-bottomed periwig, and the tragic style of their poets is always showing the disastrous influence of that portentous comet. It is the style perruque in another than the French meaning of the phrase, and the skill lay in dressing it majestically, so that, as Cibber says,"upon the head of a man of sense, if it became him, it could never fail of drawing to him a more partial regard and benevolence than could possibly be hoped for in an ill-made one." It did not become Dryden, and he left it off.

Like his own Zimri, Dryden was"all for" this or that fancy, till he took up with another. But even while he was writing on French models, his judgment could not be blinded to their defects."Look upon the'Cinna'and the'Pompey,'they are not so properly to be called plays as long discourses of reason of State, and'Polieucte'in matters of religion is as solemn as the long stops upon our organs;... their actors speak by the hour-glass like our parsons.... I deny not but this may suit well enough with the French, for as we, who are a more sullen people, come to be diverted at our plays, so they, who are of an airy and gay temper, come thither to make themselves more serious." With what an air of innocent unconsciousness the sarcasm is driven home! Again, while he was still slaving at these bricks without straw, he says:"The present French poets are generally accused that, where so ever they lay the scene, or in whatever age, the manners of their heroes are wholly French. Racine's Bajazet is bred at Constantinople, but his civilities are conveyed to him by some secret passage from Versailles into the Seraglio." It is curious that Voltaire, speaking of the Bérénice of Racine, praises a passage in it for precisely what Dryden condemns:"Il semble qu'on entende Henriette d'Angleterre elle-même parlant au marquis de Vardes. La politesse de la cour de Louis XIV., l'agrément de la langue Française, la douceur de la versification la plus naturelle, le sentiment le plus tendre, tout se trouve dans ce peu de vers." After Dryden had broken away from the heroic style, he speaks out more plainly. In the Preface to his"All for Love," in reply to some cavils upon"little, and not essential decencies," the decision about which he refers to a master of ceremonies, he goes on to say:"The French poets, I confess, are strict observers of these punctilios;... in this nicety of manners does the excellency of French poetry consist. Their heroes are the most civil people breathing, but their good breeding seldom extends to a word of sense. All their wit is in their ceremony; they want the genius which animates our stage, and therefore't is but necessary, when they cannot please, that they should take care not to offend.... They are so careful not to exasperate a critic that they never leave him any work,... for no part of a poem is worth our discommending where the whole is insipid, as when we have once tasted palled wine we stay not to examine it glass by glass. But while they affect to shine in trifles, they are often careless in essentials.... For my part, I desire to be tried by the laws of my own country." This is said in heat, but it is plain enough that his mind was wholly changed. In his discourse on epic poetry he is as decided, but more temperate. He says that the French heroic verse"runs with more activity than strength. Their language is not strung with sinews like our English; it has the nimbleness of a greyhound, but not the bulk and body of a mastiff. Our men and our verses overbear them by their weight, and pondere, non numero, is the British motto. The French have set up purity for the standard of their language, and a masculine vigour is that of ours. Like their tongue is the genius of their poets,--light and trifling in comparison of the English."

Dryden might have profited by an admirable saying of his own, that"they who would combat general authority with particular opinion must first establish themselves a reputation of understanding better than other men." He understood the defects much better than the beauties of the French theatre. Lessing was even more one-sided in his judgment upon it. Goethe, with his usual wisdom, studied it carefully without losing his temper, and tried to profit by its structural merits. Dryden, with his eyes wide open, copied its worst faults, especially its declamatory sentiment. He should have known that certain things can never be transplanted, and that among these is a style of poetry whose great excellence was that it was in perfect sympathy with the genius of the people among whom it came into being. But the truth is, that Dryden had no aptitude whatever for the stage, and in writing for it he was attempting to make a trade of his genius,--an arrangement from which the genius always withdraws in disgust. It was easier to make loose thinking and the bad writing which betrays it pass unobserved while the ear was occupied with the sonorous music of the rhyme to which they marched. Except in"All for Love,""the only play," he tells us,"which he wrote to please himself," there is no trace of real passion in any of his tragedies. This, indeed, is inevitable, for there are no characters, but only personages, in any except that. That is, in many respects, a noble play, and there are few finer scenes, whether in the conception or the carrying out, than that between Antony and Ventidius in the first act.

As usual, Dryden's good sense was not blind to the extravagances of his dramatic style. In"Mac Flecknoe" he makes his own Maximin the type of childish rant,

"And little Maximins the gods defy";

but, as usual also, he could give a plausible reason for his own mistakes by means of that most fallacious of all fallacies which is true so far as it goes. In his Prologue to the"Royal Martyr", he says:--

"And he who servilely creeps after sense
Is safe, but ne'er will reach an excellence.
But, when a tyrant for his theme he had,
He loosed the reins and let his muse run mad,
And, though he stumbles in a full career,
Yet rashness is a better fault than fear;
They then, who of each trip advantage take,
Find out those faults which they want wit to make."

And in the Preface to the same play he tells us:"I have not everywhere observed the equality of numbers in my verse, partly by reason of my haste, but more especially because I would not have my sense a slave to syllables." Dryden, when he had not a bad case to argue, would have had small respect for the wit whose skill lay in the making of faults, and has himself, where his self-love was not engaged, admirably defined the boundary which divides boldness from rashness.

What Quintilian says of Seneca applies very aptly to Dryden:"Velles eum suo ingenio dixisse, alieno judicio." He was thinking of himself, I fancy, when he makes Ventidius say of Antony,--

"He starts out wide
And bounds into a vice that bears him far
From his first course, and plunges him in ills;
But, when his danger makes him find his fault,
Quick to observe, and full of sharp remorse,
He censures eagerly his own misdeeds,
Judging himself with malice to himself,
And not forgiving what as man he did
Because his other parts are more than man."

But bad though they nearly all are as wholes, his plays contain passages which only the great masters have surpassed, and to the level of which no subsequent writer for the stage has ever risen. The necessity of rhyme often forced him to a platitude, as where he says,--

"My love was blind to your deluding art,
But blind men feel when stabbed so near the heart."

But even in rhyme he not seldom justifies his claim to the title of"glorious John." In the very play from which I have just quoted are these verses in his best manner:--

"No, like his better Fortune I'll appear,
With open arms, loose veil, and flowing hair,
Just flying forward from her rolling sphere."

His comparisons, as I have said, are almost always happy. This, from the"Indian Emperor," is tenderly pathetic:--

"As callow birds,
Whose mother's killed in seeking of the prey,
Cry in their nest and think her long away,
And, at each leaf that stirs, each blast of wind,
Gape for the food which they must never find."

And this, of the anger with which the Maiden Queen, striving to hide her jealousy, betrays her love, is vigorous:--

"Her rage was love, and its tempestuous flame,
Like lightning, showed the heaven from whence it came."

The following simile from the"Conquest of Grenada" is

as well expressed as it is apt in conception:--

"I scarcely understand my own intent;
But, silk-worm like, so long within have wrought,
That I am lost in my own web of thought."

In the"Rival Ladies," Angelina, walking in the dark, describes her sensations naturally and strikingly:--

"No noise but what my footsteps make, and they
Sound dreadfully and louder than by day:
They double too, and every step I take
Sounds thick, methinks, and more than one could make."

In all the rhymed plays there are many passages which one is rather inclined to like than sure he would be right in liking them. The following verses from"Aurengzebe" are of this sort:--

"My love was such it needed no return,
Rich in itself, like elemental fire,
Whose pureness does no aliment require."

This is Cowleyish, and pureness is surely the wrong word; and yet it is better than mere commonplace. Perhaps what oftenest turns the balance in Dryden's favour, when we are weighing his claims as a poet, is his persistent capability of enthusiasm. To the last he kindles, and sometimes almost flashes out that supernatural light which is the supreme test of poetic genius. As he himself so finely and characteristically says in"Aurengzebe," there was no period in his life when it was not true of him that

"He felt the inspiring heat, the absent god return."

The verses which follow are full of him, and, with the exception of the single word underwent, are in his luckiest manner:--

"One loose, one sally of a hero's soul,
Does all the military art control.
While timorous wit goes round, or fords the shore,
He shoots the gulf, and is already o'er,
And, when the enthusiastic fit is spent,
Looks back amazed at what he underwent."

Pithy sentences and phrases always drop from Dryden's pen as if unawares, whether in prose or verse. I string together a few at random:--

"The greatest argument for love is love."
"Few know the use of life before't is past."
"Time gives himself and is not valued."
"Death in itself is nothing; but we fear
To be we know not what, we know not where."
"Love either finds equality or makes it;
Like death, he knows no difference in degrees."
"That's empire, that which I can give away."
"Yours is a soul irregularly great,
Which, wanting temper, yet abounds in heat."
"Forgiveness to the injured does belong,
But they ne'er pardon who have done the wrong."
"Poor women's thoughts are all extempore."
"The cause of love can never be assigned,
'T is in no face, but in the lover's mind."
"Heaven can forgive a crime to penitence,
For Heaven can judge if penitence be true;
But man, who knows not hearts, should make examples."
"Kings'titles commonly begin by force,
Which time wears off and mellows into right."
"Fear's a large promiser; who subject live
To that base passion, know not what they give."
"The secret pleasure of the generous act
Is the great mind's great bribe."
"That bad thing, gold, buys all good things."
"Why, love does all that's noble here below."
"To prove religion true, If either wit or sufferings could suffice,
All faiths afford the constant and the wise."
But Dryden, as he tells us himself,
"Grew weary of his long-loved mistress, Rhyme;
Passion's too fierce to be in fetters bound,
And Nature flies him like enchanted ground."

The finest things in his plays were written in blank verse, as vernacular to him as the alexandrine to the French. In this he vindicates his claim as a poet. His diction gets wings, and both his verse and his thought become capable of a reach which was denied them when set in the stocks of the couplet. The solid man becomes even airy in this new-found freedom:

Anthony says,

"How I loved, Witness ye days and nights, and all ye hours
That danced away with down upon your feet."

And what image was ever more delicately exquisite, what movement more fadingly accordant with the sense, than in the last two verses of the following passage?

"I feel death rising higher still and higher,
Within my bosom; every breath I fetch
Shuts up my life within a shorter compass,
And, like the vanishing sound of bells, grows less
And less each pulse, till it be lost in air."

Nor was he altogether without pathos, though it is rare with him. The following passage seems to me tenderly full of it:--

"Something like
That voice, methinks, I should have somewhere heard;
But floods of woe have hurried it far off
Beyond my ken of soul."

And this single verse from"Aurengzebe":--

"Live still! oh live! live even to be unkind!"

with its passionate eagerness and sobbing repetition, is worth a ship-load of the long-drawn treacle of modern self-compassion.

Now and then, to be sure, we come upon something that makes us hesitate again whether, after all, Dryden was not grandiose rather than great, as in the two passages that next follow:--

"He locks secure of death, superior greatness,
Like Jove when he made Fate and said,
Thou art The slave of my creation."

"I'm pleased with my own work; Jove was not more
With infant nature, when his spacious hand
Had rounded this huge ball of earth and seas,
To give it the first push and see it roll
Along the vast abyss."

I should say that Dryden is more apt to dilate our fancy than our thought, as great poets have the gift of doing. But if he have not the potent alchemy that transmutes the lead of our commonplace associations into gold, as Shakespeare knows how to do so easily, yet his sense is always up to the sterling standard; and though he has not added so much as some have done to the stock of bullion which others afterwards coin and put in circulation, there are few who have minted so many phrases that are still a part of our daily currency. The first line of the following passage has been worn pretty smooth, but the succeeding ones are less familiar:--

"Men are but children of a larger growth,
Our appetites as apt to change as theirs,
And full as craving too and full as vain;
And yet the soul, shut up in her dark room,
Viewing so clear abroad, at home sees nothing;
But, like a mole in earth, busy and blind,
Works all her folly up and casts it outward
In the world's open view."

The image is mixed and even contradictory, but the thought obtains grace for it. I feel as if Shakespeare would have written seeing for viewing, thus gaining the strength of repetition in one verse and avoiding the sameness of it in the other. Dryden, I suspect, was not much given to correction, and indeed one of the great charms of his best writing is that everything seems struck off at a heat, as by a superior man in the best mood of his talk.

Where he rises, he generally becomes fervent rather than imaginative; his thought does not incorporate itself in metaphor, as in purely poetic minds, but repeats and reinforces itself in simile. Where he is imaginative, it is in that lower sense which the poverty of our language, for want of a better word, compels us to call picturesque, and even then he shows little of that finer instinct which suggests so much more than it tells, and works the more powerfully as it taxes more the imagination of the reader. In Donne's"Relic" there is an example of what I mean. He fancies some one breaking up his grave and spying

"A bracelet of bright hair about the bone,"-

a verse that still shines there in the darkness of the tomb, after two centuries, like one of those inextinguishable lamps whose secret is lost. Yet Dryden sometimes showed a sense of this magic of a mysterious hint, as in the"Spanish Friar":--

"No, I confess, you bade me not in words;
The dial spoke not, but it made shrewd signs,
And pointed full upon the stroke of murder."

This is perhaps a solitary example. Nor is he always so possessed by the image in his mind as unconsciously to choose even the picturesquely imaginative word. He has done so, however, in this passage from"Marriage à la Mode":--

"You ne'er mast hope again to see your princess, Except as prisoners view fair walks and streets, And careless passengers going by their grates."

But after all, he is best upon a level, table-land, it is true, and a very high level, but still somewhere between the loftier peaks of inspiration and the plain of every-day life. In those passages where he moralizes he is always good, setting some obvious truth in a new light by vigorous phrase and happy illustration. Take this (from"Oedipus") as a proof of it:--

"The gods are just,
But how can finite measure infinite?
Reason! alas, it does not know itself!
Yet man, vain man, would with his short-lined plummet
Fathom the vast abyss of heavenly justice.
Whatever is, is in its causes just,
Since all things are by fate. But purblind man
Sees but a part o'th'chain, the nearest links,
His eyes not carrying to that equal beam
That poises all above."

From the same play I pick an illustration of that ripened sweetness of thought and language which marks the natural vein of Dryden. One cannot help applying the passage to the late Mr. Quincy:--

"Of no distemper, of no blast he died,
But fell like autumn fruit that mellowed long,
E'en wondered at because he dropt no sooner;
Fate seemed to wind him up for fourscore years;
Yet freshly ran he on ten winters more,

Till, like a clock worn out with eating Time,
The wheels of weary life at last stood still."
Here is another of the same kind from"All for Love":--
"Gone so soon!
Is Death no more? He used him carelessly,
With a familiar kindness; ere he knocked,
Ran to the door and took him in his arms,
As who should say, You're welcome at all hours,
A friend need give no warning."

With one more extract from the same play, which is in every way his best, for he had, when he wrote it, been feeding on the bee-bread of Shakespeare, I shall conclude. Antony says,

"For I am now so sunk from what I was,
Thou find'st me at my lowest water-mark.
The rivers that ran in and raised my fortunes
Are all dried up, or take another course:
What I have left is from my native spring;
I've a heart still that swells in scorn of Fate,
And lifts me to my banks."

This is certainly, from beginning to end, in what used to be called the grand style, at once noble and natural. I have not undertaken to analyse any one of the plays, for (except in"All for Love") it would have been only to expose their weakness. Dryden had no constructive faculty; and in every one of his longer poems that required a plot, the plot is bad, always more or less inconsistent with itself, and rather hitched-on to the subject than combining with it. It is fair to say, however, before leaving this part of Dryden's literary work, that Horne Tooke thought"Don Sebastian""the best play extant."

Gray admired the plays of Dryden,"not as dramatic compositions, but as poetry.""There are as many things finely said in his plays as almost by anybody," said Pope to Spence. Of their rant, their fustian, their bombast, their bad English, of their innumerable sins against Dryden's own better conscience both as poet and critic, I shall excuse myself from giving any instances. I like what is good in Dryden so much, and it is so good, that I think Gray was justified in always losing his temper when he heard"his faults criticised."

It is as a satirist and pleader in verse that Dryden is best known, and as both he is in some respects unrivalled. His satire is not so sly as Chaucer's, but it is distinguished by the same good-nature. There is no malice in it. I shall not enter into his literary quarrels further than to say that he seems to me, on the whole, to have been forbearing, which is the more striking as he tells us repeatedly that he was naturally vindictive. It was he who called revenge"the darling attribute of heaven.""I complain not of their lampoons and libels, though I have been the public mark for many years. I am vindictive enough to have repelled force by force, if I could imagine that any of them had ever reached me." It was this feeling of easy superiority, I suspect, that made him the mark for so much jealous vituperation. Scott is wrong in attributing his onslaught upon Settle to jealousy because one of the latter's plays had been performed at Court,--an honour never paid to any of Dryden's. I have found nothing like a trace of jealousy in that large and benignant nature. In his vindication of the"Duke of Guise," he says, with honest confidence in himself:"

Nay, I durst almost refer myself to some of the angry poets on the other side, whether I have not rather countenanced and assisted their beginnings than hindered them from rising." He seems to have been really as indifferent to the attacks on himself as Pope pretended to be. In the same vindication he says of the"Rehearsal," the only one of them that had any wit in it, and it has a great deal:"Much less am I concerned at the noble name of Bayes; that's a brat so like his own father that he cannot be mistaken for any other body. They might as reasonably have called Tom Sternhold Virgil, and the resemblance would have held as well." In his Essay on Satire he says:"And yet we know that in Christian charity all offences are to be forgiven as we expect the like pardon for those we daily commit against Almighty God. And this consideration has often made me tremble when I was saying our Lord's Prayer; for the plain condition of the forgiveness which we beg is the pardoning of others the offences which they have done to us; for which reason I have many times avoided the commission of that fault, even when I have been notoriously provoked." And in another passage he says, with his usual wisdom:"Good sense and good-nature are never separated, though the ignorant world has thought otherwise.

Good-nature, by which I mean beneficence and candor, is the product of right reason, which of necessity will give allowance to the failings of others, by considering that there is nothing perfect in mankind." In the same Essay he gives his own receipt for satire:"How easy it is to call rogue and villain, and that wittily! but how hard to make a man appear a fool, a blockhead, or a knave, without using any of those opprobrious terms!... This is the mystery of that noble trade.... Neither is it true that this fineness of raillery is offensive: a witty man is tickled while he is hurt in this manner, and a fool feels it not.... There is a vast difference between the slovenly butchering of a man and the fineness of a stroke that separates the head from the body, and leaves it standing in its place.

A man may be capable, as Jack Ketch's wife said of his servant, of a plain piece of work, of a bare hanging; but to make a malefactor die sweetly was only belonging to her husband. I wish I could apply it to myself, if the reader would be kind enough to think it belongs to me. The character of Zimri in my'Absalom'is, in my opinion, worth the whole poem. It is not bloody, but it is ridiculous enough, and he for whom it was intended was too witty to resent it as an injury.... I avoided the mention of great crimes, and applied myself to the representing of blind sides and little extravagances, to which, the wittier a man is, he is generally the more obnoxious."

Dryden thought his genius led him that way. In his elegy on the satirist Oldham, whom Hallam, without reading him, I suspect, ranks next to Dryden, he says:--

"For sure our souls were near allied, and thine
Cast in the same poetic mould with mine;
One common note in either lyre did strike,
And knaves and fools we both abhorred alike."

His practice is not always so delicate as his theory; but if he was sometimes rough, he never took a base advantage. He knocks his antagonist down, and there an end. Pope seems to have nursed his grudge, and then, watching his chance, to have squirted vitriol from behind a corner, rather glad than otherwise if it fell on the women of those he hated or envied. And if Dryden is never dastardly, as Pope often was, so also he never wrote anything so maliciously depreciatory as Pope's unprovoked attack on Addison. Dryden's satire is often coarse, but where it is coarsest, it is commonly in defence of himself against attacks that were themselves brutal. Then, to be sure, he snatches the first ready cudgel, as in Shadwell's case, though even then there is something of the good-humour of conscious strength. Pope's provocation was too often the mere opportunity to say a biting thing, where he could do it safely. If his victim showed fight, he tried to smooth things over, as with Dennis. Dryden could forget that he had ever had a quarrel, but he never slunk away from any, least of all from one provoked by himself. Pope's satire is too much occupied with the externals of manners, habits, personal defects, and peculiarities. Dryden goes right to the rooted character of the man, to the weaknesses of his nature, as where he says of Burnet:--

"Prompt to assail, and careless of defence,
Invulnerable in his impudence,
He dares the world, and, eager of a name,
He thrusts about and justles into fame.
So fond of loud report that, not to miss
Of being known (his last and utmost bliss),
He rather would be known for what he is."

It would be hard to find in Pope such compression of meaning as in the first, or such penetrative sarcasm as in the second of the passages I have underscored. Dryden's satire is still quoted for its comprehensiveness of application, Pope's rather for the elegance of its finish and the point of its phrase than for any deeper qualities. I do not remember that Dryden ever makes poverty a reproach. He was above it, alike by generosity of birth and mind. Pope is always the parvenu, always giving himself the airs of a fine gentleman, and, like Horace Walpole and Byron, affecting superiority to professional literature. Dryden, like Lessing, was a hack-writer, and was proud, as an honest man has a right to be, of being able to get his bread by his brains. He lived in Grub Street all his life, and never dreamed that where a man of genius lived was not the best quarter of the town."Tell his Majesty," said sturdy old Jonson,"that his soul lives in an alley."

Dryden's prefaces are a mine of good writing and judicious criticism. His obiter dicta have often the penetration, and always more than the equity, of Voltaire's, for Dryden never loses temper, and never altogether qualifies his judgment by his self-love."He was a more universal writer than Voltaire," said Horne Tooke, and perhaps it is true that he had a broader view, though his learning was neither so extensive nor so accurate. My space will not afford many extracts, but I cannot forbear one or two. He says of Chaucer, that"he is a perpetual fountain of good sense," and likes him better than Ovid,--a bold confession in that day. He prefers the pastorals of Theocritus to those of Virgil."Virgil's shepherds are too well read in the philosophy of Epicurus and of Plato";"there is a kind of rusticity in all those pompous verses, somewhat of a holiday shepherd strutting in his country buskins";"

Theocritus is softer than Ovid, he touches the passions more delicately, and performs all this out of his own fund, without diving into the arts and sciences for a supply. Even his Doric dialect has an incomparable sweetness in his clownishness, like a fair shepherdess, in her country russet, talking in a Yorkshire tone." Comparing Virgil's verse with that of some other poets, he says, that his"numbers are perpetually varied to increase the delight of the reader, so that the same sounds are never repeated twice together. On the contrary, Ovid and Claudian, though they write in styles different from each other, yet have each of them but one sort of music in their verses. All the versification and little variety of Claudian is included within the compass of four or five lines, and then he begins again in the same tenor, perpetually closing his sense at the end of a verse, and that verse commonly which they call golden, or two substantives and two adjectives with a verb betwixt them to keep the peace. Ovid, with all his sweetness, has as little variety of numbers and sound as he; he is always, as it were, upon the hand-gallop, and his verse runs upon carpet-ground." What a dreary half-century would have been saved to English poetry, could Pope have laid these sentences to heart! Upon translation, no one has written so much and so well as Dryden in his various prefaces. Whatever has been said since is either expansion or variation of what he had said before. His general theory may be stated as an aim at something between the literalness of metaphrase and the looseness of paraphase."Where I have enlarged," he says,"I desire the false critics would not always think that those thoughts are wholly mine, but either they are secretly in the poet, or may be fairly deduced from him." Coleridge, with his usual cleverness of assimilation, has condensed him in a letter to Wordsworth:"There is no medium between a prose version and one on the avowed principle of compensation in the widest sense, i.e. manner, genius, total effect."

I have selected these passages, not because they are the best, but because they have a near application to Dryden himself. His own characterization of Chaucer (though too narrow for the greatest but one of English poets) is the best that could be given of himself:"He is a perpetual fountain of good sense." And the other passages show him a close and open-minded student of the art he professed. Has his influence on our literature, but especially on our poetry, been on the whole for good or evil? If he could have been read with the liberal understanding which he brought to the works of others, I should answer at once that it had been beneficial. But his translations and paraphrases, in some ways the best things he did, were done, like his plays, under contract to deliver a certain number of verses for a specified sum.

The versification, of which he had learned the art by long practice, is excellent, but his haste has led him to fill out the measure of lines with phrases that add only to dilute, and thus the clearest, the most direct, the most manly versifier of his time became, without meaning it, the source (fons et origo malorum) of that poetic diction from which our poetry has not even yet recovered. I do not like to say it, but he has sometimes smothered the childlike simplicity of Chaucer under feather-beds of verbiage. What this kind of thing came to in the next century, when everybody ceremoniously took a bushel-basket to bring a wren's egg to market in, is only too sadly familiar. It is clear that his natural taste led Dryden to prefer directness and simplicity of style. If he was too often tempted astray by Artifice, his love of Nature betrays itself in many an almost passionate outbreak of angry remorse.

Addison tells us that he took particular delight in the reading of our old English ballads. What he valued above all things was Force, though in his haste he is willing to make a shift with its counterfeit, Effect. As usual, he had a good reason to urge for what he did:"I will not excuse, but justify myself for one pretended crime for which I am liable to be charged by false critics, not only in this translation, but in many of my original poems,--that I Latinize too much.

It is true that when I find an English word significant and sounding, I neither borrow from the Latin or any other language; but when I want at home I must seek abroad. If sounding words are not of our growth and manufacture, who shall hinder me to import them from a foreign country? I carry not out the treasure of the nation which is never to return; but what I bring from Italy I spend in England: here it remains, and here it circulates; for if the coin be good, it will pass from one hand to another.

I trade both with the living and the dead for the enrichment of our native language. We have enough in England to supply our necessity; but if we will have things of magnificence and splendor, we must get them by commerce.... Therefore, if I find a word in a classic author, I propose it to be naturalized by using it myself, and if the public approve of it the bill passes. But every man cannot distinguish betwixt pedantry and poetry; every man, therefore, is not fit to innovate." This is admirably said, and with Dryden's accustomed penetration to the root of the matter. The Latin has given us most of our canorous words, only they must not be confounded with merely sonorous ones, still less with phrases that, instead of supplementing the sense, encumber it. It was of Latinizing in this sense that Dryden was guilty. Instead of stabbing, he"with steel invades the life." The consequence was that by and by we have Dr. Johnson's poet, Savage, telling us,--

"In front, a parlor meets my entering view,

Opposed a room to sweet refection due";

Dr. Blacklock making a forlorn maiden say of her"dear," who is out late,--

"Or by some apoplectic fit deprest

Perhaps, alas! he seeks eternal rest"; and Mr. Bruce, in a Danish war-song, calling on the Vikings to"assume their oars." But it must be admitted of Dryden that he seldom makes the second verse of a couplet the mere trainbearer to the first, as Pope was continually doing. In Dryden the rhyme waits upon the thought; in Pope and his school the thought courtesies to the tune for which it is written.Dryden has also been blamed for his gallicisms. He tried some, it is true, but they have not been accepted. I do not think he added a single word to the language; unless, as I suspect, he first used magnetism in its present sense of moral attraction. What he did in his best writing was to use the English as if it were a spoken, and not merely an inkhorn language; as if it were his own to do what he pleased with it, as if it need not be ashamed of itself.

In this respect, his service to our prose was greater than any other man has ever rendered. He says he formed his style upon Tillotson's (Bossuet, on the other hand, formed his upon Corneille's); but I rather think he got it at Will's, for its great charm is that it has the various freedom of talk. In verse, he had a pomp which, excellent in itself, became pompousness in his imitators. But he had nothing of Milton's ear for various rhythm and interwoven harmony.

He knew how to give new modulation, sweetness, and force to the pentameter; but in what used to be called pindarics, I am heretic enough to think he generally failed. His so much praised"Alexander's Feast" (in parts of it, at least) has no excuse for its slovenly metre and awkward expression, but that it was written for music. He himself tells us, in the epistle dedicatory to"King Arthur,""that the numbers of poetry and vocal music are sometimes so contrary, that in many places I have been obliged to cramp my verses and make them ragged to the reader that they may be harmonious to the hearer." His renowned ode suffered from this constraint, but this is no apology for the vulgarity of conception in too many passages.

Dryden's conversion to Romanism has been commonly taken for granted as insincere, and has therefore left an abiding stain on his character, though the other mud thrown at him by angry opponents or rivals brushed off so soon as it was dry. But I think his change of faith susceptible of several explanations, none of them in any way discreditable to him. Where Church and State are habitually associated, it is natural that minds even of a high order should unconsciously come to regard religion as only a subtler mode of police. Dryden, conservative by nature, had discovered before Joseph de Maistre, that Protestantism, so long as it justified its name by continuing to be an active principle, was the abettor of Republicanism. I think this is hinted in more than one passage in his preface to"The Hind and Panther."

He may very well have preferred Romanism because of its elder claim to authority in all matters of doctrine, but I think he had a deeper reason in the constitution of his own mind. That he was"naturally inclined to scepticism in philosophy," he tells us of himself in the preface to the"Religio Laici"; but he was a sceptic with an imaginative side, and in such characters scepticism and superstition play into each other's hands. This finds a curious illustration in a letter to his sons, written four years before his death:

"Towards the latter end of this month, September, Charles will begin to recover his perfect health, according to his Nativity, which, casting it myself, I am sure is true, and all things hitherto have happened accordingly to the very time that I predicted them." Have we forgotten Montaigne's votive offerings at the shrine of Loreto?

Dryden was short of body, inclined to stoutness, and florid of complexion. He is said to have had"a sleepy eye," but was handsome and of a manly carriage. He"was not a very genteel man, he was intimate with none but poetical men. He was said to be a very good man by all that knew him: he was as plump as Mr. Pitt, of a fresh colour and a down look, and not very conversible." So Pope described him to Spence. He still reigns in literary tradition, as when at Will's his elbow-chair had the best place by the fire in winter, or on the balcony in summer, and when a pinch from his snuff-box made a young author blush with pleasure as would now-a-days a favorable notice in the"Saturday Review." What gave and secures for him this singular eminence? To put it in a single word, I think that his qualities and faculties were in that rare combination which makes character. This gave flavour to whatever he wrote,--a very rare quality.

Was he, then, a great poet? Hardly, in the narrowest definition. But he was a strong thinker who sometimes carried common sense to a height where it catches the light of a diviner air, and warmed reason till it had wellnigh the illuminating property of intuition. Certainly he is not, like Spenser, the poets'poet, but other men have also their rights. Even the Philistine is a man and a brother, and is entirely right so far as he sees. To demand more of him is to be unreasonable. And he sees, among other things, that a man who undertakes to write should first have a meaning perfectly defined to himself, and then should be able to set it forth clearly in the best words.

This is precisely Dryden's praise, and amid the rickety sentiment looming big through misty phrase which marks so much of modern literature, to read him is as bracing as a northwest wind. He blows the mind clear. In ripeness of mind and bluff heartiness of expression, he takes rank with the best. His phrase is always a short-cut to his sense, for his estate was too spacious for him to need that trick of winding the path of his thought about, and planting it out with clumps of epithet, by which the landscape-gardeners of literature give to a paltry half-acre the air of a park. In poetry, to be next-best is, in one sense, to be nothing; and yet to be among the first in any kind of writing, as Dryden certainly was, is to be one of a very small company. He had, beyond most, the gift of the right word. And if he does not, like one or two of the greater masters of song, stir our sympathies by that indefinable aroma so magical in arousing the subtle associations of the soul, he has this in common with the few great writers, that the winged seeds of his thought embed themselves in the memory and germinate there. If I could be guilty of the absurdity of recommending to a young man any author on whom to form his style, I should tell him that, next to having something that will not stay unsaid, he could find no safer guide than Dryden.

Cowper, in a letter to Mr. Unwin (5th January, 1782), expresses what I think is the common feeling about Dryden, that, with all his defects, he had that indefinable something we call Genius."But I admire Dryden most [he had been speaking of Pope], who has succeeded by mere dint of genius, and in spite of a laziness and a carelessness almost peculiar to himself. His faults are numberless, and so are his beauties. His faults are those of a great man, and his beauties are such (at least sometimes) as Pope with all his touching and retouching could never equal." But, after all, perhaps no man has summed him up so well as John Dennis, one of Pope's typical dunces, a dull man outside of his own sphere, as men are apt to be, but who had some sound notions as a critic, and thus became the object of Pope's fear and therefore of his resentment. Dennis speaks of him as his"departed friend, whom I infinitely esteemed when living for the solidity of his thought, for the spring and the warmth and the beautiful turn of it; for the power and variety and fulness of his harmony; for the purity, the perspicuity, the energy of his expression; and, whenever these great qualities are required, for the pomp and solemnity and majesty of his style."

Chapter 8

Critical Essays

"With Honour Quit the Fort": Ambivalent Colonialism in Dryden's Amboyna

For a play called by its author"scarcely [worth] a serious perusal" and once deemed by its editors"beneath criticism" and"utterly worthless" (by Sir Walter Scott and George Saintsbury, respectively), John Dryden's Amboyna, or The Cruelties of the Dutch to the English Merchants: A Tragedy (1673) has received a good deal of critical attention in the last fifteen or so years. The reasons are related to the reason Dryden wrote the play in the first place: a wide-spread and timely fascination with colonialism and empire building. According to most modern accounts, however, Dryden applauds English empire building in his play, while readings like those of J. Douglas Canfield, Bridgett Orr, Robert Markley, and Shankar Raman deplore it.

Such readings seem to spring from a valuable deconstructive or postcolonial orientation that allows us to"read through" a text's apparent pernicious, coherently propagandistic intentions. What I would suggest instead is that Amboyna-particularly in those aspects of the play that have been neglected or confused in recent scholarship-displays Dryden's own ambivalence toward unalloyed jingoism and imperialism. My project, then, is to reassess Dryden's supposedly unilateral, if wrongheaded, propagandistic stance vis a vis his subject, and in so doing to link the relatively inconsequential Amboyna to Dryden's more famous works, to his religious evolution, and to the arc of Restoration history.

Among the aspects of Amboyna which I will revisit are these: The passage in which Dryden condemns Amboyna occurs in his dedication to Thomas Clifford, the Lord Treasurer. It reads: To this Retirement of your Lordship, I wish I could bring a better Entertainment, than this Play; which, though it succeeded on the Stage, will scarcely bear a serious perusal, it being contriv'd and written in a Moneth, the Subject barren, the Persons low, and the Writing not heightned with many laboured scenes.

Notable in Dryden's apology is his deeming his"Subject barren" and his"Persons low." This is at odds with many commentaries which have focused on the topicality of the"Subject"-read as a jingoistic rehashing of the Dutch"massacre" of English merchants in the Molucca islands in 1623--and its propagandistic relevance in the 70's when the English were engaged in the Third Dutch War. Such commentators have emphasized Dryden's strenuous efforts to elevate his merchant"Persons" by attributing to them the manners and ideals of the English gentry, as opposed to the materialistic Dutch"boors" overemphasized, I feel, since we shall see that Dryden's valorizing of the English is not absolute.

Further, in addressing his dedication to Clifford, Dryden is making his apologies to a dead man: On August 18, 1673, Clifford, a Catholic, had reportedly hanged himself in his "Retirement," having felt compelled to resign from the government after the passage in March of the Test Act requiring all office-holders to deny that transubstantiation occurs during the Eucharist. Estimates for the premier of Amboyna vary from June 1672 to May 1673, but the play was not published, with its dedication, until November 24, 1673, three months after Clifford's death. Thus, while Clifford's supposed suicide cannot have inspired Dryden's original composition of the play (though it may have had some impact on the published version), it is interesting that its tragic climax begins with a long debate between the play's hero and heroine as to whether suicide can be moral; finally, they decide it can. Their debate is deeply concerned with issues of Providence, a topic to which Dryden doggedly returns throughout his career.

Notably, however, none of the recent discussions of Amboyna have mentioned this debate, much less investigated its relevance to whatever values Dryden is espousing.

Also under- or misrepresented in recent discussions is the ambiguous handling of the play's secondary couple: the Spaniard Perez and his wife Julia. Julia, also courted by an Englishman and a Dutchman, is usually treated as a symbol of contested colonies previously Iberian, but her nationality, her worth, and her allegiance require further investigation, as do the heroism or venality of Perez, and his motives.

To show how such matters suggest that Dryden's endorsement of the colonial project is considerably less than wholehearted, let me begin by sketching the plot of Amboyna in relation to its immediate political occasion, and its relevance to the larger cultural context of its composition.

By the opening of the seventeenth century, the Dutch had driven the Portuguese out of the Moluccas (islands lying between modern Borneo and New Guinea) and were attempting to expel the English."Outgunned and out financed", the British signed a treaty in 1619 which"allowed the Dutch to have two-thirds of the trade in the east, and the English one third, both companies [the Dutch East India Company or VOC, and the English East India Company] agreeing to fight as equal partners in declared and undeclared war on the Spanish and Portuguese".

The event at Amboyna (now Ambon, the provincial capital of Seram) occurred when the Dutch accused the English there of conspiring with Japanese soldiers and Moluccan islanders (the Ternatans and Bandanese) to seize their fort, murder them, and use Amboyna as a stronghold from which to prey on VOC trade; they tortured and executed the English merchants. Dryden had read two pamphlets by a shareholder in the East India Company, Sir Dudly Digges, both published in 1624: A True Relation of the Unjust, Cruell, and Barbarous Proceedings Against the English at Amboyna (reprinted in 1651 and 1672-and hence used as propaganda to fuel the second and third wars against the Dutch as well as the first) and The Answere unto the Dutch Pamphlet, Made in Defence of the Unjust and Barbarous Proceedings against the English at Amboyna, in the East-Indies, by the Hollanders There. He had also read John Darrell's 1665 pamphlet, A True and Compendious Narration; Or (the Second Part of Amboyna) of Sundry Notorious or Remarkable Injuries, Insolences, and Acts of Hostility which the HOLLANDERS Have Exercised from time to time against THE ENGLISH NATION in the East Indies.

Dryden was motivated to dramatize the events described in his sources to gain support for the Third Dutch War (1672-74). Referring to the first earl of Shatesbury's contention that"a War was absolutely necessary and unavoidable," Blair Hoxby tells us that"What Shaftesbury strove to do in Parliament [that is, argue that a'a War was absolutely l necessary and unavoidable'], Dryden tried to accomplish on stage". Vinton Dearing, the editor of Amboyna in the California Works, remarks that Charles II's counselors wished to pass off [the war], political at root, as commercial in essence [and Dryden was following the official line. He was, after all, poet laureate and historiographer royal, and Thomas Clifford, the Lord Treasurer, who had conceived the idea of suspending treasury payments except for the war effort, saw to it that Dryden got his full salary in 1672 and 1673. It may be that the play was another of Clifford's ideas, as it was later said to be.

"Political at root" refers to the fact that Clifford was one of only two councellors to whom Charles had confided the terms of the secret Treaty of Dover with Louis XIV (1670), which withdrew England from the Triple Alliance with Holland and Sweden against France and was intended to"prepare the way for [England's] Catholicization and for French seizure of the Spanish Netherlands [modern Belgium]".

An unflattering interpretation of these facts would be that Dryden's motives for writing Amboyna as he did were strictly mercenary rather than at least partly principled. Granting that Dryden may have been engaged in political hack work, I maintain that in the play he was unable or unwilling to entirely repress counter-propagandistic positions he expresses in other, better-known works. Hoxby-alone among modern critics-argues that the play has a"divided conscience" which she sees primarily in the brutal treatment of the Amboynese heroine, a contention that I would like to amplify significantly. In any case, how far Dryden's qualifications of the"official line" in Amboyna are conscious or unconscious and how far the speed of his composition (a month) may have contributed to the ambiguity of his treatment are unclear. However, it is worth noting here one relevant detail concerning Dryden's political orientation: Though he evinced"almost unmitigated dislike" for the Dutch throughout his life, in Absalom and Achitophel (1681) Dryden would make the breaking of the Triple Alliance with Holland and Sweden (the"Triple Bond") one more crime of the Earl of Shaftesbury, who argued for it in Parliament.

So what sort of play did Dryden make of his openly propagandistic sources? Dearing writes that the historical event occurred"very much as Dryden describes it", and in relation to the"Persons Represented" he notes:

Gabriel Towerson, (John) Beamont (Beomont), (Edward) Collins, (Augustine) Perez, Harman Senior (Harman van Speult), and the Fiscal (Izaak de Brune) were real people. Their full names appear in True Relation (1624), in Answer, issued as part of True Relation, and in Acts, issued as part of Remonstrance (1632).

The play opens with Harman Senior (the Governor), the Fiscal, and Van Herring (a Dutch merchant) plotting to falsely accuse the English. The English merchants Beamont and Collins enter to announce the return of the English"General" Towerson to Amboyna after an absence of three years. Towerson has rescued Harman Junior from pirates at sea, but Harman's debt of gratitude is soon cancelled by his desire for the Amboynese woman Ysabinda, Towerson's betrothed. Perez, a Spaniard (historically a Portuguese in service of the Dutch) who has not been paid by Towerson for fighting with him against the pirates, is hired by the Fiscal to murder Towerson. Perez is reluctant to leave his wife Julia, who is being courted both by the Fiscal and by Beamont; but when he goes to Towerson's lodgings and finds his memorandum to reward Perez for his service, he leaves Towerson alive with the note"Thy Vertue sav'd thy life." The Fiscal then enlists Harman Junior in the plot to kill Towerson. After the wedding of Towerson and Ysabinda, an English woman appears to report that the Dutch have waylaid English mariners and colonists from neighboring islands and that she is the only survivor. The Dutch, of course, deny the charge. The Fiscal and Perez lure Towerson and Ysabinda separately into a wood. Perez, aware of the plot against Towerson, attacks Harman Junior, but Harman is saved by Towerson, though neither is certain of the other's identity. Harman Junior accosts Ysabinda, ties her to a tree, and rapes her. When Towerson frees her, both decide to commit suicide after their revenge has been accomplished. Towerson and Harman Junior fight and Harman Junior is killed, but Towerson is then wounded by the Fiscal. The Fiscal swears that Towerson is guilty of murder and that he and the rest of the English have conspired to capture the Dutch fort. The English (with women and children) are tortured and executed along with Perez, but Julia manages to have Beamont freed. The play ends with the condemned Towerson prophesying"Universal Ruine" for the Dutch.

Dryden's main additions to the historical event, then, are the love plots:"high," involving Ysabinda, Towerson, and Harman Junior; and"low," involving Julia, Perez, the Fiscal, and Beamont. The women of both plots are not so much invented as drastically altered and embellished from what"sources" exist. Ysabinda takes her name from Tsabinda, a Japanese soldier named in Digges'True Relation."Julia" is an invented name for an anonymous woman; of her, Dearing notes:"According to True Relation Perez'had, by the perswasion of the Dutch Gouernour, taken [a wife] in that countrey [i.e., Amboyna]; Acts says she was one of the slaves, given to him by the Dutch to engage his loyalty and repossessed by them after his death". So one thing Dryden has done is bring women centrally into the action. But to what purpose?

The obvious purpose that suggests itself is to make the play more attractive to audiences; I can think of no tragedy by Dryden-or indeed any during the Restoration-that does not include an element of love in peril and, in the case of Ysabinda, the love plot may be intended to make Towerson's doom doubly"moving," as the term was in those days. This strategy fails miserably with modern readers like Orr, who calls the Ysabinda-Towerson pairing"a degraded version of a heroic amour" or Markley, who calls it a"redaction of the Pocahontas myth". The latter phrase suggests a reason for including the women more commonly argued today, and I have already touched upon it in relation to Julia, above: that both women represent the period's contested colonies and that both prefer their English suitors (or colonizers) to any others; as Hoxby remarks,"Amboyna repeatedly equates sexual relations with commercial ones". Put plainly, possession of Ysabinda is a"synecdoche for the possession of Amboyna", and Julia represents"Iberian colonial possessions in general" now being claimed by the English and Dutch. I have reservations about such equations.

To pursue Julia first, commentators always point to her remarks on finding the Fiscal with Perez, in which she explicitly announces the emblematic nature of the subplot: If my English lover Beamont, my Dutch Love the Fiscall, and my Spanish Husband, were Painted in a piece with me amongst'em, they wou'd make a Pretty Emblem of the two Nations, that Cuckold his Catholick Majesty in his Indies

A little further on in the same scene, with Beamont's entrance, we have an exchange that seems to confirm such emblematic readings: Beam. Now Mr. Fiscall, you are the happy Man with the Ladies, and have got the precedence of Traffick here too; you've the Indies in your Arms, yet I hope a poor English Man may come in for a third part of the Merchandise.

Fisc. Oh, Sir, in these Commodities, here's enough for both, here's Mace for you, and Nutmegg for me in the same Fruit; and yet the owner has to spare for other friends too. Jul. My Husbands Plantation's like to thrive well betwixt you.

Granting the significance of such exchanges, I would like, however, to take note of some complicating factors. First, Dryden's handling of Julia's nationality (and therefore of her symbolic function) is at least ambiguous: Orr and Raman wrongly assume Julia is a Spanish woman; Canfield says that Dryden"seems to portray [her] as more European"; and Dearing, attempting to explain Beamont's reference to Spain as"your [Julia's] nation", is compelled to suggest we have three possibilities. Perhaps this is another mark of lack of"labour" on Dryden's part. Perhaps he regarded the wife as taking her husband's nationality by marriage. Perhaps there is an element of irony here, though the audience would have no sense of it unless Julia and Ysabinda were somehow costumed similarly and in some way differently from English women.

Given the difficulty modern commentators have had with Julia's nationality, it seems reasonable to suggest that audiences might not have recognized that Julia is a native of Amboyna until near the very end of the play, when Perez suddenly announces before his execution, my English friends, I'm not asham'd of death, while I have you for part'ners; I know you innocent, and so am I, of this pretended plot; but I am guilty of a greater crime; For, being married in another Country, the Governors perswasions, and my love to that ill Woman, made me leave the first, and make this fatal choice. I'm justly punish'd, for her sake I dye; the Fiscal to enjoy her has accused me.

The details of Perez's bigamy and Julia's native status are found in the True Relation, but they are dramatically a rather bizarre insertion and raise the issue of just how Julia is"ill" or whether she is indeed desirable. That Julia is desired is not at issue, but that she is desirable is called into question in the remarks the Dutch Fiscal and English Beamont whisper between themselves, comparing Julia to a"little kind of venture," a"drudgery," and a carrier of venereal disease. And since these remarks appear to satirize Julia as a Spaniard, they further problematize any clear equation between Julia and a valuable, contested colonial space. The character of Julia, her value to the various colonizers, and her valuation of them is also complicated by Julia's insisting that her condemned husband is her"dear sweet Man", that she only consents to marry the Fiscal on the condition that he spare Beamont's life, and that she parts with Perez saying"Farewel, my dearest, I may have many Husbands, but never one like thee".Orr sees in Beamont and the Fiscal's remarks at Julia's expense evidence of miscegenation:

This contempt for miscegenation, repressed in the Towerson-Ysabinda alliance (in which the heroine, though an Amboyner, is emphatically aristocratic, and hence superior to the boorish Dutch), resurfaces in the casual bonding of the North European rivals over a Spanish woman whose"easy virtue" they read as a function of her tainted blood.

The issue of how to assess Julia's value (as a representative of the colonies) in the play is indicative, perhaps, of European ambivalence toward colonial Others-simultaneous desire for and contempt for colonial persons and spaces is commonplace in texts of the period. England's expansion into"exotic or savage" cultures for profit carried with it the threat of colonists'degeneration. My point is that the character of Julia and her contested status is anything but clear cut along propagandistic, pro-colonial lines and this suggests that Dryden was at least conflicted about such lines. At the very least, Amboyna"qualifies as an attempt to register the costs and imagine the responsibities of a trade empire".

More evidence of such conflict on the playwright's part may be found in relation to the genuine representative of Spain-Perez-whose portrayal by Dryden is relatively flattering. True, Perez agrees to assassinate Towerson, and his"moral reformation" upon learning of the Englishman's intended reward might thus be seen as"a function of his sudden wealth", but this is too simple. Perez, though attempting to convince himself that his"revenge" is"noble", honorable, and fair, admits to himself that it is"Satanic" before discovering Towerson's intentions and readily repents. He says of himself: hadst thou done it, thou hadst been worse then damn'd; Heav'n took more care of me, then I of him, to expose this paper to my timely view. Sleep on thou Honourable Englishman, I'll sooner now, pierce my own breast then thine.

He then returns the blood money, and the Fiscal says Perez"had too much of honesty" for the murder. To list of positives this may be added Perez's intervention in the Fiscal-Harman Jr. attempt to kill Towerson, and his heroic farewell to his English"partners" in death, already cited.

Political readings of the Julia-Fiscal-Beamont-Perez plot are also complicated by the issue of how we are to value its English representative. In demonstrating Dryden's vilification of the Dutch, Orr misattributes a line cited above--exposing the sexual/colonial possession trope ("Y'ave the Indies in your arms")-to the Dutch villain Harman Junior, when it is in fact spoken by the English"hero" Beamont. In that exchange, the Dutch Fiscal voices the principles of"an idealized mercantile vision of an unencumbered'Traffick'" in stores of inexhaustible bounty, while the Englishman seems anxious to secure his share in a limited supply.

It seems to me that this suggests Dryden's reservations about the legitimacy of valorizing one nation's mercantile aspirations while demonizing another's. And there are other ways in which the characterization of Beamont is not unilaterally flattering to English identity or ambitions. Beamont apparently is drunk at the wedding celebration, which accounts for his fomenting bad blood on that occasion; and his besottedness, Julia believes, makes him incapable of sexual possession. Dearing argues that Beamont's drunkenness may have been suggested by that of Abel Price. Price was"a drunken debauched sot," according to Digges'Answer to the Dutch Pamphlet, an English surgeon who drank and gambled with the Japanese and"other Blacks" and threatened to burn down a Dutch home, poisoning relations between the English and the Dutch.

Markley claims that"Price is absent from Dryden's tragedy because he threatens to complicate the play's binary logic of demonizing the other as a strategy of self-definition The construction of national identity in Dryden's play thus discloses itself as an act of idealization designed to banish the Abel Prices of the world". However, insofar as Beamont is, at the very least, unimpressive in relation to the low plot, his characterization suggests that Dryden's project is not so unilaterally"an act of idealization" of the English-not simply"a stoic hero in the tradition of Hercules". The"low" plot does not unproblematically heroicize colonialism or the English role in it; a critical attitude toward the colonial project may be fostered in the play not despite Dryden's (unsuccessful) attempts to whitewash it, but because of Dryden's own ambivalence toward it.

By contrast to his character in the low plot, however, Beamont's behaviour in the high plot appears so different as to be nearly schizophrenic, and Dryden's handling of this plot-the Ysabinda-Towerson-Harman triangle and the"massacre" itself-seems to aim at entirely different effects. Let me now turn, then, to examine these sections of the play.

Raman identifies a"buried tension" in the high plot:"Gabriel Towerson, who bears the burden of English honour and the English colonial cause, is as much a merchant as any of the Dutch against whom he contends"; Towerson is thus"inappropriate for heroic representation". Canfield notes that Towerson"was at best a ship's purser". Yet, Markley argues, in order to portray a"manichean politics of Dutch vice and English virtue," to stage the essential clash between"gentlemanly virtue and lower-class money-grubbing," Dryden"conflates the values of absolute honour and mercantile compromise in the person of a hero dedicated to the gentlemanly extension of English power. This hybrid, the heroic merchant, both constitutes and is constituted by the discourse of nationalism".

Looked at this way, Beamont would be essential to Dryden's project of elevating Towerson. In the high plot, and according to convention, Beamont becomes the hero's friend and panegyricist-Dollabella to Towerson's Antony, Cleanthes to Towerson's Cleomenes. We first hear of Towerson from Beamont-in quite a different rhetoric than that Beamont is given in the Julia-Fiscal scenes:

Were I to chase of all mankind, a Man, on whom I would rely for Faith and Counsel, or more, whose personal aid I would invite, in any worthy cause to second me, it should be only Gabriel Towerson; daring he is, and thereto fortunate: yet soft and apt to pitty the distress'd; and liberal to relieve'em:

I have seen him not alone to pardon Foes, but by his bounty win'em to his love: if he has any fault,'tis only that to which great minds can only subject be, he thinks all honest,'cause himself is so, and therefore none suspects.

Beamont is also available to support the testimony of the abused Englishwoman, to protest Towerson's innocence from the charge of murdering Harman, to suffer torture stoicially (until he begs to die at the very end, and, upon being freed, to hear Towerson's heroic leave-taking:"A long and last farewel; I take my death with the more chearfulness because thou livst behind me Last, there's my heart, I give it in this kiss-[Kisses him.] Do not answer me; Friendship's a tender thing, and it would ill become me now to weep". Beamont, then, is a hinge that links the low to the high plot, and his drastic inconsistency may be an index of the deeply ambivalent stance Dryden takes toward his material.

To elaborate, let me return to the"woman as land" trope, here in relation to Ysabinda. In relation to the"high" love plot, Raman explains: the"Indian woman" becomes a site of a direct struggle between the two European powers who have taken over the mantle once worn by Spain/Portugal. The struggle between Towerson and Harman for Ysabinda aims, first, to make explicit the qualitative difference between their respective desires, and, second, to establish the ethical superiority of the English position.

Raman cites the East India Company's claims that the natives of two Moluccan islands had surrendered their lands to England"entirely [by] their own motion" and outlines the process'three principal components:"first, the [temporal] priority of England's colonial rights; second, the voluntary surrender on the parts of the natives; and finally, symbolic confirmation." All three are satisfied in regard to Towerson's contract with Ysabinda, which was established three years before, has included Ysabinda's voluntary conversion to Christianity, and is confirmed by their marriage ceremony.

The analogy of woman and land is made explicit in readings of lines like those in which the Dutch Harman Junior rationalizes his rape:

You are a Woman; have enough of Love for him [Towerson] and me; I know the plenteous Harvest all is his: he has so much of joy, that he must labour under it. In charity you may allow some gleanings to a Friend.

But several commentators have argued that-despite Dryden's intentions--such lines rebound upon the English colonizer hero as well as the Dutch villain. Canfield feels that Harman's speech"sounds eerily like Towerson's rationale for shared trade":

what mean these endless jars of Trading Nations?'tis true, the World was never large enough for Avarice or Ambition; but those who can be please'd with moderate gain, may have the ends of Nature, not to want: nay, even its Luxuries may be supply'd from her o'erflowing bounties in these parts; from whence she yearly sends Spices, and Gums, the food of Heaven in Sacrifice: And besides these, her Gems of richest value, for Ornament, more than necessity.

Orr adds that Dryden's hero Towerson tries to deny the synecdochical relation Harman Jr. identifies between Ysabinda and the island ("You've the Indies in your arms") by disclaiming any pecuniary motives for his marriage Nevertheless after the rape he reassures Ysabinda that she is still"Paradise,""still as fragrant as your Eastern Groves".

Raman elaborates on what he sees as Dryden's failure to distinguish adequately between Towerson and Harman Jr.- between"England's legitimate marriage with the (Christianized and assimilated) Eastern other and her brutal rape at the hands of the Dutch colonialist" by focusing on the epithalamium sung at the wedding, which utilizes the marriage-as-rape trope, and the depiction of Ysabinda's actual rape by Harmon:"[The epithalamium conceals the implicit English rape of the colonized by explicitly assigning it elsewhere". In short, such arguments suggest that Dryden tries to construct a"Manichean politics of English virtue and Dutch vice", but his attempts are, at least to modern readers, unsuccessful.

I have already suggested that, at least in relation to the English Beaumont (who calls Julia"the Indies"), an uncomplicated"Manichean politics" does not seem to be precisely what Dryden is after, and I would like to adjust readings like those above. First, as regards the epithalamium, Dearing notes that Dryden based it"On the Latin of Joannes Secundus (Jan Everaerts, a Dutchman), first as appropriate to a celebration provided by Harman [Senior], and second, in its picture of the groom raping the bride, as appropriate to Harman Junior's character and foreshadowing what he will do". Secondly, the impropriety and brutality of the Dutch song is underscored by Beamont, who says"Come let me have The Sea Fight, I like that better than a thousand of your [my emphasis] wanton Epithalamiums". Towerson worries that the song celebrating an English naval victory will"breed ill blood," and in fact it does. Harman Junior grumbles,"See the insolence of these English, they cannot do a brave Action in an Age, but presently they must put it into Meter, to upbraid us with their benefits". The scene, then, seems intended to underscore the difference between the two nations through these samples of their art. However, as I have already pointed out, Beamont's request is a drunken and antagonizing one, and I might add that the difference is only between sexual and martial lustiness, and after all, lust is lust-a truism, by now, of postcolonial studies, and one Dryden seems to have recognized in relation to his low plot.

To pursue what Orr calls"the linkage between love and acquisition, love and location", I would note that in his defence against Harman's second attempted assault, Towerson claims," this Sword Heaven draws against thee, and here has plac'd me like a fiery Cherub, to guard this Paradice from any second Violation". Whereas Harman Junior depicts Ysabinda as a"Harvest," Towerson names her a"Paradice"-an attempt on Dryden's part, some argue, to distinguish between the rapacious commercial nature of Dutch colonialism and the (supposedly) pious stewardship of the English. If that were his strategy-which I question-it would be no great success since depictions of colonized lands and peoples as Edenic, accompanied by admissions of willingness to exploit these"Edens" are common in colonial literature. One thinks, for instance, of Aphra Behn's description of the Indians of

Surinam in Oroonoko as"like our first Parents before the Fall", and a few paragraphs later, remarking that these same Indians"supply the parts of Hounds" to the English colonizers.

More obviously, however, Towerson's claim is just one instance of Dryden's characteristic interest in religious matters, an interest that manifests itself in this play in the action surrounding Ysabinda's rape.

The theme of the role of Providence in the fates of individuals and of nations is first announced when Ysabinda greets Towerson after their three year separation:"Now I shall love your God, because I see that he takes care of Lovers". Her reliance on Providence is emphasized in the rape scene, when she calls on assistance from Heaven four times in thirty lines and urges Harman to"tremble at a power above, who sees, and surely will revenge it". Granting that a possible parallel between the villain and the hero may lurk in this exchange--Ysab. Does thou not fear a Heaven?

Harm. No, I hope to find one in you. (4.3.55-56) -more forcefully Dryden wishes to call attention to issues of divine justice, when, for instance, Towerson frees Ysabinda:

Ysab. [Harman] forc'd me to an Act, so base and Brutall, Heaven knows my Innocence:but, Why do I call that to Witness? Heaven saw, stood silent: Not one flash of Lightning shot from the Conscious Firmament to shew its Justice: Oh had it struck us both, it had sav'd me! Towers. Heaven suffer'd more in that then you, or I: Where-fore have I been faithful to my trust, true to my Love, and tender to th'opprest? Am I condemn'd to be the second man, who e'er complain'd, he vertue serv'd in vain? (4.5.24-32)

Of Towerson's lines, Dearing remarks,"Exactly what Towerson has in mind is not clear; perhaps he feels that God's reputation has suffered, or perhaps he means that a loving God feels the sorrows of his world even more than it does" and"Apparently'the second'means'another'(OED), though the normal meaning of'who ever'goes awkwardly with such an interpretation". On the points Dearing raises, I am equally puzzled, but more interesting to me in this exchange is Dryden's clear interest in a higher court of"justice" than those man-made ones, inevitably tainted by extra-legal private agendas, that come into conflict in the play's denouement, when Towerson insists to the Dutch governor"you have no right to judge me". Dearing calls this"a major theme of the play", one also sounded in, and adds that the matter of which nation's law should govern in Amboyna was very much at issue historically, with each side claiming its law should govern. This scene raises that theme to a metaphysical level, as Towerson and Ysabinda debate the intention and judgement of"th'Eternal Mind".

Concerning suicide, Dryden's handling of it throughout his career-in Aureng Zebe (1676), All for Love (1678), Don Sebastian (1690) and Cleomenes (1692), for instance--seems to suggest that his view is the one voiced by Towerson:"Self-homicide, which was in Heathens honour, in us is only sin". In this play, though, the Christians finally decide that in their case, too, suicide is"honorable" and no sin. Ysabinda argues that as God has"given us will to choose, and reason to direct us in our choice why should he tie us up from dying, when death's the greater good". Towerson counters with the"greatest Law" of nature,"to preserve our beings". Then Dryden has Ysabinda say something rather remarkable: I grant, it is its great and general Law: But as Kings, who are, or should be above Laws, dispence with'em when levell'd at themselves; Even so may man, without offence to Heaven, dispense with what concerns himself alone.

This is noteworthy since Dryden's habitual position seems to be that the monarchy itself is bound by law and that this principle underlines monarchical right and the rights of those governed. As he puts it in Absalom and Achitophel,"Laws are vain, by which we Right enjoy, / If Kings unquestiond can those laws destroy". Just as remarkable is Towerson's reply. After weakly suggesting that"Heaven may give [Ysabinda] succor yet," he points to himself, and Ysabinda dismisses this ("'Tis too late, you shou'd have come before"). Towerson then concedes that suicide, even for Christians, is justified:

You have convinc'd my reason, nor am I asham'd to learn from you. To Heavens Tribunal my appeal I make; if as a

Governor he sets me here, to guard this weak built Cittadel of Life, when'tis no longer to be held, I may with honour quit the Fort. But first I'll both revenge my self and you.

The term"quit the Fort" calls attention to itself as"the fort" is the site of dispute in Amboyna and since Towerson's status as a"Public Person, entrusted by my King and my Employers" was earlier produced by him as justification for refusing to hazard his life in a duel with Harman. His speech upon being condemned by the Dutch likewise focuses on the obligations incurred by one"set" in a position of national trust:"give to my brave Employers of the East India Company, the last remembrance of my faithful service; tell'em I Seal that Service with my Blood".

One might add that Towerson takes leave of Ysabinda"in haste" since"time would divide my Love'twixt Heaven and you" and that he urges Ysabinda to survive him; she resolves on death not by active means but by starvation. As with Ysabinda's speech above, the metaphysical questing has occasioned secular theorizing at odds with Dryden's apparent positions elsewhere. It is surely curious that in this play our merchant hero should provide, couched in religious terms, a rationale to"quit the fort." But religious and political issues (here, especially in relation to trade) are inevitably intertwined in Dryden's work-in this instance in a way that links the relatively inconsequential Amboyna to three of Dryden's more famous poems, and to his religious development in the context of Restoration history.

Dryden's Amboyna, linked to the Third Dutch War, was, on some level, meant to serve as a piece of topical and royalist anti-Dutch propaganda (undercut, I believe, by Dryden's inability to wholeheartedly prostitute himself); to a lesser extent, so was the more ambitious Annus Mirabilis, The Year of Wonders, 1666 (1667), linked to the Second Dutch War. Edward Niles Hooker and H. T. Swedenberg, Jr. describe the latter as"a piece of inspired journalism, written to sway public opinion in favour of the royal government, which dreaded a revolution Dryden suggested at every point through the poem that heaven and Providence had favored the King's party". In

Annus Mirabilis, Dryden suggests a theory of the"mercantile state" which Hooker and Swedenberg sum up thus: A healthy state seeks power and wealth; wealth flows in from the expansion of foreign trade; trade is the means of enriching the public treasury, and the nation's treasury alone has the resources to wage modern war; a strong king is needed to foster and protect trade, and to lead his people in war; and by victory in war the expansion of wealth and power is guaranteed.

In other words, whether synergy, a vicious cycle, or both, Dryden's theory of the mercantile state is an extension of his staunch royalism and allegiance to the Stuarts, the same allegiance that likely led him to compose Amboyna.

Securing support for the Third Dutch War was important to Charles II. In June 1672 Louis XIV's army had invaded Holland, resisted by Prince William of Orange; also in that month was published a pamphlet revealing the true contents of the secret Treaty of Dover (1670) negotiated between Charles and Louis, which"withdrew England from the Triple Alliance [with Holland and Sweden against France] and was intended to prepare the way for its Catholicization". When Amboyna and other attempts to secure support failed, Charles was forced by Parliament, in exchange for financial war supplies, to withdraw the Declaration of Indulgence which he had issued earlier that year and which had suspended all laws previously enforced against Dissenters and Catholics.

Encouraged by success, the Parliamentary majority passed the Test Act, for which Shaftesbury argued, and which led to Clifford's resignation and, soon after, to his suicide. As Winn explains,"On Easter Sunday, the day after Parliament recessed, the Duke of York [later James II] failed to take Anglican communion, in effect officially declaring his Catholicism; since he remained the heir apparent, the Anglican interests now victorious in the Parliament had to face the prospect that a Papist would eventually inherit the throne". It is this prospect, of course, that led to the Exclusion Crisis and to Absalom and Achitophel. The Test Act is also integral to the occasion of Dryden's equally famous and longest poem, The Hind and the

Panther (1687). Earl Miner calls that poem, published"more or less under James [II]'s aegis," a"salvo in the controversy of the day". James had"vainly expected the Anglican bishops to nullify" the Test Act, and began to seek the support of Dissenters with his own Declaration of Indulgence in 1687;"the question became one of whether the King or the bishops could persuade the Sects that they shared common interests, and on whose side James's son-in-law, William of Orange, would come down". History tells us, of course, on whose side-Dutch William of Orange became William III of England; and Dryden, Catholic since 1685, lost his public posts, putting him, as Winn believes Dryden was acutely aware, in the position of Clifford fifteen years earlier. Dryden's response, in Don Sebastian, Amphitryon, and Cleomenes, was to continue writing plays that radically explore the role of Providence in human history.

It is interesting, then, that in The Hind and the Panther, Dryden returns to a charge against the Dutch and the English leveled in Amboyna. In the prologue, and the epilogue of the play, Dryden"specifically refutes the arguments of those reluctant to attack the Dutch on the grounds of a common religion", but he does it by accusing both the Dutch and the English of irreligiousity; he says to his English audiences that the Dutch"have no more Religion, faith-than you". In the later poem, he says the Dutch"on gain, their onely God, rely. / And set a publick price on piety", but just as Dryden's charge in the prologue to Amboyna rebounds upon his own countrymen, so he savages British colonialism in The Hind and the Panther:

Our sayling ships like common shoars we use,
And through our distant colonies diffuse
The draughts of Dungeons, and the stench of stews;
Whom, when their home-bred honesty is lost,
We disembogue on some far Indian coast:
Thieves, Pandars, Palliards, sins of ev'ry sort,
Those are the manufactures we export;
And these the Missionaires our zeal has made:
For, with my country's pardon be it said,
Religion is the least of all our trade.

I have argued that Dryden's stance toward colonialism in Amboyna is not as unilaterally-if wrongheadedly-pro-English as recent commentators have presented it to be. I would close with an observation by Canfield that does, I think, come close to representing the effect of the play-with this crucial difference: Canfield sees Amboyna as a"paean to Brittania" and what he regards as a single exceptional moment he believes to be unintentional; I see Dryden's attitudes as expressed in the entire play as considerably more ambivalent. Canfield remarks that sticking out like a sore thumb is Ysabinda's plea to Towerson after her rape:"For my sake, fly this detested Isle, where horrid Ills so black and fatal dwell, as Indians cou'd not guess, till Europe taught."Europe" includes not only the cruel Spanish and Dutch but the English as well. A minor note, surely not intended by Dryden to undercut his paean. Yet it as surely sounds, however diminished, in the ear of the attentive spectator. The difference amounts to this: as an"attentive spectator," I believe that in Amboyna, Dryden once again demonstrates-however intentionally--his characteristic complexity of mind, here, in relation to the propagandistic purposes he was under pressure to serve.

"A play, Which I Presume to Call Original": Appropriation, Creative Genius, and Eighteenth- Century Playwriting

That invention is the first great leading talent of a poet has been a point long since determined, because it is principally owing to that faculty of the mind that he is able to create, and be as it were a MAKER.... But surely there are many other powers of the mind as fully essential to constitute a fine poet, and therefore, in order to give the true character of any author's abilities, it should seem necessary to come to a right understanding of what is meant by GENIUS, and to analyse and arrange its several qualities. This once adjusted, it might prove no unpleasing task to examine what are the specific qualities of any poet in particular, to point out the talents of which he seems to have the freest command, or in the use of which he seems, as it were, to be left-handed. In this plain fair-dealing way the true and real value of an author will be easily ascertained; whereas in the more confined method of investigation, which establishes, at the outset, one giant-quality, and finding the object of the enquiry deficient in that, immediately proceeds to undervalue him in the whole, there seems to be danger of not trying his cause upon a full and equitable hearing. Arthur Murphy's sensible exposition of the grounds for assessing literary merit, among which invention is an important but by no means the determining factor, found few candid adherents in late eighteenth-century England. Though most practicing playwrights, like Murphy himself, would have no doubt agreed with the proposition that invention is merely one of several qualities that make a good playwright, they felt compelled outwardly to endorse the doctrine of original genius that was rapidly gaining the status of critical orthodoxy and to reproduce the rhetoric that came with it."By the 1750's," as Walter Jackson Bate has noted,"some of the least original minds of the time were beginning to prate constantly of `originality'". What were the consequences of the near-universal acceptance of originality as a criterion of literary value for the status of plays and playwriting? How did the imperative to produce new and original literary artifacts that could aspire to match the compositions of that quintessential British genius, Shakespeare, tally with the commercial demands of the theatrical marketplace?

Modern scholars look upon the mid- to late eighteenth century as a period of an almost unrelieved dramatic decline. They attribute the erosion of dramatic standards to the long-term effects of the Licensing Act of 1737, which confirmed the monopoly of the two London patent companies and for decades stifled the production of new plays. The repertories at Drury Lane and Covent Garden consisted largely of old favorites, both companies catering to the steady increase in audiences by periodically expanding the capacity of their playhouses. Scholars further blame the mediocrity of theatrical offerings upon the widespread adoption of French-derived ideas of correctness and dramatic decorum that led to the appearance of numerous stodgy tragedies,4 and they castigate the playwrights'determination to supply performance vehicles for star actors to the detriment of the plays'structural unity.'The manifestations and causes of the decay of drama as a literary form have been amply documented; what has received far less attention is how authors of all those"bad" plays conceived of themselves and of their work. Did their authorial self-fashioning mimic those of Restoration and early eighteenth-century playwrights, or did they depart from their predecessors'views and rhetoric of playwriting?

The half-century following the Restoration of the Stuart monarchy in 1660 witnessed a significant shift in conceptions of dramatic authorship. The key manifestation of that shift was the emergence of the notion of literary property. Playwrights were increasingly seen as"owners" of their scripts, while indebtedness to earlier texts, particularly plays, was condemned as theft. Charges of plagiarism multiplied as the demand for creative independence and solo composition grew stronger. By the beginning of the eighteenth century, the drama was established as a literary form with serious artistic claims; its cultural stature had solidified. That process led to, and was assisted by, first, the development of dramatic criticism; second, the publication of collected editions of both Renaissance and post-- Restoration plays; and, third, the improvement in the economic situation of playwrights, whose literary ambitions found expression in substantial prefatory epistles and accounts of whose lives and works were being written and disseminated with increasing frequency.

Although Shakespeare was beginning to be accorded an esteem higher than that of Jonson or Beaumont and Fletcher, he was by no means seen as superior to later playwrights such as Dryden, Wycherley, or Congreve. The dramatic canon in the first two decades of the eighteenth century was principally a modern one, with works by post-Restoration playwrights enjoying greater popularity on the stage and on the page than those by their Elizabethan and Jacobean predecessors. One might have expected these trends-which so powerfully enhanced the position of drama and playwriting by the end of the seventeenth century-to develop and continue. Yet, when we look at the situation a century later, in the 1780s and 90s, we find a very different picture. Many, if not most, of the new and successful plays were now adaptations and translations, not independent compositions. Playwriting no longer possessed the cultural centrality it had attained in the first decade or so of the eighteenth century; its literary pretensions had been virtually abandoned. This regression is surprising. Why did the stature of drama decline so drastically? More specifically, how was that process affected by the changing practice and rhetoric of appropriation?

To understand eighteenth-century conceptions of playwriting, we need to reconstruct the conventions governing the use of sources. We have to investigate the modes of acknowledgement of plays'textual foundations and to assess the corresponding justifications of literary borrowing, adaptation, and translation. In the Restoration, although occasionally the original author's name was mentioned in the prologue or epilogue spoken in the theater, the most common form of source acknowledgement was an extended preface outlining the reasons for the revision of the borrowed materials. In the mid-eighteenth century, that convention is altered. The lengthy preface is replaced by a brief, non-descriptive"advertisement," which offers a bare list of sources without elaborating on their transformation. Such advertisements are prefixed both to singly printed plays as well as to plays included in collections. For example, the text of George Colman the Elder's comedy The Jealous Wife (1761) in his Dramatic Works of 1777 is preceded by the following Advertisement:

The use that has been made in this comedy of Fielding's admirable novel of Tom Jones, must be obvious to the most ordinary reader. Some hints have also been taken from the account of Mr. and Mrs. Freeman, in No. 212, and No. 216, of the Spectator; and the short scene of Charles's intoxication, at the end of the third act, is partly an imitation of the behaviour of Syrus, much in the same circumstances, in the Adelphi of Terence. There are also some traces of the character of The Jealous Wife, in one of the latter papers of the Connoisseur.

Colman scrupulously documents the hints and sources

behind textual minutiae Similar advertisements are prefixed to plays by David Garrick, Isaac Bickerstaffe, Hannah More, Elizabeth Griffith, Elizabeth Inchbald, Frederick Reynolds, and many others. To illustrate: Garrick confesses that"the hint of Miss in her Teens is taken from... La Parisienne of D'Ancourt"; Bickerstaffe admits that his farce The Sultan, or A Peep into the Seraglio"is taken from Marmontel"; More acknowledges that her tragedy Percy derives from"The French Drama, founded on the famous old Story of Raoul de Coucy"; Griffith specifies that"the hint of [The School for Rakes] was taken from a much admired performance of Monsieur Beaumarchais, soled Eugen"; Inchbald declares that in The Widow's Vow she"is indebted for the Plot of her Piece, and for the Plot only, to L'Heureuse Erreur, a French Comedy of one Act, by M. PATRAT"; Reynolds states that his operatic drama The Virgin of the Sun"is founded on Marmontel's Incas, and Kotzebue's Rolla, or Virgin of the Sun, and forms the first part of the Tragedy called Pizarro"

The only cases where the acknowledgement is more discursive are a few adaptations of native plays by Shakespeare, Jonson, Beaumont and Fletcher, and Wycherley, such as Colman's version of Philaster; a few renditions of French and German plays into English, such as Inchbald's immensely popular Lovers'Vows taken from Kotzebue: and the infrequent attempts to transplant Greek drama to England, such as William Mason's turgid Elfrida, A Dramatic Poem. Written on the Model of The Ancient Greek Tragedy. By and large, however, the extensive prefatory justification disappears. Playwrights usually admit borrowing directly but make little or no effort to justify it. One reason for-and manifestation of-this state of affairs is the reduction of claims to authorship and literary stature made by contemporary dramatists. Where Restoration playwrights asserted authorship in their plays based on novels, romances, and history, as well as their adaptations of foreign and native drama, their eighteenth-century successors are a lot more cautious and modest. In their advertisements, they repeatedly style themselves editors and alterers rather than authors.

Possibly the earliest instance of the reviser describing himself as editor occurs in Lewis Theobald's preface to The Double Falsehood (1728), his redaction of a supposed Shakespearean original. Theobald previously had publicized his ambition (and qualifications) to supply a new edition of Shakespeare's works by mounting a fierce attack on Pope's edition of 1723-5 in Shakespeare restored: or, A Specimen of the Many Errors, As well Committed, as Unamended, by Mr. Pope In his Late Edition of this Poet. Designed Not only to correct the said Edition, but to restore the True Reading of Shakespeare in all the Editions ever yet publish'd (1726). The preliminaries to The Double Falsehood entail a notion of editorial procedure strikingly different from that implicit in Theobald's arraignment of Pope. In Shakespeare restored, Theobald's chief aim is to reconstruct Shakespeare's"True Reading."13 By contrast, though he claims to have approached the managers of Drury Lane with a copy of The Double Falsehood"as an Editor, not an Author," Theobald professes to have"with great Labour and Pains, Revised, and Adapted the STAGE.

That double sense of editing-as judicious restoration and as more or less radical adaptation-was to persist throughout the eighteenth century. Successive editions of Shakespeare attest to the former strain;15 Colman the Elder's playwriting illustrates the latter. Colman reworked plays by Jonson, Fletcher, and Shakespeare, and his versions found their way into the collected edition of his plays of 1777. They were included in"Volume the Third; containing Alterations of Philaster King Lear, Epicoene; Or The Silent Woman." Although printed in Colman's Dramatick Works, individual title pages ascribe the plays to the original authors, while in the advertisements such as the one prefixed to Philaster, Colman refers to himself as the editor:"To remove the objections to the performance of this excellent play on the modern stage, has been the chief labour, and sole ambition, of the present editor"."It is impossible," he continues,"for the severest reader to have a meaner opinion of the editor's share in the work than he entertains of it himself'. Garrick, who in any event frequently omitted to bill his revisions as such or to put his name to them if the work were published, employs virtually identical rhetoric in the advertisement to The Country Girl (1766), an adaptation of Wycherley's salacious comedy The Country Wife: ... Tho'near half of the following Play is new written, the Alterer claims no Merit, but his Endeavour to clear one of our most celebrated Comedies from Immorality and Obscenity... and if this Wanton of Charles's Days is now reclaimed, as to become innocent without being insipid, the present Editor will not think his Time ill employed.

In the same year, Bickerstaffe calls himself the editor of Doctor Last in his Chariot, a comedy derived from Moliere: The following piȩce is a translation of Le Malade Imaginaire, one of Moliere's most celebrated productions in the farcical kind. Some scenes which could not possibly succeed upon the English stage, have been removed, and those substituted, in which the character of Doctor Last is introduced; and, for that character only, the editor has to answer; nothing else in the subsequent scenes, being entirely his.

By the latter half of the eighteenth century, then, the appropriative nature of playwriting had come to be widely accepted; but the urgency and passion with which Restoration and early eighteenth-century playwrights had asserted their authorial credentials and repudiated charges of plagiarism were mostly gone. The dramatists'self-esteem and confidence in the artistic value of their productions seem to have been eroded and replaced by self-consciousness, even self-depreciation.

Those negative sentiments are particularly in evidence in the work of professional men of the theater-actors, managers, prompters-who supplied a high proportion of contemporary theatrical offerings, chiefly lightweight pieces including farces, musical comedies, and ballad operas. Such play-- doctors freely admit that their extensive remodeling of earlier texts is due not only to haste and desire for profit but to plain lack of invention and talent."That I am indebted to Mr. Ramsay's GENTLE SHEPARD, (a Scotch Pastoral Comedy, wrote Originally in Five Acts) for the greatest Part of the following Piece," says the actor Theophilus Cibber in the preface to Patie and Peggy: or, The Fair Foundling. A Scotch Ballad Opera,"was not owing to my Idleness, but a Doubt of my Abilities to produce any Thing entirely New of this kind, that might plead so much pretence to Favour". Charles Dibdin (house-composer at Drury Lane in the 1770s) is equally frank about the origin of his ballad opera The Waterman. He put it together so as to recycle"the different pieces I have composed for Ranelagh and the Theatre... which have been but little heard." Having cited the source of"the dialogue necessary to work up these materials into a Ballad Farce," Dibdin states: I am resolved to acknowledge at all times from whence I collect any matter for the trifles I may have an opportunity of presenting to the public. I must be an egregious egotist indeed, and little entitled to the indulgence they have hitherto favoured me with, if I could be so unconscious of my own inability as to suppose I ever can present them with any thing worthy their notice without assistance of this sort.

The Waterman proved a taking afterpiece, and its concocter went on to cobble together many more shows like it and to compose music for them, being content to reap profits from the theater without staking claims to literary stature.

The decline in assertions of authorship further manifests itself in the wording of contemporary title pages and in the content and typography of theatrical playbills. Where Dryden, Shadwell, D'Urfey, and others had proudly placed their names on the title pages of their appropriative plays (thus Troilus and Cressida; or, Truth Found too Late was printed as"Written by Mr. Dryden," and The History of Timon of Athens, the Man-Hater was touted as having been"Made into a Play. By Tho. Shadwell"), Garrick, Colman, Bickerstaffe, and other eighteenthcentury playwrights either refrained from doing so or conspicuously cited the name of the original author alongside their own, thereby reinforcing the impression that theirs was merely a cut-and-paste job." A good illustration is the adaptation of an unacted play by James Thomson, Edward and Eleonora. It was acknowledged as such not only on the title page of the printed edition: Edward and Eleonora, A Tragedy... Altered from James Thomson. And new adapted to the Stage by Thomas Hull (1775) and in the prologue spoken in the theater ("T'onight your Favour and your Praise we claim, / For lo! the Page, bears Thomson's honour'd Name")," but also in a playbill for a touring production:

By His MAJESTY'S SERVANTS.

At the NEW THEATRE in LANCASTER,

On MONDAY the 11th of AUGUST, 1777,

Will be performed a new Piece, (written originally by Thompson, Author of the Seasons, altered and properly adapted to the Stage by Mr. Hull) called Edward and Eleonora.

The success of this adaptation on the London stage explains not only why it was taken on tour but also why the names of both the original author and the reviser were touted on the playbill. Over the course of the eighteenth century, playbills grew in size, yet, as David Gowen has pointed out,"[even with the extra room, bills announcing new plays customarily omitted the playwright's name." Gowen speculates that the omission may have been"a precaution against undesirable recognition in the event of a poor reception" . Whatever the reason, the absence of the author's name from an elaborately decorated playbill that advertised a premiere performance of his or her work (and that supplied plentiful information about the venue, the company, the actors, the prices, etc.) is itself a sign of a deepening depreciation of authorial stature.

The pedantic nature of the acknowledgements of sources, especially those included in the paraphernalia of printed play texts, created the sense that modern playwrights'productions were slight and inconsequential. For what is one to make of the authorial credentials of Isaac Bickerstaffe on the basis of the following title page:"The Hypocrite: A Comedy... Taken from Moliere and Cibber, By the Author Of the Alterations of the Plain-Dealer"? Bickerstaffe's claim to fame is to have adapted Wycherley's The Plain Dealer, which qualifies him for the task of altering Cibber and Moliere! Among other examples are new versions of old plays by Garrick and Richard Brinsley Sheridan. Garrick was responsible for Isabella: or, The Fatal Marriage. A Play. Altered from Southern, The Gamesters: A

Comedy. Altered from Shirley, and Every Man in his Humour A Comedy. Altered from Ben. Johnson;" Sheridan for A Trip to Scarborough... Altered from Vanbrugh's Relapse; or, Virtue in Danger (1781). On the evidence of such title pages, eighteenth-century readers could not have felt but that theirs was entertainment based essentially on recycled wares.

One could ask, of course, why such revampings were produced and printed. The answer is simple. Most of the originals behind them had been for decades successful repertory pieces, and theaters wanted to keep them there. The acting company's chief concern was profit, not literary value. If a popular play was beginning to show age-whether on account of its outmoded or indecorous language, irregular construction, or lax sexual mores-a modest amount of retouching was all that was needed to ensure its continued stage viability. Having a vast stock of proven scripts at their disposal, the theaters repeatedly issued commissions for revision rather than risking their capital by mounting new shows. Concomitant with the decline in the proprietary claims made by eighteenth century playwrights was the reduction of their artistic claims.

While amateur appropriators such as Sir William Killigrew and Sir Robert Howard in the 1660s, and professional ones such as John Dryden, Elkanah Settle, Aphra Behn, and Thomas D'Urfey in the 1670s and beyond, invariably prided themselves on having improved whatever they took from the scripts they set out to adapt, eighteenth-century revisers such as Garrick, Colman, Bickerstaffe, Inchbald, and many others largely refrained from doing so. The reason for this disparity was the fundamental difference between the motives for appropriation that prevailed in the later seventeenth century and those dominant throughout most of the eighteenth century. Aesthetic justifications of adaptation put forward by Restoration writers were gradually replaced by ethical justifications proposed by Garrick and his contemporaries. However we may judge of their productions, a Dryden or a Vanbrugh believed that both language and manners had become refined since the pre-Civil War era and, that in order to make Shakespeare or Fletcher stageable, the linguistic and stylistic obsolescence of their plays ought to be eliminated. To give Miranda a sister and to add a man who has never seen a woman to the cast of the Shakespearean Tempest, as Davenant and Dryden did in their version performed in 1667, was to create a better play. A new version of a pre-Civil War piece was superior to the original by virtue of the removal of obsolete diction or indecorous and/or improbable action; a new rendition of Corneille or Moliere surpassed the too-scanty original owing to the addition of a subplot, new characters, and new incidents.

Eighteenth-century adapters were not so confident. As the century went on, the belief that earlier drama could be improved was losing its hold. True, both Renaissance and Restoration plays were being substantially revised and altered for stage representation, but the new versions were no longer touted as artistically superior to the originals on which they were based. Rather, they were advertised as morally superior, having been purged of sexually explicit language and action. The decisive change occurred around mid-century, by which time many of the salacious favorites had been subjected to a thorough-going reformation. Indeed, there were those who believed that not only pieces intended for the stage but also published play texts should be reformed.

Thomas Seward, one of the editors of Beaumont and Fletcher's Works of 1750, actually undertook to expunge from their scripts what he called"gross and indecent Expressions" and: a great many Indecencies... which, when I began my Part of the Work for the Press, I had actually struck off, as far as I could do without injuring the Connection of the Context; but the Booksellers press'd, and indeed insisted upon their Restoration: They very sensibly urged the last-mentioned Plea, and thought that the bare Notion of a curtail'd Edition would greatly prejudice the Sale of it.

In such a case, the publishers'commercial interests stood in the way of the editor's righteous zeal. The theater managers' commercial interests, by contrast, positively required censorship of sexual impropriety at the level of both plot and language. As Garrick phrased it in the Prologue to Sheridan's redaction of Vanbrugh's The Relapse,

Those writers well and wisely use their pens,
Who turn our Wantons into Magdalens;
And howsoever wicked wits revile'em,
We hope to find in you, their Stage Asylum.

Yet turning"Wantons into Magdalens" was hardly an inspired or inspiriting task. Where late seventeenth-century adapters occasionally held up their versions as less vulgar than the originals or insisted-as did Tate when he restored Lear to the throne and had Cordelia wed Edgar that they fulfilled the ideal of poetic justice by rewarding the good and punishing the bad, for the most part the arguments in favour of adaptation were aesthetic rather than moral. Indeed, many Restoration adaptations were far more licentious than their sources, the cause celebre being the Dryden-Davenant Tempest. By contrast, mid- and late-eighteenth-century adapters proclaim themselves guardians of the nation's morals, implicitly (and sometimes explicitly) conceding the inferiority of their versions, as did Colman in his revision of Philaster and Garrick in his bowdlerization of The Country Wife.

They hold up their works as more decorous and proper than their sources:"There seems indeed an absolute Necessity for reforming many Plays of our most eminent Writers," wrote Garrick,"For no kind of Wit ought to be received as an Excuse for Immorality, nay it becomes still more dangerous in proportion as it is more witty." The upshot of such repeated bowdlerization was to beget the impression that modern plays, even if exhibiting greater propriety, were simply less good than older ones.

As we have seen, eighteenth-century appropriators made claims less ambitious and less grand than those of their late seventeenth-century predecessors. Now, I wish to turn to two other indicators of the diminution in the literary standing of plays: the pattern of dramatic publication and the subject matter of dramatic criticism. By the latter part of the eighteenth century, the contrast between old and new drama was not easy to perceive on the stage since most of the indecent favorites had slipped from the repertory or been supplanted by expurgated versions, but the printed page afforded ample opportunities for comparison-above all, with Shakespeare. Here again, in the realm of printed drama, we can notice the reversal of trends that had characterized the earlier period. The proliferation of handsome collected editions of plays in the first two decades of the eighteenth century had contributed to the elevation of plays'literary status and enhanced their authors'reputations." It is thus surprising to note that, in the mid- to late eighteenth century, there were so few collected editions of plays by modern playwrights.

Only Garrick, Lillo, Fielding, More, Colman the Elder, and Murphy could boast a collection. Theirs were as a rule less typographically ambitious or lavish collections than the impressive folio of Dryden's brought out in 1701 or the elegant octavo volumes Congreve saw through the press in 1710. Moreover, the prefatory statements, whether authorial or editorial, to be found in those collected editions were often less than complimentary about the contents. Thus, the prefaces to Garrick's collections of 1768 and 1798, respectively, displayed a condescending attitude to his dramatic exertions-the former describing them as"little productions," the latter as"little things." Arthur Murphy's introductory essay to the four-volume edition of Fielding's Works (1762), which contained plays, novels, and other pieces, judged Fielding's playwriting considerably inferior to his comic fiction:"he confessedly did not attain to pre-eminence in this branch of writing." Thomas Davies's enthusiastic assessment of George Lillo's dramatic output in the preliminaries to the two-volume Works of 1775 was therefore quite exceptional in being accorded to a near-contemporary (Lillo died in 1739). Davies goes so far as to rate Lillo's Fatal Curiosity-"this master piece of fine writing"-alongside Shakespearean tragedy:

In all Dramatic Poetry, there are few scenes where the passions are so highly wrought up, as in the third Act of the FATAL CURIOSITY... LILLO need not be ashamed to yield to Shakespeare, who is superior to all other writers; but excepting the celebrated scenes of murder in Macbeth, these in the

FATAL CURIOSITY, for just representation of anguish, remorse, despair, and horror, bear away the palm. But there was more to Lillo's playwriting than his magisterial portrayal of passions in The Fatal Curiosity and The London Merchant. Davies was impressed by the generic novelty of Lillo's tragedies, which, in contrast to most serious drama of his day, focused on the private sphere and dramatized the predicament of lower-class figures, moving beyond the earlier attempts at domestic tragedy by Otway and Rowe."The World is indebted to this writer," Davies observes,"for the invention of a new species of dramatic poetry, which may properly be termed the inferior or lesser tragedy."

The most imposing collected edition by a living playwright was The Works of Arthur Murphy, Esq. (1786), in seven volumes, which the author himself saw through the press. It featured not only plays, each one of them subjected to"a careful revisal," but also Murphy's contributions to The Gray's Inn Journal. Neither Murphy's nor Lillo's nor Colman's collection was reprinted before the end of the century. Fielding's Works reappeared in an expanded twelve-volume set in 1783 (with the addition of The Fathers; or, The Good-natured Man) and continued to be reprinted in the nineteenth century, no doubt on account of his novels rather than plays. By far the greatest commercial hit was Hannah More's collection of closet pieces, Sacred Dramas; Chiefly Intended for Young Persons: The Subjects Taken from the Bible (1782), which had gone through eighteen editions by 1815 and which was also reprinted in America. Eighteenth-century Theater and literary drama went their separate ways.

The energies of editors and textual scholars-from Rowe and Pope through Theobald, Hanmer, Warburton, Johnson, Capell, and Steevens to Edmond Malone-were devoted to Shakespeare and, to a lesser extent, to Jonson, Massinger, and Beaumont and Fletcher. Instead of author-centered collections of modern plays, the eighteenth century saw a proliferation of anthologies setting forth the plays as"regulated from theatrical promptbooks," thus emphasizing their connection with the stage.35 The format, layout, and typography of such anthologies evince their lower status with respect to author-based editions of older drama. Their print is very small, dozens of plays being crowded into each volume, and they frequently lack their own individual title pages and engraved illustrations. The lowering of plays'literary status as evidenced by altered patterns of publication is paralleled by changes in dramatic criticism. It is evinced, too, by the directions of theater reviewing that developed in the late 1740s and gathered momentum in the 1780s and 90s. Eighteenth-century criticism assumed a variety of forms, including book-length treatises, pamphlets, prefatory essays by authors and editors, and newspaper and journal articles.

Early in the period, shorter forms prevailed; in the second half of the eighteenth century, serious studies began to proliferate. Yet whereas previously both Renaissance and post-- Restoration plays furnished subject matter for discussion, now earnest critics focused on old rather than new drama. Newspapers and journals, it is true, published reviews of newly premiered shows as well as revivals; however, those commentaries largely focused on performance, not literary quality. They customarily provided a plan or plot summary of the new offering, a convention that made the repetitive and derivative nature of modern playwriting all the more obvious. Most substantial critical projects concentrated on Shakespeare and other old playwrights.

Those that did take the story further dwelt on the"progress" of the English stage from the age of Elizabeth to that of Charles, and on its"decline and fall" in the age of the Georges. Why should that have been the case? What curtailed authorial ambitions? Most interestingly, why did the artistic collapse occur at a time when the remuneration for new scripts was actually rising? The reasons, let me suggest, were partly economic. The disappearance of genuine theatrical competition following the Licensing Act of 1737 and the ensuing collusion between the two patent houses, Drury Lane and Covent Garden, led to the rapid fall in the number of new plays as both companies relied heavily on revivals. To keep their repertories up-to-date, they regularly had old plays retouched.

For the playwright, such a commission would have been more than welcome: the market for the product was guaranteed, and the financial risk involved in writing an original play was eliminated. Admittedly, script revision was not as profitable as a successful new show, but it required less work and provided insurance against failure.

With the expansion of the star system, theatrical scripts came increasingly to be seen as vehicles for leading performers. It was no longer the play that mattered but the player. The theater's commercialization likewise manifested itself early in the eighteenth century in the popularity of entr'acte entertainments and later in the introduction of afterpieces-short play lets usually of comic or farcical character, pantomimes, and musical shows-which followed the play proper. The increasing number of actor-benefit afterpieces concocted especially for the occasion and later abandoned suggests that managers were prepared to countenance such shows for variety even as they remained conservative in their preference for tried main pieces. The resulting fragmentation of the theatrical experience could not but have affected the audience's perception of the play.

Seeing Othello or Hamlet on its own is a very different proposition from seeing it followed by a farce or a burlesque.41 Besides exploding the unity of the night's entertainment, the popularity of and demand for afterpieces led to playwrights cobbling such pieces fast by reusing all manner of materials, including earlier main pieces. The very existence of the afterpiece contributed to the erosion of the status of the drama. But another reason, one that accounts for the intense self-consciousness and often self-denigration of playwrights, was the growing valorization of creative originality.

Subjectivity, uniqueness, and inspiration were certainly easier to achieve-and their lack more difficult to detect-in poetry, perhaps even in prose fiction, than in the drama. It was one thing for a Dryden or a Behn to profess to have improved the source text and assert ownership of the resulting play script by detailing their alterations; it was quite another for a Colman or a Cumberland to claim originality in a play that he felt bound to acknowledge was based on another. Colman playfully canvassed the current theories of literary creativity in the prologue and epilogue to his comedy The Man of Business (1774). The Prologue is spoken by a disappointed"Author, with a manuscript" railing against the manager-Colman-who has rejected his play in order to stage his own derivative piece:

See here, good folks, how genius is abus'd!
A play of mine, the manager refus'd!
And why?-I knew the reason well enough--
Only to introduce his own damn'd stuff.
His play to-night, like all he ever wrote,
Is pie-ball'd, piec'd, and patch'd, like Joseph's coat;
Made up of shreds from Plautus and Corneille,
Terence, Moliere, Voltaire, and Marmontel;
With rags of fifty others I might mention,
Which proves him dull and barren of invention:
But shall his nonsense hold the place of sense?
No, damn him! damn him, in your own defence!"

The Epilogue has two speakers: a critic and a lady. The critic high-handedly condemns appropriative playwriting and clamors for originality:

What are the riff-raff of our modern plays?
Their native dullness all in books intrench:
Mere scavengers of Latin, Greek, and French,
Sweep up the learned rubbish, dirt, and dust,
Or from old iron try to file the rust.
Give me the bard whose fiery disposition
Quickens at once, and learns by intuition;
Lifts up his head to think, and, in a minute,
Ideas make a hurly-burly in it;
Struggling for passage, there ferment and bubble,
And thence run over without further trouble;
'Till out comes play or poem, as they feign
Minerva issued from her father's brain!
Be all original! struck out at once;
Who borrows, toils, or labours, is a dunce:
Genius, alas! is at the lowest ebb;

And none, like spiders, spin their own fine web.
Old books, old plays, old thoughts, will never do:
Originals for me, and something new!

He is immediately answered by the female spectator who is obviously up-to-date with recent critical developments and the Lockean notion of tabula rasa:

`New? (cries the lady) Prithee, man, have done!
We know there's nothing new beneath the sun.
Weave, like the spider, from your proper brains,
And take at last a cobweb for your pains!
What is invention?'Tis not thoughts innate;
Each head at first is but an empty pate.
'Tis but retailing from a wealthy hoard
The thoughts which observation long has stor'd,
Combining images with lucky hit,
Which sense and education first admit;
Who, borrowing little from the common store,
Mends what he takes, and from his own adds more,
He is original; or inspiration
Never fill'd bard of this, or other nation,
And Shakespeare's art is merely imitation.
For'tis a truth long prov'd beyond all doubt,
Where nothing's in, there's nothing can come out.

However facetious, Colman's prologue and epilogue illustrate the incompatibility of concepts such as solitary genius, inspiration, and originality with the commercial demands of the contemporary theater. The clash between critical ideas and commercial realities underlies the contradictory rhetoric of Richard Cumberland's preface to Joanna of Montfaucon (1800). The printed title page advertises it as"A Dramatic Romance of the Fourteenth Century... Formed upon the Plan of the German Drama of Kotzebue: and Adapted to the English Stage by Richard Cumberland." Despite the acknowledged reliance on the foreign source, Cumberland fervently insists on his own offering's originality in the preface:

It has so rarely been my habit to write upon any plot but of my own fabrication and invention, that what I assert in the Prologue is most strictly true; viz.

"All, who cou'd judge my labour, wou'd confess
"Originality had made it less."

Yet his assertion of originality is undermined by the very wording of his title page acknowledgement. Cumberland, of course, had been ridiculed as Sir Fretful Plagiary in Sheridan's The Critick (1779); but, given Sheridan's own wideranging use of textual materials-both native and foreign-we may feel that the pot was calling the kettle black. Indeed, during the first run of Cumberland's Joanna in January, 1800, daily receipts at Covent Garden were lower by half than those at Drury Lane where Sheridan's Pizarro (a version of Kotzebue's Die Spanier in Peru) was enjoying a hugely successful revival. The rage for adaptations of the German's work drew fire from a number of commentators. Sheridan, whose position as author-manager made him a particularly convenient target, was singled out for attack in a satirical skit More Kotzebue! To be upbraided for plagiaristic proclivities must have been acutely galling to a dramatist who had asserted in the preface to his debut-piece, The Rivals, that his"first wish in attempting a Play, was to avoid every appearance of plagiary." How the mighty had fallen.

As we have seen, the theatrical milieu characterized by a strong demand for script revision and adaptation, foreign novelties, and effective afterpieces was hardly congenial to original playwriting. We have noted, too, that those writers who were connected with the playhouse mainly in their capacity as actors, managers, or prompters as a rule refrained from making serious claims about the artistic merit of their self-confessedly derivative scripts, preferring, instead, to emphasize their theatrical potential. By contrast, those few writers-some professionals, some amateurs-who strove to assert the literary value of their plays felt constrained to adopt the critical vocabulary of originality, invention, imagination, and genius made current by treatises such as Hurd's, Young's, Duff's, and Gerard's.46 We may scoff at Cumberland's confused justification of Joanna or Murphy's meandering apologies for Alzuma and The Rival Sisters, but what about those plays for which no immediate textual source can be identified? After all, not every late eighteenth-century play was a translation or an adaptation. Which dramatic form-comedy or tragedy-provided greater scope for originality, and what were the strategies adopted by writers to achieve it?

The eighteenth century did not invent"originality." Yet it was in that period that originality, hitherto conceived as an attribute of the literary work, came to be defined in terms of the creative process that produced it. This shift of emphasis from work to author, from the literary artifact to the mind behind it, stimulated interest in the psychology of artistic creation. There appeared a series of treatises exploring the nature of original genius and illustrating its workings (or lack thereof) with reference to ancient and modern writings. Among the best known are: Joseph Warton's Essay on the Writings and Genius of Pope (1756), Young's Conjectures on Original Composition (1759), Duff's Essay on Original Genius; and its Various Modes of Exertion in Philosophy and the Fine Arts, Particularly Poetry (1767) and his Critical Observations on the Writings of the Most Celebrated Geniuses in Poetry. Being a Sequel to the Essay on Original Genius (1770), and Alexander Gerard's Essay on Genius (1774).

Despite differences of method and focus, these studies share a number of theoretical premises and often use the same examples, notably Homer, Milton, and Shakespeare. For my purposes, the evaluation of Shakespeare's genius is of particular interest not only because he was a modern, a Briton, and a professional dramatist, but also because his appropriative playwriting-as documented, for example, by Charlotte Lennox in Shakespeare Illustrated& or The Novels and Histories, On which the Plays of Shakespeare are Founded, Collected and Translated from the Original Authors (1753)-presented the champions of originality with a formidable difficulty. They strove to overcome it by avoiding direct engagement with the evidence of Shakespeare's textual debts amassed by Lennox and others, or, alternatively, by maintaining that he refined even"the basest materials." They also adopted two distinct if complementary ways of reconceptualizing originality so as to accommodate and excuse those debts. One common ploy was to make a firm distinction between sentiments and expression."The most original writer," Richard Hurd argues,"is allowed to furnish himself with poetical ideas from all quarters." According to this line of argument, Shakespeare's use of ready-made plots is irrelevant, for his originality consists wholly in the singularity and uniqueness of style. Again, Hurd's formulation is the most succinct: You will best understand of what importance this affair of expression is to the discovery of imitations, by considering how seldom we are able to fix an imitation on Shakespeare. The reason is, not, that there are not numberless passages in him very like to others in approved authors, or that he had not read enough to give us a fair hold of him; but that his expression is so totally his own, that he almost always, sets us at defiance.

Another tactic was to reverse the Aristotelian hierarchy, with its primacy of fable over any other element of the dramatic structure, and to accord priority to the invention of characters over the invention of plots. Arthur Murphy asserts that"Fable is but a secondary Beauty; the Exhibition of Character, and the Excitement of the Passions, justly claiming the Precedence in dramatic Poetry." William Duff concurs:"The invention of characters... is unquestionably the greatest effort of original Genius." Since Shakespeare was the acknowledged master of characterization, his recourse to preexisting stories could be conveniently downplayed and his originality upheld:"If Shakespeare therefore excelled in the last more difficult effort of Genius, he might doubtless have excelled in the first, if he had thought it proper to have attempted it." There was a fair amount of rhetorical ingenuity, even outright contradiction, involved in such arguments. For one thing, Shakespeare's near-verbatim transcription of some of his sources was common knowledge.

For another, the hankering after absolute originality could neither be allayed nor fully satisfied by the claim that he invented"original" characters but inserted them into"unoriginal" plots. As Duff himself admits,"A Poet endued with a truly original Genius, will... be under no necessity of drawing any of the materials of his composition from the Works of preceding Bards" Granted that by mid-eighteenth century"truly original" composition was held up as an ideal, contemporary playwrights need not have suffered debilitating anxiety of influence on account of Shakespeare. On the contrary, they could draw comfort from the example of a universally acclaimed modern genius who was also a wide-ranging appropriator.

Moreover, within the framework of the contemporary dramatic poetics, some materials were less objectionable than others. That is to say, though one's credentials as an original writer could be in jeopardy if specific textual debts had been incurred, historical sources were routinely accepted as legitimate foundations for plays."The most celebrated characters of all ages and nations," wrote Thomas Wilkes,"the most remarkable events lie open to the creative genius of the dramatic poet, under whose hands they rise to light, with additional luster of strong fancy, and harmonious numbers to embellish them". William Duff, too, conceded that:

A Poet possessed of the most sublime and extensive original Genius, finding either in the records of history, the traditions of his country, or the events of his own times incidents great and surprising enough to captivate the imagination, will sometimes rest satisfied with these (without giving himself the trouble to invent others), and think only of displaying them to the utmost advantage in poetry. This tolerance of the use of historical sources led to a paradoxical situation, for tragedy-a form at once more dignified and more challenging than comedy-- was also one in which originality was easier to come by.

There were many reasons why eighteenth-century playwrights selected historical subject matter for representation in their tragedies-to address the political concerns of the day, to glorify the native past, or to cater to the audience's interest in far-off lands and climes stimulated by the British empire's expansion yet the dramatists were also keen to capitalize on the wealth of characters and storylines that could be gleaned from native or foreign history in the knowledge that the genre of historical tragedy held out the prospect of gaining credit for invention and originality.

Foreign pasts were more promising in this respect than native lore. One could score points simply by choosing unfamiliar historical setting and story. The novelty then could be underscored through a contrast with the overworked Greek and Roman themes. The Prologue to Young's Busiris reminds the audience of the stale wares with which they have been treated of late-"Long have you seen the Greek and Roman Name, / Assisted by the Muse, renew their Fame"-so as to alert them to the freshness of the Egyptian tale about to unfold:"Yet ne'er has Albion's Scene, though long renown'd, / With the stem Tyrants of the Nile been crown'd." Young's pretensions were instantly mocked by an anonymous pamphleteer: "notwithstanding what the Prologue says, he had better contented himself with the Heroes of Greece and Rome, than to have travelled to Egypt to form a greater Monster than the Nile produced". Even so, later dramatists were not deterred from experimenting with a variety of remote settings, the comparison between exotic and classical history itself soon becoming a cliché. John Home's Prologue to Alexander Dow's Zingis (1769) ("taken from the Tarich Mogulistan, or History of the Mogul Tartars") and Arthur Murphy's Prologue to his own Alzuma (1773) (based on"the history of the Spanish conquests in AMERICA") are typical of this trend. Following the predictable jibe at classical tragedy-"Too much the Greek and Roman chiefs engage / The Muses care,-they languish on our Stage," Home extolls Dow's creative acumen evident in his dramatization of Tartar history.

To fill the scene, to night our Author brings
Originals at least,-warriors and kings--
Heroes, who like their gems, unpolish'd shine,
The mighty fathers of the Tartar line;
Greater than those, whom Classic pages boast,
If those are greatest, who have conquer'd most.

Bensley's Prologue to Murphy's Alzuma is written in the same formula:"While GREECE and ROME swell'd our theatric state... only classic heroes could be great. / This night our author, an advent'er grown, / Dares trace the virtues of the Torrid Zone".

The exoticism of later eighteenth-century historical drama, a genre predicated on the assumption that"the intermixture of recorded facts tends to augment the interest of works of imagination, provoked a reaction in favour of English themes. Joseph Warton's wish"that our writers would more frequently search for subjects, in the annals of England, which afford many striking and pathetic events, proper for the stage,"61 did not go unheeded. Indeed, as James Lynch has pointed out,"more plays using themes and characters drawn from English history reached the stage during the eighteenth century than ever before or since". In the last quarter of the century, this quasi-antiquarian preoccupation with the native past, especially with the medieval period, received a strong boost from the rising tide of gothic romance, resulting in a proliferation of fake histories permeated by an atmosphere of doom, gloom, and foreboding.

The historical inauthenticity of gothic plays was in large measure a function of their obsessive concentration on the highly wrought personal relationships among a small cast of characters. In this respect, gothic drama looks back to domestic tragedies of Rowe and Lillo rather than to historical plays of Shakespeare. As a new form, gothic drama might have afforded late eighteenth-century playwrights greater scope for the exercise of invention and originality than the established genres, however formulaic its conventions may seem to us.63 Yet, as the production history of Hannah Cowley's Albina, Countess Raimond demonstrates, the author's"original" ideas could be, as it were, intercepted and put into circulation in others'scripts even before the play from which they were taken reached the stage.

Albina's theatrical misfortunes are quickly told. Cowley showed her script-then called Edwina-to Garrick before his retirement and later attempted to secure production first at Covent Garden then at Drury Lane. After a protracted wait, Cowley had her play rejected in turn by the colluding managers of both winter houses, Harris and Sheridan. Albina was finally produced in July, 1779, by George Colman the Younger at the Haymarket Theater where it proved a moderate success. There is nothing extraordinary in an author's failing to get a script accepted by either of the patent houses and having to settle for a showing at the Haymarket, many would-be playwrights despairing of performance even at that venue. The case of Cowley's Albina is of special interest, for it throws into sharp relief the conflict between the playwright's aspirations to individuality and originality and the material conditions of theater production-- the process of script acceptance, revision, and rehearsal-which fostered conformity, collaboration, and ultimately the surrender of authority on the part of the playwright.

At the Crossroads: Gendered Desire, Political Occasion, and Dryden and Lee's Oedipus

Let me begin with three common observations about the 1678 Oedipus of Dryden and Lee. First, more than their predecessor versions by Sophocles, Seneca, and Corneille, the Restoration playwrights emphasize the erotic nature of the incestuous relationship between Oedipus and Jocasta.1 Second, Creon is transformed from the relatively ambitionless playboy prince of Sophocles'original to the physically and morally twisted precipitator of the crisis, analogous to"the figure of Shaftesbury seen through royalist eyes and representations". Third, as the previous suggests, Dryden and Lee's play, while offering no strict allegory, has relevance to contemporary events-the Popish Plot and the gathering Exclusion Crisis-not least in that, with its added subplot, their version focuses more than others on issues of legitimacy and succession.

My focus here is the link between the first observation-the exaggerated eroticism of the play-and the others, a link that exists since a patriarchal, monarchical society transmits its power and property through the body of a woman. That eroticism has usually been attributed to Lee's tendencies toward the sensationalistic, by contrast to Dryden's judicial and metaphysical emphases.4 Insofar as that may be true, and I will severely qualify its applicability, I would argue that in the collaboration, especially in the depiction of Jocasta, if these are Lee's means, they nevertheless serve-in a complex way-Dryden's ends. We should begin by placing the composition of Dryden and Lee's Oedipus in its historical context. Max Novak has written that in 1678"the political theater of the Popish Plot had distracted theatergoers from the beauties of the legitimate stage". The Popish Plot, of course, was a series of alleged Catholic-backed plots that involved the planned assassination of Charles II by Jesuits, the installation of James on the throne, and a Catholic invasion. The Earl of Shaftesbury led the Whigs in exploiting the supposed danger by pressing for the exclusion of James from the succession and the legitimization of the Duke of Monmouth, Charles's bastard-and Protestant-son. The larger issue, of course, was a Parliamentary struggle to reverse the flow of power, to restructure both constitutional laws and historic notions of kingship, which was accomplished, finally, with the Glorious Revolution.

But Novak's term the"legitimate stage" posits a drama untainted by politics-arguably untrue of all theater, as indeed of all art. A most explicitly political work is Dryden's own Absalom and Achitophel, published in 1681during Shaftesbury's trial, the climax of the"Plot." Dryden first published it anonymously-a transparent attempt at distancing himself from his argument, but an attempt all the same. The relation of Oedipus to contemporary events is more oblique. In choosing to adapt so well known a play, Dryden and Lee could do implicitly what Dryden later did explicitly in the later political crisis, the Glorious Revolution, when he claimed, somewhat disingenuously, that his plays were not political commentaries but"plain stories". Dramatically, the collaborators would wait until 1683, with The Duke of Guise and its"Vindication," to make contemporary relevance more plain. Yet Oedipus does have at least broad relevance to the Popish Plot in that guilt is unexpectedly uncovered and innocence falsely accused. (It may be telling, too, that Dryden's next play, Troilus and Cressida [1679], is subtitled The Truth Found Too Late.)

Since Dryden, according to his own declaration, composed the whole design of Oedípus as well as writing Acts I and III, it is worthwhile to review his personal involvement in contemporary events. In 1681, he claimed that he had"seen through" the Plot from the start. Be that as it may, as early as 1677, Dryden would have been aware and personally concerned with its developing implications. He would have followed the marriage of William of Orange to Mary, with its potential repercussions to adherents of James II, and in the dedication of All for Love he attacks Shaftesbury and Buckingham, asserts that"subverters of Governments" are no friends to the arts and equates Shaftesbury with Satan-a strategy he would return to in Absalom and Achitophel. In 1673, enemies had damned one of Dryden's plays as a"Catholic intrigue"; and in 1676 Catholic mass was said illegally only steps from Dryden's home.

An actor who might have expected to participate in Oedipus, Matthew Medbourne, a Roman Catholic, was committed to Newgate on Titus Oates's testimony and died there in March"Commentary to Oedipus"). Dryden's brother-in-law Charles, second Earl of Berkshire, who had written compromising letters to a"conspirator," fled to France in 1678 and died there in 1679. Also in 1679, Dryden himself was beaten senseless with cudgels by three thugs, in all probability for a"lampoon" touching upon some members of the Opposition-which he had not even authored.

And certain specific passages in Oedipus's apparatus do indicate Dryden's orientation to the issues raised by the plot. In the prologue, for example, he urges that audiences not"pell-mell to damning fall, / Like true born Brittains who ne'er think at all" and, more pointedly, warns against headlong, potentially disastrous commitment to action, like William of Orange's assault on Mons relevant since England was close to being drawn into a war with France and Holland, with Shaftesbury arguing strenuously for a war Charles opposed. The prologue closes with a similar caution against the"private spirit" of"Fanaticks", that"numerous Host of dreaming Saints" Dryden describes in Absalom and Achitophel as joining with the Whigs in pressing for the exclusion of James. Similarly, the epilogue tells audiences,"We know not what you can desire or hope, / To please you more, but burning of a Pope". Odai Johnson describes the Pope-Burning Pageants between 1673 and 1682 as"Whig theater that sought by performative strategies to politicize the crowd as a stable subject of the Whig Party a propagandized extension of the Whig party". Dryden's strategy too is to camouflage politics in aesthetics, but that is a gauzy tactic when aesthetic matters are political matters and, in the 1670s, 80s, and 90s, dovetail with religious and metaphysical matters-a point to which I will return later. Let us turn now to examine two of the broader analogues between politics and play: the representation of the Theban citizenry and of Creon. In Sophocles and in Seneca, the Theban chorus are almost unshakably loyal to their king.

In Sophocles, at the peak of Oedipus's paranoiac rage against Creon, the Chorus only tells him"Sir, I have said before and I say again-be sure that I would have been proved a madman, bankrupt in sane council, if I should put you away"6 Even after the truth of parricide and incest is revealed, the chorus's response is more empathie than condemnatory:"To speak directly, I drew my breath / from you at the first, and so now I lull / my mouth to sleep with your name". In Dryden and Lee's play, the citizenry is portrayed quite differently. They are a"people prone, as in all general ills / To sudden change", like the"headstrong race" of the Jews (English) in Absalom and Achitophel.

When Tiresias chides them for"Rebellion" and reminds them of their oath of loyalty to Oedipus, one citizen grumbles,"This is true; but it's a hard World Neighbors, if a mans Oath must be his master". As Oedipus has become king of Thebes"By publick voice elected", so in Absalom and Achitophel the citizenry whose"Humour more than Loyalty exprest, / Now, wondered why, so long, they had obey'd / An Idoll Monarch which their hands had made". Their characterization, with the characterization of the English in the prologue and epilogue, reminds us that the propagandized posturing surrounding the Popish Plot was"responsible for the creation of a popular political entity outside the court-the crowd-not as a subject produced by the monarch (the rabble), but as participants of the Whig party a construct of the Whigs designed to publicly demonstrate against the king the City of London's popular support of Exclusion" The head of the drive toward Exclusion is Shaftesbury in history, Creon in the play, and Achitophel in the poem.

As Shaftesbury's ostensible opposition was to the succession of Charles's brother James, so Creon initially and necessarily opposes not the king himself, but Oedipus's likely successor, his"step-daughter," Eurydice, who resists marriage to Creon, which would make him the next king of Thebes. Novak considers the representation in Creon of"the figure of Shaftesbury seen though royalist eyes and representations" Dryden and Lee's"crucial" alteration of their sources. In Act I, Creon describes his deformity thus:

Am I to blame if Nature threw my body
In so perverse a could? Yet when she cast
Her envious hand upon my supple joints,
Unable to resist, and rumpled'em
On heaps in their dark lodging, to revenge
Her bungled work she stamped my mind more fair:
As for Chaos, huddled and deformed,
The God strake fire, and lighted up the Lamps
That beautify the sky, so he informed
This ill-shaped body with a daring soul:
And making less than man, he made me more. (1.1.145-55) This passage certainly forecasts Dryden's description in Absalom and Achitophel of Shaftesbury's"huddled Notions," his"Pigmy Body" reproduced in his son,"born a shapeless lump, like Anarchy". Creon, of course, aims to rule himself, and Dryden makes the same accusation against Achitophel,"Resolved to Ruin or to Rule the State". The most interesting parallel between Creon and Achitophel extends the emphasis upon those characters'twisted bodies. Creon admits"My body opens inward to my soul, /And lets in day to make my Vices seen / By all discerning eyes, but the blind vulgar", so Creon's ambition is not really a compensation for

his deformity, but an extension of it. Likewise, in his relentless plotting, Achitophel"Punished a Body which he [can] not please". Creon's frustration manifests itself in misogynist statements like this:

These Women are such cunning Purveyors!
Mark where their Appetites have once been pleased,
The same resemblance in a younger Lover
Lyes brooding in their Fancies the same Pleasures,
And urges their remembrance to desire. (1.1.66-70)

Or this:"That thoughtless Sex is caught by outward form / And empty noise, and loves it self in man". Achitophel is likewise misogynistic, arguing that Charles"By Force wishes to be gained, like women's Lechery". Where Creon plans to take Eurydice by blackmail or force, and afterwards to discard her, Achitophel urges Absalom to"commit a pleasing rape upon the Crown". Charles's petitioners are"Unsatiate as the barren Womb or Grave". In the villains of both Oedipus and Absalom and Achitophel, sexuality is either debased, sterile, or brutal. Problematized representations of sexuality, however, are certainly not limited to the villains-not in this play-which leads us to consider Dryden and Lee's depiction of Oedipus himself and, especially, Jocasta. Specifically, I want to emphasize two points: first, Dryden's contributions in Acts I and III and the whole"design" accentuate the psycho-sexual complexities especially apparent in this version of the Oedipus story as much as, if not more than Lee's; second, these complexities, too, are particularly relevant to the political context of the collaboration.

There is a tremendous emphasis on carnality, even animality, from the outset of play. Act I.i, written by Dryden, insists on the drive-often brutal-toward sex and procreation. Alcander recommends that Oedipus (absent)"bring the Wives and Children / of conquer'd Argians to renew his Thebes". Creon says Jocasta remarried in haste since she"Fear'd to lye single", and he attempts to seduce Eurydice"For when the Gods destroy so fast,'tis time/ We should renew the Race" even"in the midst of horrour". Eurydice retorts by describing Creon's monstrous birth, at which"The Midwife stood aghast And knew not, if to burn thee in the flames / Were not the holier work", calling him only fit to mate with monsters like himself. Further, Act I introduces two occasions for incest, not one: the consummated incest of Oedipus and Jocasta, mother-son incest; and the potential, though ultimately unperformed, incest between Creon and Eurydice, uncle-niece incest. Likewise, there are two triangles: Oedipus/Lajus/Jocastaand Creon/Adrastus/Eurydice. The obvious difference is that Creon's rival is not his kin, whereas Oedipus's is. Oedipal incest, of course, involves the replacement of father with son; or, to put it another way, the son, in seeking to displace and replace his sire, to some degree becomes his sire, becomes husband/father. Thus, the Oedipal version of parricide and incest conflates identification and difference; they meet at the crossroads, if you will.

Dryden represents this meeting, the doubled nature of the incestuous desire, in two early and crucial rhetorical moments: the plague and its consequent meteorological manifestations is described in a figure that would seem to conflate Oedipus with Lajus, and Oedipus's earlier career with his ultimate fate:"Blind Winter meets the Summer / In his Midway, and seeing not his livery, / Has driven him headlong back". Let me unpack these lines. Every one of the spectators, and each of us readers, though not the characters at this moment, would recognize in the passage the image of Oedipus driving Lajus back at the crossroads, not having recognized his"Livery"-that is, his status as king and father (positions analogous in the contemporary, though embattled, political theory of Dryden's time). It is not going too far to see in Oedipus's and Lajus's jostling for primacy to pass through the"narrow way", the"verge" (perhaps recalled in the famous line Lee gives Oedipus at his moment of discovery:"Gods meet Gods, and justle in the dark! the contest for primacy in the passage to Jocasta's womb. As Jeffrey Rusten has detailed,"the juncture of three roads (double into single) figures the female genital region"; the Greek word that designates"crossroads" is etymologically closely related to the word for"crack," defined as"the vulva" in Rufus of Ephesus On Medical Terminology, and Rüsten traces such associations in, for instance, Aristophanes's Wasps. Thus, Rusten concludes,"the crossroads may double as a designation for sexual territory, territory that is simultaneously the threshold of emergence into life and of accession to political power. That a woman's body may become the terrain of sexual and generational rivalry is especially overt in the case of Jocasta".

This initial impression of how the lines mean, however, is complicated, in that the Oedipal figure is"Blind," a forecast, also easily recognizable, of Oedipus's literal blindness to come. Essentially, the figure overlays the image of Oedipus in the play's past (at the crossroads) with the image of Oedipus in the play's future (blinded). And this rhetorical palimpsest goes further in that Oedipus, the youthful son, would here be"Blind Winter" (my emphasis), while the older Lajus would be"Summer." A later image similarly conflates Oedipus with Lajus, particularly in the attribution of blindness, not to the young but to the old. Oedipus sees an omen:

A young Stork,
That bore his aged Parent on his back;
Till weary with the weight, he shook him off,
And peck'd out both his eyes. (3.1.384-87)

The effect of such complex figures (Dryden's, I would remind us) is to hint at the problematic identification/ difference paradox at the heart of the Oedipal crisis.The second rhetorical moment I think crucial will position Jocasta at the Oedipus/Lajus juncture, and this moment involves Creon's theorizing with his supporters about feminine desire:

More straightforwardly than the previous passage, these lines stress the identification of Lajus and Oedipus and particularly injocasta's perception, wherein"remembrance" is confused with"desire." But they also hint at the association of female sexual desire with narcissism, another version of the confusion of other with self, which Creon makes clearer in his reading of Eurydice's desire for Adrastus:"That thoughtless Sex is caught by outward form / And empty noise, and loves itself in man". In Act III, when Eurydice is condemned (since the murderer is supposed to be"the first of Lajus'blood" and

Oedipus's paternity is not yet known), Creon's description of what death will bring further emphasizes what he sees as female narcissism. Eurydice's spirit will enter

What is notable here is that while the"object of desire" in these lines is Eurydice's body and those who desire it in the play are Creon and Adrastus, this image makes the one desiring as well as the desired Eurydice herself. She is agent and object; female eroticism, here even after death, is auto-eroticism. My point in all of this is to suggest that the insistent identification/difference trope in relation to Oedipus and Lajus-their permeability, or interchangeability-ultimately impacts on Jocasta, as does the issue of narcissism, the latter as Jocasta, not Eurydice, is the primary object of the play's examination of female desire, and thus even utterances not about her per se accrue to her characterization. More than other versions, Dryden and Lee's play obsessively returns to the question, as a colleague of mine phrased it,"What does Jocasta know, when did she know it, and what has she been telling herself all these years?"

For in Dryden and Lee's version, Jocasta's culpability is certainly more at issue than in Sophocles, Seneca, or Corneille, and more likely to be condemned than Oedipus's own. In his preface, Dryden, claiming that ne follows Sophocles's example, takes Corneille's version to task particularly for"miserably failing in the Character of his Hero": if he desir'd that Oedipus should be pitied, he shou'd have made him a better man. He forgot that Sophocles had taken care to shew him in his first entrance, a just, a merciful, a successful, a Religious Prince, and in short, a Father of his Country: instead of these, he has drawn him suspicious, designing, more anxious of keeping the Theban Crown, than solicitous for the safety of his People: Hector'd by Theseus, contem'd by Dirce, and scarce maintaining a second part in his own Tragedie.

Dryden's self-proclaimed faithfulness to Sophocles's conception of Oedipus's character is not dogged, however. Whereas Sophocles's Oedipus is groundlessly hostile toward Creon, Dryden's Creon is groundlessly hostile toward his Oedipus. In so reversing the flow, Dryden diverts at least part of the culpability of his hero toward his villain and his cronies, who busy themselves in attempts to destroy all of the major admirable characters in both plots, which, Novak feels, makes Oedipus's tardiness in solving the mystery of his birth more plausible ("Commentary to Oedipus" 459-60). Dryden further mitigates the guilt that might accrue to his hero for the sins he does commit in all versions (murder and incest) by including the ghost of Lajus. Dryden provides Lajus with a warning before the birth of Oedipus. Lajus says the gods.

In providing this detail, Dryden allots some of the guilt to Lajus by his own admission and reinscribes Oedipus's virtuous nature and his victim hood. In fact, Dryden later wondered if he had made Oedipus"too good a man".

The guilt, then, is partly extenuated in relation to Oedipus, but, I would argue, exacerbated in relation to Jocasta. At her first entrance, Jocasta's wish that Heaven"bring the effects of these [Oedipus's] pious prayers / On you, and me, and all" is ill-timed as Oedipus has been cursing the murderer of Lajus, and his"Unkind" rebuke to her evokes this, the first of many explicit references to their incest (not to be found in sources). Such lines may be thought to work paradoxically. They keep the horror and revulsion toward their incest that the characters will have to admit in the forefront of our reckoning of their guilt; yet they suggest that Oedipus's and Jocasta's actions are, in fact, unwitting and thus-insofar as that matters to us-innocent. For why should the remarks on physical likeness and the incestuous rhetorical figures be so glibly and publicly given voice by the couple and their enemies if the implications of these were consciously recognized?

But insofar as this is how these lines work, they work less efficiently in term of Jocasta, since immediately after this exchange Jocasta sues that Oedipus allow the marriage of Creon and Eurydice. Oedipus, at least, sees the uncle/niece union as incestuous and forbids even mention of it ("I know not why, it shakes me / When I but think on Incest", to which Jocasta reluctantly agrees. Jocasta's understanding of the prohibition against incest is, at least in the case of Creon and Eurydice, more elastic than that of her husband. Moreover, since, I have argued, the moral and psychological valence of Eurydice also impacts upon Jocasta as the play's major representative of female desire (and"like mother, like daughter"), it is relevant that Eurydice does not seem to consider a union with Creon incestuous, only unwelcome-she never raises the issue of kinship in her rejections of him. We might also note that in the passage above, despite the problematic terms, Oedipus characterizes his love for Jocasta as"pious," she characterizes hers as"tender" and speaks of his being"in [her] arms." More of the implications of forbidden desire accrue to Jocasta than to her husband. We might pause for a moment to consider that Eurydice was promised to Creon by Jocasta early, when her daughter was"at Nurse" and that after Lajus's death Jocasta"Fear'd to lye single."

The latter suggests a voracious female sexual appetite combined with timidity at being alone, but also latent in these details is the matter of the succession to the throne of Thebes. Creon and his followers seem to assume that if Jocasta had remained unmarried, Creon would have ascended to the throne after Lajus's death. As Diocles remarks,"Had merit, not her dotage, been consider'd, / Then Creon had been King". The implication is that Jocasta, unmarried, would not have been permitted to rule alone; her power would have been effaced. Under these circumstances, one motive for the hasty marriage to Oedipus, then, may have been the preservation of Jocasta's position as queen.

It is instructive to remember that up to Dryden and Lee's day, with the exceptions of Elizabeth I and"Bloody" Mary I, all British monarchs had been male. The cultural moment for a female monarch would not arrive until Mary II (and the operative monarch, her husband, William III) and following her, Ann, in 1685 and 1702, respectively. If in the details of the Restoration Oedipus we choose to ascribe such a motive to Jocasta-the preservation of female monarchical power-the response to such a motive during Dryden and Lee's day would likely have been negative. From politically based suspicion to visceral horror is but a short step in this play, and Lee takes it immediately in opening Act II with prodigies:"blood on the moon" and gigantic figures of Oedipus and Jocasta against the sky. While the other spectators comment on the astronomical manifestations as astronomical (shooting stars, comets, lightning and so on), Oedipus sees a monstrous birth, one in which he will assist:

Ha! My Jocasta', look! The Silver Moon!
A selling Crimson stains her beauteous Face!
She's all o're Blood! And look, behold again,
What mean the mistick Heav'ns, she journeyes on?
A bast Eclipse darkens the labouring Planet.
Sound there, sound all our Instruments of War;
Clarions and Trumpets, Silver, Brass, and Iron,
And beat a thousand Drums to help her Labour.

The monstrous birth recalls, of course, Oedipus's own and the"birth" to come of his recognizing his true identity. He offers his life as a sacrifice to the angry gods, but when Jocasta enters and the prodigies vanish, he retreats into erotic (and, he insists, innocent) imaginings:

Yes, I will dye, O Thebes, to save thee!
Draw from my heart my blood, with more content
Than e're I wore the Crown. Yet, O Jocasta
By all the indearments of miraculous love,
By all our languishings, our fears in pleasure,
Which oft have made us wonder; here I swear
On thy fair hand, upon thy breast I swear,
I cannot call to mind, from budding Childhood
To blooming youth, a Crime by me committed,
For which the awful Gods should doom my death.

What is interesting about this is that in the midst of denying criminality, Oedipus mentions misgivings about sexual pleasure and attributes these to Jocasta as well as himself. Jocasta takes the opportunity to sooth Oedipus's fears and proclaim his and her own innocence; her"perhaps" is notable:"Were you, which is impossible, the man, / Perhaps my Ponyard first should drink your blood; / But you are innocent, as jour Jocasta". Oedipus, however, elaborates on his habitual aversion to (as well as attraction to) sexual intercourse with Jocasta after sending her reluctantly to bed:

Nay, she is beauteous too; yet, mighty Love!
I never offer'd to obey thy Laws,
But an unusual chillness came upon me;
An unknown hand still check'd my forward joy,
Dashed me with blushes, tho'no light was near:
That ev'n the Act became a violation.

In the next scene, Oedipus is seen sleepwalking, dreaming that the Jocasta he approaches in bed is his supposed mother, Merope, and that he has killed his supposed father, Polybus, two acts whose criminality he clearly ranks:

Yet what most shocks the niceness of my temper,
Even far beyond the killing of my Father,
And my own death, is, that this horrid sleep
Dashed my sick fancy with an act of Incest:
I dreamt, Jocasta, that thou were my Mother

Jocasta's response is interesting. Essentially, she accuses Oedipus of loathing her ill-timed, distracting, and"vile" sexual appetite; and her effect is to determine Oedipus to"act [his] joys".

In the next Act, Dryden elaborates a hint in Sophocles to damning affect. As in Sophocles, Jocasta attempts to counter mounting evidence by discounting prophecies, but the brevity, the peremptoriness of her responses to Oedipus's anguished questions is striking. To the rumor that Oedipus was not Polypus's son, she says only"T'was somewhat odd"; to the Delphic prophecy of parricide and incest,"Vain, vain oracles"; to Oedipus's determination to avoid these, only"Too nice a fear". (Notably, Jocasta's later discounting of oracles has something of a feminist cast, when she says"If we must pray / Let Virgin hands adorn the Sacrifice; / And not a gray-beard forging Priest come near. It does not help that Jocasta has just emphasized to Oedipus his suspicious physical resemblance to Lajus:

JOCASTA: bate but his years, You are his picture
OEDIPUS aside: Pray Heaven he drew me not!-Am I his picture?
JOCASTA: So I have often told you.
OEDIPUS: True, you have (3.1.537-540)

We may add to this Jocasta's extreme reluctance to produce Forbes, the shepherd who was supposed to murder the infant Oedipus. Jocasta recognizes the truth about the murder and marriage even before Forbes is, finally, produced and, having recognized it, seeks to dissuade Oedipus from questioning him-presumably she would continue in the incestuous relationship if her son remained ignorant of its true nature. Or is recognition not so much of the truth as it is recognition of the imminence of exposure of a fact she has suspected or even known all long? The play maintains ambiguity, but the weight of evidence in Dryden and Lee's version allows, perhaps even impels spectators and readers to suspect the latter. In fact, looked at this way, the motto for Oedipus's and Jocasta's relationship may be found in his line to her,"O, thou wilt kill me with thy Love's excess!".

"Thy Love's excess"-the lines return us from what Jocasta knew to what Jocasta is: a woman. I have already argued in relation to Eurydice that other characters'psychological/moral valence accrues to Jocasta as she is the play's primary study of female desire; now I would like to reverse the flow and suggest that jocasta's psychological/moral valence accrues to other characters-to begin with, to Oedipus's supposed mother, Merope. When the news arrives that Polypus has died of natural causes, Oedipus's consideration of his supposed mother's widowhood undergoes an extreme shift:

AEGEAN: Your Royal Mother Merope, as if She had no Soul since you forsook the Land, Waves all the neighboring Princes that adore her.

OEDIPUS: Waves all the Princes! Poor heart! For what? O speak. AEGEAN: She, tho'in full-blown flower of glorious beauty, Grows cold, even in the Summer of her Age: And, for your sake, has sworn to dye unmerry.

OEDIPUS: How! For my sake, dye, and not marry! O My fit returns.

AEGEAN: This Diamond, with a thousand kisses blest, With thousand sighs and wishes for your safety, She charged me give you, with the general homage Of our Corinthian Lords.

OEDIPUS: There's Magic in it, take it from my sight; There's not a beam it darts, but carried Hell, hot flashing lust, and Necromantick Incest: Take it from these sick eyes, Oh hide it from me.

As we recognize, and as Oedipus is informed, Merope is not his mother and thus not guilty of"Necromantick Incest," but the emphasis on her languishing, on her desirability, on her"thousand kisses" all make the charge of"hot lust" at least momentarily plausible and add to the play's depiction of the insatiability and transgressiveness of female sexuality. We also hear that Merope has"had no Soul," which leads us to consider the play's handling of the laws of Heaven versus the appetites of Earth, or, In another formulation, the Apollonian versus the Dionysian, the latter term of both formulations being identified as female.

In Tiresias's oracular terms, Heaven"sees" while Earth births:"Then hear me Heaven, / For blushing thou hast seen it: hear me Earth, /Whose hollow womb cou'd not contain this murder". Accordingly, the ceremony in the grove that brings Oedipus's guilt to light is earthbound, performed in a trench, rather than at an altar; the sacrifice involves a"barren Heyfer," who, when opened in Seneca"proves to contain a fetus even though it is unmated allegorically representing the incestuous issue of Oedipus and Jocasta"; the grove is dedicated to the furies, violent female deities transformed and demoted by the Olympian Apollo in TheEunpides. Oedipus, one might say, seeks to ally himself with law and with heaven against these feminized forces, to deny them in himself. In Act I, considering the plague and the murder of Lajus, he rails at the Corinthian crowd: Novak explains that this is partly because Thebes was the birthplace and a cult centre of Dionysus, a god of the earth and underworld. Oedipus supposes himself of Corinth, whose principle cultwas that of Olympian Aphrodite. The opposition between underworld and Olympian deities recurs in Oedipus'.

Novak further, in commenting on Jocasta's murder of all her children ("swift and wild, / As a robb'd Tygress bounding o're the Woods), points out that Dryden and Lee may have in mind Seneca's Oedipus,"where Jocasta's final entrance is marked by likening her to another Theban matron, Agave, who killed her son in a frenzy..., and did so on the wooded slopes of Mount Cithaeron, where she and her fellow Bacchants roamed with and like animals. After the discovery, Oedipus vacillates between cursing Jocasta as"thou far worse than worst / of damning Charmers" and yearning toward her:

For her part, Jocasta alternates between deferring to Lajus's prohibitive ghost and attempting to"fright" the Gods and reclaim her husband (whom she alternately imagines as Oedipus and Lajus). Oedipus wishes for sight to see her"mouth the Heav'ns, and mate the Gods...". Novak glosses"mouth" as"declaim against" and"mate""in the sense of rival or vie with, especially presumed superiors". I would add that the phrase keeps intact Jocasta's defiance of Apollonian law and her voracious sexuality. And, if Dryden and Lee had contemplated writing a sequel, the suicides of Oedipus and Jocasta and the murders of the rest of the royal family would have made impossible an Antigone, in which the Apollonian laws are upheld by a woman.

Novak and others have pointed out Dryden's making Oedipus"too good a man" may have stemmed from his acceptance of certain principles of Thomas Rymer: We are to presume the greatest vertues, where we find the highest of rewards; and though it is not necessary that all Heroes should be Kings, yet undoubtedly all crown'd heads by Poetical right are Heroes. This Character is a flower, a prerogative, so certain, so inseparably annex'd to the Crown, as by no Poet, no Parliament of Poets, ever to be invaded,". Hence, the problem Oedipus would pose for a Restoration playwright: Oedipus both kills a king and is a king; he commits parricide and incest but must be a"Heroe." And it is a truism by now that political theory during the Restoration (and modern literary criticism-particularly New Historicism) exploits the analogies of state and family, of father and king. At the time Dryden and Lee were writing, moreover, contemporary political theory as well as the brute facts of government and power were in crisis. In relation to Absalom and Achitophel, Susan Greenfield explains,

Political theorists assume that discourses about the body and state overlap, and they recognize that any representation of conception is thus a political act. This sense of integration was obviously influenced by their own system of government, figured in the body of a ruler who passed his power through genetic descent. At the same time, though, recent historical events-most importantly the execution of Charles I-had proved that the royal succession could be broken. The classic seventeenth-century patriarchalism that linked monarchal and paternal creative power would not endure.

Richard A. McCabe has discussed the relevance of incest to such embattled political theorizing in his Incest, Drama and Nature's Law: 1550-1700:"Perversions in the sexual politics of the family provide ready analogies for corruptions in the power politics of the state or the ideological politics of church and academy". J. Douglas Canfield is more specific: The majority of Restoration political tragedies polemically defend Stuart monarchial theory of hereditary succession, especially at the time of the most severe political crisis of the era, 1678-88, from the Popish Plot through the Exclusion Crisis to the Glorious Revolution. A handful of plays offer a counter ideology-or at least expose the fatal Oedipal crisis lurking at the heart of monarchial ideology.

Given the dilemma inherent in the Oedipus story they had inherited and given Dryden's (at least) staunch royalist convictions, Dryden and Lee could do neither one of these, exactly. The uneasy nature of what they did do has been largely explained by commentators insisting on the strict division of labour, forte, and intention between Dryden and Lee. McCabe, for instance, says that"Dryden is intent upon the tragedy of fate Lee upon a tragedy of desire":

Lee was interested in the psychological Oedipus, Dryden in the political, in the virtuous"Father of his Country" overcome by circumstance, and his part of the play duly reflects the moral and political confusion of the age through the strategy of oblique allusion at which he excelled In this play, if anywhere, Dryden evokes something of Sir Robert Filmer's atavistic respect for the king as patriarch. So, according to McCabe, Lee's additions"[undermine] Dryden's insistence upon [Oedipus's] purity of motive in wedding Jocasta". But, as my analysis of the play has shown, Dryden's parts too question"purity of motive"; Dryden too is interested in the"tragedy of desire" and the"psychological Oedipus." There is more coherence in the two playwrights'efforts than divisionary analyses suggest.

Moreover, both playwrights are interested in"purity of motive,""desire," and the"psychological" in relation to Jocasta as much as, perhaps even more than, in relation to Oedipus. The role of Jocasta, and by extension the depiction of woman, does much of the cultural work that would be required of royalist playwrights. Greenfield has argued in relation to Absalom and Achitophel that the poem's"emphasis on [David's] promiscuity has been effaced by increasing references to a feminine sexual desire and productivity so dangerous that the king appears reliable by contrast". Jocasta's characterization in Oedipus functions similarly: in deflecting much of the attention, perhaps condemnatory attention to issues of desire and agency as depicted in the female, the playwrights do not excuse Oedipus, who is, when all is said and done, inexcusable; but they do manage to mitigate it as much as possible under the circumstances. As Greenfield concludes in relation to Absalom and Achitophel,

In many respects Dryden at first seems remarkably sensitive to the mothers, reflecting what James Winn has described as his"more than occasion insight into the hard lot of... women." But this insight is, as Winn notes of other works, also balanced by Dryden's tendency to lapse into misogynistic conventions. Ultimately by the end only the standard negative implications about female sexuality persist. As much as I would like to soften this judgment in relation to Dryden and Lee in regard to Oedipus, it seems to me disturbingly true.

Translating difference: The Example of"Dryden's Last Parting of Hector and *Andromache*"

It is one of the ironies of the recent phase of eighteenth-century studies that, within a discipline that has responded so interestingly to new theoretical and new historical ways of reading, emphasizing the discursiveness of institutions and the materiality of historical experiences, the practice of translation-so pervasive a discourse in the period 1660-1800-still remains to be theorized and fully historicized.

For most of the eighteenth century, Dryden's and Pope's translations were regarded as major works; for example, Johnson's lives of Dryden and Pope, while registering the particular shape and temper of each poet's output, also develop an underlying argument as to the preeminent place of translations in their respective poetic oeuvres and in the construction of a national literature. Substantial scholarly work has been done on the trope and the genre of translation in the years 1660-1800, from H. A. Mason's To Homer Through Pope (1972) to Howard Weinbrot's Britannia's Issue: The Rise of British Literature from Dryden to Ossian (1993), yet recent theoretical developments and skepticism of the philosophical and cultural claims of the Enlightenment (and of the concurrent scholarship) seem to have eclipsed the idea of translation as a serious form of writing in the eighteenth century. It is easy to see why this might be so.

When Dryden claims in his various acts of translation to be representing"the spirit which animates the whole" of the original, the suggestion for many is of a privileged and transparent correspondence between the contemporary text and the Classical or other pre-existent authority, embodying (supposedly) an essential and universal claim to cultural authority that is anathema to the discursive and material emphases of postmodernism and new historicism. For John Bender, the sign of such essentialist and universalist qualities in the Enlightenment is an unreflexiveness, a philosophical innocence with regard to the function of language that he sees as recapitulated (until very recently) in criticism of eighteenth-century literature.6 Their frame of reference, according to Bender, was based in the supposition that reason, nature, and truth were accessible to the enlightened individual, thereby assuming an unproblematic and accessible relation between literature and reality, such as Pope might be supposed to reveal when in the"Essay on Criticism" he writes how he discovered Homer and Nature to be the same. If"new," theoretically oriented eighteenth-century scholarship-such as was inaugurated by Felicity Nussbaum and Laura Brown's New Eighteenth Century (1987)-is based on an inextricable interconnectedness between the very categories of politics (including the politics of gender), history, and literature, and if postmodern theories emphasize the function of narrative forms and cultural contexts to question and (indeed) to create the"truths" that were habitually ascribed to the representation of history by eighteenth-century writers, then I wish to suggest that the discourse of translation signifies for the eighteenth century a pure yet paradoxically self-reflexive and luminal form of literary and historical representation.

Gerald MacLean explains that"For political, social and cultural historians, the Restoration constitutes a complex intersection of changing practices and ideas that are central to our understanding of early-modern Britain, and what was to pass for civility in much of the modern world", yet the volume of essays to which this comment is an introduction has no room for translation as a cultural form of great popularity within which a complex, differential notion of historical and material experience is developed as part of eighteenth-century knowledge and civility. By way of investigating the proposition that translation is central to eighteenth-century historiography, that is, to eighteenth-century ways of conceptualizing and rendering history, I shall consider Dryden's pronouncements about translation, concentrating on his version of a passage from the Iliad Bk.VI,"The Last Parting of Hector and Andromache," from Examen Poeticum (1693), the third part of Miscellany Poems published by Jacob Tonson.

I also draw on Pope's and Johnson's versions of the same passage, and briefly place these eighteenth-century translations in the context of our present concerns about language, legitimacy, authority, and history. Dryden's purity is, of course, engagingly and distinctively hybrid-a deliberate and strategic textuality that points towards the liminality of Augustan thinking about the world even while it claims for itself cultural centrality and authority. During the period 1660-1740, translation was a mode of writing par excellence that generated its knowledge through a structural, historical, and philosophical difference in which language was understood as both essential and inessential for the intended effect.

The critical discussion of translation in the seventeenth century (from Johnson to Cowley, Denham, Oldham, Behn, and Rochester), employed neo-Aristotelian, neoclassical ideas of representation to position the translated text between two basically different kinds of relation to the original and in relation to language. These types of translation were what, in the 1680 Preface to Ovid's Epistles, Dryden called meta phrase and imitation. According to Dryden, Ben Jonson's"Ars Poetica" exemplified the first while Cowley's Pindaric Odes the second form. For Dryden, however, both of these methods were unsatisfactory (notwithstanding his great admiration for the poetry of both Cowley and Jonson) because they forced the translator to make an impossible choice between what one might call language or form and spirit or content.

Recent commentators on translation (including George Steiner, Jacques Derrida, and Douglas Robinson) have remarked on the sterility of the traditional dichotomy in translation studies between language and spirit. For Steiner,"Fidelity is not literalism or any technical device for rendering'spirit'. The whole formulation, as we have found it over and over again in discussions of translation, is hopelessly vague." But for Steiner (echoing the rather dogged older versions of Dryden's neoclassical"moderation"), Dryden could not have had his kind of insight.

In Steiner's view,"The whole of Dryden's literary thought aims for the middle ground of common sense.... In regard to translation he sought to trace a via media between the word-for-word approach demanded by purists among divines and grammarians, and the wild idiosyncrasies displayed in Cowley's Pindarique Odes of 1656.... No less than the classic poet, the modern translator must stand at the clear, urbane centre". Samuel Johnson, however, understands Dryden's"common sense" to be vigorously animated by a genius,"that power which constitutes a poet," an"energy which collects, combines, amplifies, and animates," and that informs Dryden's whole poetic oeuvre, including (perhaps especially) the translations. In the Preface to Ovid, Dryden discusses-and demonstrates in his poetry in this and later collections-that metaphrase and imitation, as modes of translation, imply a naive theory of language, and therefore of translation, because both tended to treat English as equivalent to the"original" or source language (whether Latin, Greek, French, Italian, or Middle English): metaphrase by locating meaning in the words of the original, and imitation by locating meaning in the escape from the words of the original text. In the Preface to Sylvae (1685), Dryden conceptualizes the sensitive and successful rendition of the"spirit" of the original in metaphorical terms of the body:"I dare assure them readers that a good poet is no more like himself in a dull translation, than his carcass would be to his living body."

For Dryden, language (the"dress of thought") and spirit were, though clearly not the same, implicit in each other in translation (as they were in all good poetry), and their nexus pointed to a material experience for which the human body (as locus for spirit) was the metaphor. Below I shall discuss the relationship between this idea of Dryden's and a similar argument in Walter Benjamin's important essay,"The Task of the Translator." For the moment, however, I wish to suggest that the notion of translation offered by these quite typical pronouncements of Dryden's is quite other than the traditional (and still usual) understanding of neoclassical ideas of language and form as expressive and timeless.

Dryden's proposition about translation is not in accordance with Steiner's statement that"all translation from the canon, all imitation, restatement, citation is... synchronic", but rather a diachronic (and dialogical) understanding of discourse as constitutive of a reality that is also always outside and other. Dryden's"paraphrase"-the successful and creative mode of translation that he developed in the 1680s, yet a manifestly insufficient critical term for the performativity and historical nuances of his poetry-recognized a discreetness-in-continuity and a structural difference in the relation of languages to cultures in history. Translation for Dryden is the quintessentially differential mode of discourse. On the differential nature of translation, as pertaining to Dryden's practice, John Johnston, discussing Benjamin's"The Task of the Translator," remarks:

Benjamin argues that the difference between languages that translation must somehow necessarily overcome cannot and should not be suppressed, for translation lives on (or in) this difference; a particular translation will be valuable according to how it alludes to or dissimulates this difference, or, more positively, reveals and accentuates it. And it is in this positive sense of difference that we are to gauge an individual work's'translatability.'For Dryden, translation is the medium, above all, of language, and language the medium of history.

Though Dryden might talk, in the Preface to Fables, of translation as the"transfusion" of one poet's spirit into another or in more religio-mythic terms, echoing Milton's"heavenly Muse" and"Spirit" (Paradise Lost I, 6-17), of the spirit from one poet into another-all of his translations, from the Ovidian and Horatian poems of the early 1680s to the complete Virgil and the Fables at the end of his career, explicitly and variously enact the intersections of language and history.

What I have done, imperfect as it is for want of health and leisure to correct it, will be judged in after-ages, and possibly in the present, to be no dishonour to my native country, whose language and poetry would be more esteemed abroad, if they were better understood. Somewhat (give me leave to say) I have added to both of them in the choice of words, and harmony of numbers, which were wanting, especially the last, in all our poets, even in those who, being endued with genius, yet have not cultivated their mother-tongue with sufficient care; or, relying on the beauty of their thoughts, have judged the ornament of words, and sweetness of sound, unnecessary.

Compare this with the following from Milton's"The Reason of Church-Government Urg'd Against Prelaty": I began thus fame to assent both to them [Italian academicians] and divers of my friends here at home, and not lesse to an inward prompting which now grew daily upon me, that by labour and intent study (which I take to be my portion in life) joyn'd with the strong propensity of nature, I might perhaps leave something so written to aftertimes, as they should not willingly let it die.... I apply'd my selfe to that resolution which Ariosto follow'd against the perswasions of Bembo, to fix all the industry and art I could unite to the adorning of my native tongue; not to make verbal curiosities the end, that were a toylsom vanity, but to be an interpreter & relater of the best and sagest things among mine own Citizens throughout this Iland in the mother dialect.

Dryden's understanding of"spirit," in the context of his thinking about translation as a poetic mode, is inseparable from his understanding of history, and his historical consciousness of language enables Dryden to conceptualize his relation to his originals as he does. Those relationships-as articulated in the prefaces to Ovid (1680), Sylvae (1685), Examen Poeticum (1693), the Aeneid (1697), and Fables (1700)-are all rendered as being at once material and spiritual; to wit: Dryden feels an essential connection to the"character" (or the various"characters") of the original poet, as manifested in that poet's verse, and it is on the basis of this connection, as well as the attendant sense of some continuity between himself and the original, that Dryden is able to change his original; Dryden feels penetrated by the character, energy, or fire (he uses various metaphors here) of the original, and it is this penetration that frees Dryden to write poetically and, at the same time, in the way his original poet would have done had he been alive now; Dryden changes his original in order to keep him the same-represents him in what he calls a"double likeness" but at the same time to give him currency at this different, latter-day historical moment; and the English language at this particular historical juncture requires the infusion of the original language in order to fulfill its teleology, its linguistic purpose and national identity, and to become the vehicle for the cultural, political, social, religious, and personal experience that Dryden makes it. It is out of such a nexus of different, contending demands and perspectives-- the otium and negotium of circumstance and language, in Geoffrey Hill's words that Dryden develops his patriarchal and fraternal notion of poetic families (of fathers and sons related to each other, with the occasional daughter, such as Anne Killigrew, thrown in) and of a common human nature (though not necessarily male gendered) that exists through temporal changes and historical differences. As Dryden (famously) expresses his sense of recognizing Chaucer's characters when rendering The Knight's Tale (and others) anew:

We have our forefathers and great-grand-dames all before us, as they were in Chaucer's days: their general characters are still remaining in mankind, and even in England, though they are called by other names than those of Monks, and Friars, and Canons, and Lady Abbesses, and Nuns; for mankind is ever the same, and nothing lost out of nature, though every thing is altered.

The fictive and imagined aspect of these ideas of family and continuity is, as Johnson registers in his discussions of Dryden's prose in the"Life of Dryden," something that Dryden himself implicitly acknowledges in the deliberateness and the metaphoric nature of his critical prose. Paradoxically, this fictiveness enhances rather than diminishes the significance and the experience of commonality in Dryden's writing. For Dryden, commonality is what asks to be translated, and-as for Walter Benjamin-it is in the translatability of the text that its authority lies. But this situation does not prompt Dryden to try to"reproduce" or even to"transform" anything originlly. Rather than terms of verbal fidelity to or verbal freedom from a pre-existing, permanent Classical presence-terms that imply a traditional neoclassical notion of verisimilitude Dryden's notion of translatability engages that aspect of the original text that is transmitted to the present in acts of textual appropriation (sometimes, of expropriation), and it also recognizes and honors those aspects of the original text that are unreachable. Acts of translation"repeat" the original text's difference-the relation (in Benjamin's formulation) between the text's content and language and also identify some aspect of it that (as Derrida argues in explicating Benjamin's essay) seeks survival, that is historically continuous. In fact, Johnson sees such poetic and textual appropriation as a linguistic and historical process indicative of all good translation. In discussing Pope's Iliad (for Johnson, the single greatest translation in the language, and therefore one of the most significant poems of all time), and the central function of translation in Dryden's poetic achievements, Johnson sees the problematics of translation as entailing precisely such play with historical and linguistic differentials:

The chief help of Pope in this arduous undertaking was drawn from the versions of Dryden. Virgil had borrowed much of his imagery from Homer, and part of the debt was now paid by his translator. Pope searched the pages of Dryden for happy combinations of heroic diction, but it will not be denied that he added much to what he found. He cultivated our language with so much diligence and art that he has left in his Homer a treasure of poetical elegance to posterity.... Homer doubtless owes to his translator many Ovidian graces not exactly suitable to his character; but to have added can be no great crime if nothing be taken away.

Elegance is surely to be desired if it be not gained at the expence of dignity. A hero would wish to be loved as well as to be reverenced.... Pope wrote for his own age and his own nation: he knew that it was necessary to colour the images and point the sentiments of his author; he therefore made him graceful, but lost him some of his sublimity. As this passage suggests, the cultural and poetic authority of Homer and Virgil is, for Dryden and for Pope, partly found and partly invented by their various acts of poetic translation: Pope"added much to what he found" and"he therefore made him Homergraceful." Of his Aeneid translation, Dryden says,"some things too I have omitted, and sometimes have added of my own. Yet the omissions, I hope, are but of circumstances, and such as would have no grace in English; and the additions, I also hope, are easily deduced from Virgil's sense." One deduction from these observations by Johnson on Pope and Dryden on Virgil is that, while the"original" text may be the occasion for translation, it is not originary in any essential and final way, and the event of translation encompasses and surpasses its origin. Not only does the original, as Derrida argues, reach forward to be translated and form a new language with the later version, but the original is itself, at the same time, created by the translation. Although Dryden and Pope (and other eighteenth-century translators and Classical scholars) are more or less schooled in Greek, in a sense Homer only exists for them through various acts of memory.

But, this retrospective act of invention that is memory is no mere metalepsis; it is a recollection that mediates and therefore historicizes the relationship between the original and the competing and interlinked versions. The instance of such historicization on which I would like to focus is the episode of the last parting of Hector and Andromache from the sixth book (lines 391-503 in the Greek) of the Iliad as rendered by Dryden in Examen Poeticum (1693), the third part of Tonson's Miscellany Poems. This famous episode in the Iliad comes at a strategic, dramatic, and formal moment in the poem, and also represents Homer's deep human understanding.

Unlike Achilles, Hector is defined by a web of communal relations rather than by an identity that realizes itself in solitude and defiance of social norms. In the poem, Homer has been at pains to establish Hector as a sympathetic individual, and his behaviour in Bk.VI involves encounters with his mother, his brother (Paris), his sister-in-law (Helen), his wife (Andromache), and their child (Astyanax). It also comes at a crucial, pivotal moment in the action and reaches both backwards and forwards in the poem, recalling the origins of the Trojan war and looking forward to the death of Hector and the fall of Troy.

In the scene itself, Hector meets Andromache accidentally, as they rush to seek each other before his returning to battle. The setting anticipates their conversation, which turns on the paradox that Hector cannot stay at home precisely because he values his home so highly. Like Hecuba and Helen, Andromache wants to keep Hector from fighting, and her attempt at restraining him gains poignancy from the fact that

Hector is all she has left in the world-her father and brothers have been killed by Achilles, and her mother, captured and ransomed, died shortly afterwards. The history of Andromache sets up the expectations that Achilles, who deprived her of everything else, will also deprive her of Hector. Hector's response to Andromache's plea, far from allaying her fears, actually confirms them, for his reply assumes that Troy will fall. Nonetheless, he must fight, not only to avoid the reproaches of the Trojans but also to live up to the commands of his"self":"since I have learned to be valiant and always to fight among the foremost ranks of the Trojans, winning great glory for my own self, and for my father". Hector's clairvoyance is full of poignant feeling and regret, manifesting itself in the vision of the enslaved Andromache that closes his speech. This is Dryden's version of that speech:

The fatal Day draws on, when I must fall;
And Universal Ruine cover all.
Not Troy itself, tho'built by Hands Divine,
Nor Priam, nor his People, nor his Line,
My Mother, nor my Brothers of Renown,
Whose Valour yet defends th'unhappy Town,
Not these, nor all their Fates which I foresee,
Are half of that concern I have for thee.
I see, I see thee in that fatal Hour,
Subjected to the Victor's cruel Pow'r:
Led hence a Slave to some insulting Sword:
Forlorn and trembling at a Foreign Lord.
A spectacle in Argos, at the Loom,
Gracing with Trojan Fights, a Grecian Room;
Or from deep Wells, the living Stream to take,
And on thy weary Shoulders bring it back.
While, groaning under this laborious Life,
They insolently call thee Hector's Wife;
Upbraid thy Bondage with thy Husband's name;
And from my Glory propagate thy Shame.
This when they say, thy Sorrows will encrease
With anxious thoughts of former Happiness;
That he is dead who cou'd thy wrongs redress.

But I opprest with Iron Sleep before,
Shall hear thy unavailing Cries no more.
("Last Parting" lines 116-40)

From this devastating image of the actual (but as yet unrealized) future, Hector turns to the present moment and indulges in the wish of an imagined (but very real) future for his son. Father-son relationships are important though usually fractured in the Iliad, but this one between Hector and Astyanax takes the form of a domestic idyll and is, as Martin Mueller notes, a powerful instance of the clash between the heroic and the domestic that pervades Bk.VI. There is both pathos and irony here: not only does the child's fear of the father's helmet join husband and wife in a moment of gentle laughter, but the father's conventional prayer for heroic succession is obviously vain, since it receives no response from any of the gods and, since we know, from our point of historical retrospection, that Astyanax will in fact die soon after the fall of Troy. But in words of the purest factualness, designed to comfort Andromache, Hector leaves for battle committed to whatever will happen:

Think not it lies in any Grecian's Pow'r,
To take my Life before the fatal Hour.
When that arrives, nor good nor bad can fly
Th'irrevocable Doom of Destiny.
("Last Parting" lines 179-182)

Dryden's lines convey something of the double sense in the Greek of constraint and freedom. The Greek (lines 487-9) registers the knowledge of what will happen-because the gods have already decreed it-as well as the uncertain human drama in which Hector faces the unknown with vulnerability. John Alvis observes that"Hector is a victim of a delusion inasmuch as he cannot know he has been set a fixed term of grace by Zeus.... Nevertheless, Hector's fate also proceeds from his free decisions. These decisions cooperate with Zeus's plan, but they are not inspired by the god, who in respect to Hector works just as he acts with respect to Achilles and Patroclus, in accord with character". Dryden's lines absorb into the consciousness of Hector this sense in the Greek of the simultaneity of the personally willed and the divinely inevitable. As Felicity Rossalyn remarks, when describing Pope's version of Hector, the"rules of conduct" are not a matter of choice, according to temperament, but of necessity; they are embedded deep in the nature of things.... Aidos cannot do away with suffering, but it can convert it into resignation at the last, and though it cannot prevent death, it wrests some meaning from it. Hector dies because he feels aidos towards the Trojans, and his responsibility for them overcomes his longing for safety; his death has a purpose, and Zeus looks down on him with favour.

Andromache returns home, not to her weaving, as she was bid ("Return, and to divert thy thoughts at home, / There task thy Maids, and exercise the Loom"), but to mourn her husband as if he were already dead:"Those loud Laments her echoing Maids restore, / And Hector, yet alive, as dead deplore" ("Last Parting" lines 194-95). As Michael Anderson remarks, in her lament over the dead body of Hector in Bk.XXIV, Andromache simultaneously foresees the fall of Troy as a consequence of Hector's death and implicitly links the future destruction of the city with the death of her child, Astyanax (lines 728-30 in the Greek). Andromache's recapitulation in Bk.VI of the loss of her family during the sack of Thebes at the hands of Achilles (lines 414-26 in the Greek) looks back upon a past that, as Anderson says,"the poets have created in the image of Andromache's future" .

Homer, echoed by Dryden, forges an explicit narrative between the close of the Iliad itself and this important episode in Book VI, and seems to magnify and incorporate into Bk.VI the element of formal leave-taking that only becomes explicit and elegiac in Andromache's lament in Bk.XXIV, as if Dryden were translating Bk.VI with a consciousness of Bk.XXIV. This episode of the last parting, together with Priam's supplication to Achilles over Hector's dead body in Bk.XXIV, were for many in the eighteenth century a touchstone for pathos and a natural style.40 In terms of their critical pronouncements, Dryden and Pope differ in their assessment of Bk.VI. For Dryden-at least, as he writes in the Preface to Examen Poeticum (1693) Homer's heroes are"ungodly man-killers" given to the"destruction of

God's images," and the feelings generated by his epic are"rage" and the"irascible appetite" rather than the gentler and humane feelings of grief and pity, which are more Virgil's forte (in, for example, the Dido and Aeneas episode of the Aeneid). If the reader's compassion is moved by Homer, Dryden writes, it is only by the death of Hector, and then the pathetic effect is mostly due to Congreve, whose translations of these passages appeared in the Examen Poeticum along with Dryden's"Last Parting":

If this last [Priam's lamentation over the death of Hector] excite compassion in you, as I doubt not but it will, you are more obliged to the translator [Congreve] than the poet";

Pope thought differently. In the Preface (1715) to his version (1715-20), he remarks on the impeccable pitch of Homer's style, the"great Secret... [of] when to be plain, and when poetical and figurative," and in a note to Bk.VI (1716), drawing on some hints by the Jesuit Rend Rapin, he discourses at length on Homer's capacity to"touch the Heart with Tenderness":

He was the only Poet who had found out Living Words;... Yet his Expression is never too big for the Sense, but justly great in proportion to it:'Tis the Sentiment that swells and fills out the Diction, which rises with it, and forms itself about it.... Homer undoubtedly shines most upon the great Subjects, in raising our Admiration or Terror: Pity, and the softer Passions, are not so much of the Nature of his Poem, which is formed upon Anger and the Violence of Ambition. But we have cause to think his Genius was no less capable of touching the Heart with Tenderness, than of firing it with Glory, from the few sketches he has left us of his Excellency in that way too.

In the present Episode of the Parting of Hector and Andromache, he has assembled all that Love, Grief, and Compassion could inspire. The actual translations of Dryden and Pope, however, complicate their critical pronouncements. Pope is generally agreed to respond to the epic dimension in Homer in one of two ways, either by developing a mock-epic style (of the kind he does most impressively in Clarissa's speech in the"Rape of the Lock," a creative parody of

Sarpedon's speech to Glaucus in Bk.XII of the Iliad), or by attempting to recreate Homer's moral and religious grandeur.46 The consequence of Pope's poetic choices in the particular passage under consideration is that his rendition of the parting of Hector and Andromache is unable to reconcile the simple (pathetic) and the heroic (sublime) in their actions and their words, qualities that are uniquely combined in Homer. For example, though Pope recognizes that much of the power of Homer's scene lies in the simple, domestic details,47 his poetry seems inevitably to raise Hector above the material and experiential reality of the moment, while sentimentalizing Andromache's response. Johnson observes that Pope had"a mind active, ambitious, and adventurous, always investigating, always aspiring; in its widest searches still longing to go forward, in its highest flights still wishing to be higher; always imagining something greater than it knows, always endeavouring more than it can do," and these qualities are perhaps entirely borne out in the scene of the last parting

Andromache! my Soul's far better Part,
Why with untimely Sorrows heaves thy Heart?
No hostile Hand can antedate my Doom,
Till Fate condemns me to the silent Tomb.
Fix'd is the Term to all the Race of Earth,
And such the hard Condition of our Birth.
No force can then resist, no Flight can save,
All sink alike, the Fearful and the Brave.
No more-but hasten to thy Tasks at home,
There guide the Spindle, and direct the Loom:
Me Glory summons to the martial Scene,
The Field of Combate is the Sphere for Men.
Where Heroes war, the foremost Place I claim,
The first in Danger as the first in Fame.
(Pope, Iliad, VI, lines 624-37)

While Pope identifies Dryden's version as being flawed at certain points, Pope's translation itself is indebted to Dryden's: I must not forget, that Mr. Dryden has formerly translated this admirable Episode, and with so much Success, as to leave me at least no hopes of improving or equalling it. The utmost I can pretend is to have avoided a few modern Phrases and Deviations from the Original, which have escaped that great Man. With regard to the imaginative focus of the passage, Pope's delicacy and politeness do not fully register that Hector's choice of death-the sense in lines 486-- 93 of the Greek that Hector will continue in the battle because he knows that Troy will fall-is achieved with full consciousness and in the face of everything domestic that makes life valuable. Instead, Pope's note to the passage moralizes Homer's sentiment:

The Reason which Hector here urges to allay the Affliction of his Wife, is grounded on a very ancient and common Opinion, that the fatal Period of Life is appointed to all Men at the time of their Birth; which as no Precaution can avoid, so no Danger can hasten. This Sentiment is as proper to give Comfort to the distress'd, as to inspire Courage to the desponding; since nothing is so fit to quiet and strengthen our Minds in Times of Difficulty, as a firm Assurance that our Lives are expos'd to no real Hazards, in the greatest Appearances of Danger. In missing the peculiar imaginative resonance and edge of the Homeric scene, Pope's version fails to grasp that the scene encapsulates the essential structure of the whole Iliad, linking this ultimate moment of parting with the beginning and end of the action.

Whatever the weaknesses of Dryden's version of Bk.VI- and he has been accused of everything from crassness to burlesque -his version of this scene, I would argue, understands that the last parting of Hector and Andromache is precisely that part of the Iliad on which the structure of the poem turns. He sees also that the scene opens a door to Homer's imaginative world as well as to the historical world of the Ilioupersis -that series of ancient, inter-linked texts deriving from the story of the fall of Troy and culminating, for Western literature and culture, in Virgil's Aeneid-a work that itself stimulates a further series of historical reflections and re-creations. Dryden's insight into the nature of Homer's scene and poem becomes clear when one considers how he translates the significance of the episode of the child and Hector's handling of the irrevocableness of his decision to return to the war.

Though it might be conceded that Dryden does not capture the simplicity of the child's response to the fearful-looking father, his use of the unHomeric epithet"illustrious" (lines 154, 174) to describe the child suggests that Dryden has conceptualized the child symbolically as looking to a conspicuous, eminent, and noble future, terms that do not usually apply to a child. The moment contrasts significantly with the"last parting" of Aeneas, Creusa, and their child Ascanius in the Aeneid Bk.II. In his translation of that episode, Dryden also dramatizes the presence of the child-"For while I held my Son, in the short space, / Betwixt our Kisses and our last Embrace" but entirely without the symbolic resonance of the Iliad episode.54 This may be because the narrative of the Aeneid has a different illustrious purpose for Ascanius, in contrast to the fated purpose of Astyanax in the narrative of the Iliad, and so Dryden feels no need to write him up.

In any case, the teleology of Dryden's"Last Parting" is not present in Homer's words, which say, simply, that Hector"kissed his dear son, and fondled him in his arms" and that Andromache took the child"to her fragrant bosom, smiling through her tears". But Dryden's attempt to give"point" to the child is important in the light of the pivotal function of this scene in the structure of the whole poem-a structure that moves inevitably forward to the death of Hector, the fall of Troy, and the death of the child himself. From Dryden's perspective as a seventeenth-century reader, the child looks to the future, yet is also already dead. This superimposition of temporal perspectives, though not precisely Homer's, does generate its own powerful human and historical poignancy. This is enhanced by the turn Dryden gives to Hector's acceptance of the inevitable, in the lines already quoted but that bear reconsideration.

My Wife and Mistress, drive thy fears away;
Nor give so bad an Omen to the Day:
Think not it lies in any Grecian's Pow'r,

To take my Life before the fatal Hour.
When that arrives, nor good nor bad can fly
Th'irrevocable Doom of Destiny....
At this, for new Replies he did not stay,
But lac'd his Crested Helm, and strode away.
(lines 177-82, 188-89)

"Doom of Destiny" is a Virgilian formulation, or, rather, a typical Drydenian formulation in his translation of Virgil. In his version of Aeneid Bk.II, for example, variations of"doom,""destiny," and"fate" are used repeatedly to signal the remembered fall of Troy:"The fatal Day, th'appointed Hour is come, / When wrathful Jove's irrevocable Doom / Transfers the Trojan State to Grecian Hands". In Dryden's Homer passage,"Doom of Destiny" suggests not only the universal significance of the fall of Troy and its repetition throughout Western history, but also looks to the particular future that Virgil envisages for the fall, through the foundation of Augustan Rome as depicted in the Aeneid. At the end of Bk.II of the Aeneid, Dryden has the spirit of Creusa look forward to a time when Aeneis will no longer weep for her, which is also the time of the founding of Rome:

Where gentle Tiber from his Bed beholds
The flow'ry Meadows, and the feeding Folds....
There Fortune shall the Trojan Line restore;
And you for lost Creusa weep no more.

While Astyanax perishes at Troy, Ascanius, Aeneis's child, survives and fathers a line that eventually rules Rome. As Steven Zwicker remarks of Dryden's Virgil,"the poet both directly and obliquely argued the connections of Trojan, Roman, and English histories".

In Dryden's"Last Parting," therefore, the human actors stand at the verge of one kind of history, reminiscent of the conflict and the continuity in Homer of the heroic and the domestic world, a domestic world-the relationship of man, woman, and child-made especially poignant and resonant for the fact that it stands alone against the inevitability of a history that is acknowledged as always already having happened and as exceeding the individual will.56 Sowerby remarks that"Dryden's empathy with the whole range of Homeric epic is something rare in any age, but particularly remarkable in a period notorious for its taste for Roman gravity and decorum". Pope's Hector, by contrast, speaks-- or rather, declaims-with a reassuring Roman expansiveness and gravity:

Andromache! my Soul's far better Part,
Why with untimely Sorrows heaves thy Heart?
No hostile Hand can antedate my Doom,
Till Fate condemns me to the silent Tomb.
Fix'd is the Term to all the Race of Earth,
And such the hard Conditions of our Birth.
No Force can then resist, no Flight can save,
All sink alike, the Fearful and the Brave.

Johnson's Hector, in his early version of this passage, speaks like a Christian stoic in a rhetoric that re-emerges at the end of The Vanity of Human Wishes:

Ah! let not tears down that fair countenance roll,
Restrain your sorrows, calm your troubled soul.
Your sighs are spent in vain; if fates withstand
Hector shall perish by no warriour's hand.
But if by their irrevocable doom
My death is now decreed my death will come.
The bravest hero and the fearfull'st slave
Shall sink alike into the gloomy grave.

Dryden's Hector, by contrast, manages to retain the rhythms of the speaking voice, while at the same time giving the impression of an individual mind expanding to meet the facts of the moment charged with the significance of history. Hence, the appropriateness of Johnson's writing of Dryden's poetry in general that the power that predominated in his intellectual operations was rather strong reason than quick sensibility. Upon all occasions that were presented he studied rather than felt, and produced sentiments not such as Nature enforces, but meditation supplies. With the simple and elemental passions, as they spring separate in the mind, he seems not much acquainted, and seldom describes them but as they are complicated by the various relations of society and confused in the tumults and agitations of life. In the case of

Dryden's version of Iliad Bk.VI, I would suggest that the"elemental passions" and the"complications" mentioned by Johnson are inextricably mingled as Dryden remembers and re-envisions Homer's heroic world and explicitly conceptualizes its human drama within historical terms of interest to himself in 1693. For the vision of the universal doom of the fall of Troy signifies for Dryden the continuity-the after-life that every text seeks in translation-- represented by the founding of Augustan Rome, in a political epic, the Aeneid, that came to be the most important Classical text in English culture in the Restoration, and that underlies Dryden's (and other writers') conceptualization of a civilized politics in the 1690s.

That future history, so to speak, is what Dryden anticipates in the"English palace"-in his poem addressed to the Earl of Roscommon-that English translators build out of the ruins of ancient Troy and Augustan Rome:

Roscommon, whom both Court and Camps commend,
True to his Prince, and faithful to his friend;
Roscommon first in Fields of Honour known,
First in the peaceful Triumphs of the Gown;
Who both Minerva's justly makes his own.
Now let the few belov'd by Jove, and they,
Whom infus'd Titan forma of better Clay,
On equal terms with ancient Wit ingage,
Nor mighty Homer fear, nor sacred Virgil's page:
Our English palace open wide in state;
And without stooping they may pass the Gate.

The imperial impulse, as David Kramer has demonstrated, is never far in Dryden from the human and the emotional: the theme of familial relationship in the Homer translation echoes Dryden's similar concerns in other poems of the period, particularly in those addressed to Oldham and to Congreve, whose version of the Iliad Bk.XXIV is cited by Dryden (in the Preface to Examen Poeticum) as a necessary complement to his own rendition of Bk.VI. It is as if the relationship between Congreve and Dryden envisaged in"To my Dear Friend Mr. Congreve" (1694) pertains obliquely to their respective translations of Homer in the Examen Poeticum of the year before."Difference" is a resonant term in the context of Dryden's translations, also referring to several different discursive realities in translation as a general mode of discourse: Dryden's rendition of Homer, in relation to other versions (like Chapman's, Congreve's, Pope's, and Johnson's) and to other mediating structures of thought (such as Virgil's Aeneid) explicitly recognizes his historical lateness and thereby also reflects on the nature and structure of temporality; Dryden's translation recognizes the necessity of having to negotiate with the cultural, philosophical, and linguistic gaps between the moment of the original text and that of his own; Dryden's poetic language in translating Homer creates its own meanings in response to his poetic understanding of the needs of his own culture, the English language, and his own personal experience; and Dryden's prefaces repeatedly draw attention to the temperamental, stylistic, and philosophical differences between himself and the poets he translates, while his translations themselves find in that difference occasion for some of his best and most characteristic poetry.

One of Dryden's terms for all these differential relationships is harmony. Yet harmony is a problematic term on which to end, since most readers-even specialist Restoration scholars-assume that the largest reality to which the term can refer is the sound and sense of the heroic couplet. My suggestion, however, is that the term operates for Dryden within the same register of poetic, linguistic, and philosophical meaning as it does for such theorists (and practitioners) of translation as Derrida and Benjamin.

In"The Task of The Translator," Benjamin argues that there is something in the"nucleus" of the original text at which the translation aims but that"does not lend itself to translation". However, this something in the"nucleus" of the original, the transfer of which can never be total, is essential to the problematics of translation because, for Benjamin (though not necessary for Dryden-or for Derrida), it implies the larger metaphysical purpose of translation,"the reconciliation and fulfillment of languages." The reason why the"nucleus" of the"original" text does not lend itself to translation (though essential to the process itself) is explained by Benjamin using two metaphors: Unlike the words of the original it [the nucleus] is not translatable, because the relationship between content and language is quite different in the original and the translation. While content and language form a certain unity in the original, like a fruit and its skin, the language of the translation envelops its content like a royal robe with ample folds.

In"Des Tours de Babel," Derrida points out that Benjamin's"nucleus" and"fruit" are not the same. In the metaphoric relationship between fruit and skin or between content and language, the"nucleus" is not the tenor in the metaphor but the relationship between tenor and vehicle, between fruit and skin. The"nucleus" of the original text, therefore, is situated or constituted between or within the relationship between skin and fruit. Benjamin's second metaphor, however, sees the relationship between language and content in the translation as that between a royal cape with large folds and the king's body. The king's body here is not that of the original text but the tenor of the translated text-the fruit in Benjamin's first metaphor.

But, as Derrida remarks,"the king has indeed a body... but this body is only promised, announced and dissimulated by the translation. The clothes fit but do not cling strictly enough to the royal person. This is not a weakness; the best translation resembles this royal cape. It remains separate from them to which it is nevertheless conjoined". But, for Derrida, it is in the relationship between these two sets of metaphoric relationships-one natural and one artificial-that truth lies. Derrida himself uses the word"truth"; but truth here is not the representational correspondence between the original and the translation-that essential and universal paradigm assumed to pertain to translation with which I began-nor the primary adequation of original to some object exterior to it.

It is to this relationship or truth-paraphrasing Benjamin's identification of the object of translation as"pure language"-that Derrida gives the term"harmony": It is among these modes that the translation should seek, produce or reproduce, a complementarily or a"harmony." And since to complete or complement does not amount to the summation of any worldly totality, the value of harmony suits this adjustment, and what can here be called the accord of tongues.... As long as this accord does not take place, the pure language remains hidden, concealed, immured in the nocturnal intimacy of the"core." Only a translation can make it emerge. These are not quite Dryden's terms, nor does Dryden have any explicit concern with"pure language," yet Benjamin's depiction of the problematics of translation, and Derrida's exposition, bears closely on Dryden's views and practice as I have described them. As for Benjamin, the harmony of translation for Dryden resides in those double relationships, double likenesses, between modern and classical languages, between Dryden himself and poets such as Homer, Lucretius, Horace, and Virgil, and between the body (both human body and textual body) and the"spirit which animates the whole":

Translation is a kind of drawing after the life; where every one will acknowledge there is a double sort of likeness, a good one and a bad.'Tis one thing to draw the outlines true, the features like, the proportions exact, the colouring itself perhaps tolerable; and another thing to make all these graceful, by the posture, the shadowings, and chiefly by the spirit which animates the whole.... I dare assure them [readers] that a good poet is no more like himself in a dull translation, than his carcass would be to his living body. Notwithstanding the linguistic and historical difficulties of approaching what Benjamin calls the"nucleus" and Dryden calls the"spirit which animates the whole" of the original, these writers understood the central contribution to the process of civilization implied by acts of translation. They would not have disagreed with Frederic Will's conclusion:

Translation must always be of the past-it is the present. The past it's of is only questionably knowable, and therefore translation exists as a never guaranteed effort to know and re-establish its object. In fact the translator's effort provides the ideal testing-ground for determining whether the past is knowable. If translation is impossible-cannot truly revive the interior of the past-then it looks as though history-writing as a whole will be impossible.

For Dryden (as much as for the more explicitly theoretical modern commentators), translation reveals the aporetic nature of language whose law is the very revelation of the ontological and historical truths that always, rationally, remain elusive, impenetrable, and different, but that actually justify the whole endeavor.65 In different ways, commentators agree that translation, standing simultaneously inside and outside the representative circle of language and operating at once as both essence and supplement, is directly about and incorporates into itself the play of difference in a way that other genres do not. Derrida and Foucault's whole deconstructive enterprise might be seen as an exercise in and animadversion on the Western cultural process of translation.

Johnson's"Life of Dryden" (1779)-and perhaps the entire Lives of the Poets (1779-81), itself (like Benjamin's essay and Derrida's grammatology) a kind of translation in its prefatory nature, relatedness, and nuanced and layered engagement with the absences and presences of memory-is structured by the knowledge that Dryden found the English language brick and, through translation, left it marble. Any suggestion that such translations and critical awareness are nothing more than unconscious rationalizations of the Enlightenment's preeminence in our system of knowledge might give us an illusory superiority over the past, but we thus effectively flatten out the eighteenth-century's inflected and luminal sense of its own historical knowledge, and reveal the relative inflexibility and unhistoricity of our own.

The Grounds of Criticism in Tragedy

With this attempt, which must be classed among Dryden's dramatic failures, was printed the remarkable Preface concerning the Grounds of Criticism in Tragedy, which, although not actually the last of Dryden's contributions to dramatic criticism, may be said to complete their cycle. Here, at last, we find a plain and reasonable application of the fundamental Aristotelian theory of tragedy to the practice of the English drama. Shakespeare and Fletcher-the former in particular-are set down as deficient in"the mechanic beauties" of the plot, but, in the"manners" of their plays, in which the characters delineated in them are comprehended, the two great masters of the English drama are extolled at the expense of their French rivals. Although exception must be taken to the distinction between Shakespeare and Fletcher as excelling respectively in the depiction of the more manly and the softer passions,"to conclude all," we are told,"Fletcher was a limb of Shakespeare"-in other words, the less is included in the greater. Thus, though neither of much length nor very clearly arranged, this essay signally attests the soundness of Dryden's critical judgment, with his insight into the fact that the most satisfactory dramatic theory is that which is abstracted from the best dramatic practice.

It was not given to him to exemplify by his own dramatic works the supreme freedom claimed by the greatest masters of the art; but he was not to end his theatrical career without having come nearer than he had as yet approached to his own ideals. From this point of view, two tragedies may be passed by in which the unbalanced, but not wholly uninspired, powers of Lee co-operated with the skill and experience of Dryden. Oedipus (acted 1678), though provided with an underplot, threw down a futile challenge to both Sophocles and Corneille. In The Duke of Guise (acted in December, 1682), Dryden's share seems to have been mainly confined to the furbishing up of what he had written many years before.

Whatever he might say in the elaborate Vindication of the Duke of Guise (printed in 1683), the political intention of the play, as a picture of the now discomfited intrigues of Shaftesbury in favour of Monmouth, was palpable, and not disproved by the fact that the authority of Davila had been more or less closely followed, or by the other fact that the parallel might, in some respects, have been pressed further than would have been pleasing to king Charles. In Albion and Albanius, Dryden committed himself to a still lower descent-hardly to be excused by the"thought-depressing" quality of opera mentioned by Dryden (who, on this head, agreed with St. Évremond) in the interesting preface which gives a short account of the early history of musical drama. After many delays, the chief of them being due to the death of Charles II, in compliment to whom the opera had been first put together, it was at last performed on 3 June, 1685. Ten days later, the news arrived of Monmouth's landing at Lyme, and the unlucky piece, with its jingling rimes, French music and all, was finally withdrawn. Saintsbury describes it as, to all intents and purposes, a masque; but it lacks all the beauties of which that kind of composition is capable, and which are not made up for by the grotesquely ridiculous supernatural machinery to which here, as in The Duke of Guise, the author condescended to have recourse.

Dryden was not, however, deterred from carrying out his intention of writing the"dramatic opera" of King Arthur or The British Worthy, to which Albion and Albanius had been designed as a prelude. It was produced in 1691, with music by Purcell; but, notwithstanding the claim put forth in the preface, little or no proof is furnished of Dryden's familiarity with Arthurian romance; and, in spite of the magic, there is not much fire in the piece, while the figure of the blind Emmeline is an unpleasing experiment. Perhaps, as the tag suggests, the poet was, for once, almost losing heart.

Critical Reception

The eighteenth-century English author Samuel Johnson regarded Dryden as a poet who crystallized the potential for beauty and majesty in the English language by effectively shaping rough words into refined verse. Dryden first began developing his poetic style while writing his early, laudatory verses, experimenting as he wrote them with the traditional hexameter form. Although recognized for their artistic promise and innovation, these poems have since been faulted for misplaced or excessive conceits and similes. Ultimately, the best of this early poetic period is represented by Annus Mirabilis, an inspirational, heroic treatment of the great fire in London and of the AngloDutch naval war. Years later, with

Absalom and Achitophel, Dryden displayed his mastery of the heroic couplet and the suitability of his streamlined verse for political satire. Cloaked in allusive language and based on the biblical story of King David's rebellious son, this mockheroic poem addresses the explosive political climate of the time through a string of character portraits, narrative, and speeches. Dryden's portrayals of Charles II, an inveterate philanderer; his illegitimate son Monmouth, who planned to dethrone his father; and Shaftesbury, the chief orchestrator of the Popish Plot; are admired by critics not only for their liveliness but for the judicious manner in which they are presented. Scholars have remarked that the relentless movement of the poem, its delightful yet pointed commentary on the crucial situation, and its timeless appeal establish it as one of the highest achievements in the heroic couplet form.

That Dryden was an exemplary poet of public events and was able to infuse even the most ordinary incident with dignified, original art is not disputed. However, his poems have been charged with displaying a disturbing impersonality. Nevertheless, several modern critics have detected a clear, confessional tone in Dryden's later poems, *Religio Laici* and *The Hind and the Panther*. Although the theological viewpoints in them are disparate, critics have observed that both these works forcefully document the poet's personal reactions to the political milieu as well as to the power of religious faith in his era.

Bibliography

The Cambridge Companion to *John Dryden. Ed.* Steven *N. Zwicker*. (Cambridge University Press, 2004).

John Dryden 1631-1700: His Politics, His Plays, and His Poets. Claude Julien Rawson & Aaron Santesso. Univ of Delaware Press, 2004).

John Dryden: Tercentenary Essays. Paul Hammond & David Hopkins. (Oxford Univ Press, 2000).

John Dryden: Selected Criticism. G. A. Parfitt & James Kinsley. (Oxford University Press, 1999).

Ancient Faith and Modern Freedom in *John Dryden's* the Hind and the Panther. Anne Barbeau Gardiner. (Catholic Univ of Amer Press, 1998).

"When Beauty Fires the Blood": Love and the Arts in the Age of Dryden. *James Anderson Winn*. (University of Michigan Press, 1998).

Dryden and the Problem of Freedom: The Republican Aftermath 1649-1680. *David B. Haley*. (Yale Univ Press, 1997).

Critical Essays on *John Dryden. Ed.* James Anderson Winn. (G K Hall, 1997).

Dryden in Revolutionary England. *David A. Bywaters*. (University of California Press, 1991).

John Dryden and His World. James Anderson Winn. (Yale Univ Press, 1988).

John Dryden (Modern Critical Views). Ed. Harold Bloom. (Chelsea House Publishing, 1987).

Dryden: The Poetics of Translation. Judith Sloman. (Univ of Toronto Press, 1985).

Dryden: The Public Writer. George McFadden. (Princeton Univ Press, 1978).

Dryden As an Adapter of Shakespeare. *Allardyce Nicoll.* (AMS Press, 1978).

Contexts of Dryden's Thought. *John Phillip Harth.* (University of Chicago Press, 1978).

A Preface to Dryden. *David Wykes.* (Longman Group, 1977).

Politics and Poetry in Restoration England: The Case of Dryden's Annus Mirabilis. *Michael McKeon.* (Harvard Univ Press, 1975).

Tragic Theory in the Critical Works of Thomas Rymer, John Dennis, and *John Dryden. Joan C. Grace.* (Associated Univ Press, 1975).

Dryden's Classical Theory of Literature. *E. Pechter.* (Cambridge University Press, 1975).

Dryden's Political Poetry: Typology of King and Nation. Steven Zwicker. (University Press of New England, 1972).

The Intellectual Design of *John Dryden's Heroic Plays. Anne T. Barbeau.* (Yale Univ Press, 1970).

John Dryden and the Poetry of Statement. *K. G. Hamilton.* (Michigan State Univ Press, 1969).

Art of *John Dryden. Paul Ramsey.* (University Press of Kentucky, 1969).

Twentieth Century Interpretations of All for Love: A Collection of Critical Essays. *Bruce Alvin King.* (Prentice Hall, 1968).

Dryden's Poetry. Earl Roy Miner. (Indiana University Press, 1967).

Dryden's Heroic Drama. Arthur C *Kirsch.* (Gordian Press, 1965).

John Dryden's Imagery. A. W. Hoffman. (University Press of Florida, 1962).

Life of *John Dryden.* C.E. Ward. (Univ of North Carolina Press, 1961).

John Dryden: A Study of His Poetry. Mark Van Doren. (Indiana University Press, 1960).

Homage to *John Dryden. T. S. Eliot.* (Hogarth Press, 1924).